BEARING
THE WEIGHT OF
SALVATION

BEARING THE WEIGHT OF SALVATION

THE SOTERIOLOGY OF IGNACIO ELLACURÍA

MICHAEL E. LEE

FOREWORD BY GUSTAVO GUTIÉRREZ

A Herder & Herder Book
The Crossroad Publishing Company
New York

The Crossroad Publishing Company
www.cpcbooks.com
www.crossroadpublishing.com

In continuation of our 200-year tradition of independent publishing, The Crossroad Publishing Company proudly offers a variety of books with strong, original voices and diverse perspectives. The viewpoints expressed in our books are not necessarily those of The Crossroad Publishing Company, any of its imprints or of its employees. No claims are made or responsibility assumed for any health or other benefit.

Cover photo: by Christopher Broughton. Detail from a San Salvador mural near the location of Archbishop Oscar Romero's assassination. Romero appears to the right. The people around him, pictured, bear the stigmata of bullet holes and nail holes, representing what Ignacio Ellacuría called "the crucified people."

Printed in the United States of America on acid-free paper

The text of this book is set in 10/12 Sabon. The display face is Amerigo.

Library of Congress Cataloging-in-Publication Data

Lee, Michael Edward, 1967-
    Bearing the weight of salvation : the soteriology of Ignacio Ellacuria /
  Michael E. Lee ; foreword by Gustavo Gutierrez.
        p. cm.
    "A Herder & Herder book."
    Includes bibliographical references and index.
    ISBN-13: 978-0-8245-2421-0 (alk. paper)
    ISBN-10: 0-8245-2421-7 (alk. paper)
    1. Salvation – Catholic Church. 2. Ellacuría, Ignacio. 3. Liberation
  theology. 4. Christian sociology – Catholic Church. I. Title.
  BT755.L44 2008
  234.092 – dc22

                                    2008043034

In loving memory of
Waldemar Edward Lee
(1934–2005)

Contents

Foreword

Ignacio Ellacuría, a philosopher and theologian who holds a distinctive place in the theology of liberation, expressed himself in sharp and relevant essays that might have been further developed. He never got the opportunity to do so; the full meaning of his writings was revealed in another manner: with his martyrial witness. The outstanding work of Michael Lee goes to the source of Ellacuría's thought, and, from there, tackles its various elements. He says with precision, "This book takes [the] meeting of Ellacuria's martyrdom and apologetics as its starting point." And so it is.

This allows the author of this book to penetrate the significance that Ellacuría assigns to salvation in history. Lee helps us to see that the profound immersion in historical reality, of Ellacuría's thought and life, is owed precisely to that role that Ellacuría attributes to the transcendence of God the liberator. In the midst of the difficult situation of conflict in his country, where he decided to live (and die), Ellacuría was able to nourish the hope of a crucified people, as he said. According to Paul Ricoeur, theology is born of the intersection between a space of experience and a horizon of hope. The keen, mature analysis of Michael Lee, which expounds a complex system of thought with great clarity, places the theology of Ignacio Ellacuría in that perspective.

— *Gustavo Gutiérrez*

Acknowledgments

WRITING ON THIS remarkable and committed person put me in contact with many remarkable and committed people. Among these, I would first like to thank my mentor, J. Matthew Ashley. He introduced me to Ellacuría's work, and his intelligence, careful reading, and thoughtful questions have made this book. They are overshadowed only by his effect on me as a person: his character, compassion, and deep commitment. I am also deeply indebted to Crossroad Publishing Company, particularly John Jones, John Eagleson, and Catherine Osborne, for their expertise. The final manuscript is only a dream without their skilled eyes and careful reading.

Many thanks are due to other readers as well: to Mary Catherine Hilkert, whose conscientious pedagogy and close reading continue to teach me; to David B. Burrell, whose critical questions have deepened my thought and made me a more honest scholar; to Gustavo Gutiérrez, whose stories, insights, and friendship I consider one of the great honors of my life; and to David Tracy, who expanded my intellectual horizons like no one else. They have taught me how humility and sanctity coincide with the vocation of theologian.

My work benefited greatly from the financial support of several sources. Along with the encouragement from my wonderful colleagues at Fordham University that allowed me to see this project through to publication, I would like to acknowledge the generous support of the Graduate School and Theology Department of the University of Notre Dame that made doctoral studies a possibility, the Nanovic Institute for European Studies, whose grant afforded me travel to Spain and the Basque country. Thanks also to the Hispanic Theological Initiative, whose dissertation fellowship, networking, and *comunidad* were a great source of sustenance. Many thanks also to James F. Fetscher and the support of the St. Louis Catholic Community in Miami.

Research has taken me to three continents where people have been affected by Ellacuría's legacy. In Spain, I owe a debt of thanks to the Fundación Xavier Zubiri, especially Antonio González. Thanks also to the hospitality of Juan José Tamayo Acosta. In El Salvador, I owe thanks to the members of the Universidad Centroamericana José Simeón Cañas, and particularly for conversations with Dean Brackley and Jon Sobrino. They put a human face on an imposing thinker. I am also grateful for the continuing work of the Casa de Solidaridad. In the United States, I would like to thank Robert Lassalle-Klein for wonderful conversation and advice, and Kevin F. Burke, whose input and friendship make him an older brother of Ellacuría studies.

I would like to acknowledge the four people without whom this book would never have been written. To Waldemar and Virginia Lee, who by word and example taught me that faith and faithfulness are lived in small, daily acts of self-sacrifice. To my son, Will, who daily teaches me the joy and challenge of unconditional love. Finally, to my beloved wife, Natalia, whose selflessness in serving so many roles with this project — as soundboard for ideas, as set of eyes for revision, as reference for impossible Spanish phrases — is just a microcosm of the great collaboration that is our life together. *Muchas gracias, mi amor.*

Abbreviations

ECA	*Estudios Centroamericanos*
EF	*Escritos filosóficos*, 3 vols., Ignacio Ellacuría
EP	*Veinte años de historia en El Salvador (1969–1989): Escritos políticos*, 3 vols., Ignacio Ellacuría
ET	*Escritos teológicos*, 4 vols., Ignacio Ellacuría
FMF	*Freedom Made Flesh: The Mission of Christ and His Church*, translation of *Teología política*, Ignacio Ellacuría
FRH	*Filosofía de la realidad histórica*, Ignacio Ellacuría
HD	*El hombre y Dios*, Xavier Zubiri
IL	*Inteligencia y logos*, Xavier Zubiri
IRA	*Inteligencia y razón*, Xavier Zubiri
IRE	*Inteligencia sentiente: Inteligencia y realidad*, Xavier Zubiri
ML	*Mysterium Liberationis: Conceptos funadamentales de la teología de la liberación*, ed. Ignacio Ellacuría and Jon Sobrino (Madrid: Editorial Trotta, 1990). English translation: MLT.
MLT	*Mysterium Liberationis: Funadamental Concepts of Liberation Theology*, ed. Ignacio Ellacuría and Jon Sobrino (Maryknoll, NY: Orbis Books, 1993). Translation of ML.
NHD	*Naturaleza, historia, Dios*, Xavier Zubiri
NHG	*Nature, History, God* (translation of NHD), Xavier Zubiri
SE	*Sobre la esencia*, Xavier Zubiri
SI	*Sentient Intelligence*, Xavier Zubiri
TP	*Teología política*, Ignacio Ellacuría

Service:

BOOK

support@book.com

173267740

0

FLD2

Item Price	Total
31.65	31.65

If you are not satisfied with your order, you may return it within 14 days of the delivery date. For your convenience, items may be returned to the address on the packing slip or returned to your local Barnes & Noble store (check the local store refund policy for details).

Choose a return reason below and include this slip with the item in your package. Please cut out label on dotted line and affix to carton being returned.

[ ] **Wrong Quantity**

[ ] **Defective or Damaged in Transit**

[ ] **Wrong Merchandise Received**

[ ] **Other (please explain)** _____

Pay Method: **Credit Card#:**

✂

From:
Otha Gilyard
1380 South Roosevelt Ave
Columbus, OH 43209
USA

To:
**Barnes & Noble.com
B&N.COM Customer Returns
1 Barnes & Noble Way
Monroe Township, NJ 08831
USA**

830702279

OU FOR YOUR ORDER!

99050000000913253646

11/14/2014 12:00 AM   (EAD)

11/11/2014 5:35 AM   (PRINT)

BARNES&NOBLE
www.bn.com

Sold To:
BN Inc. SHIP TO HOME
1380 South Roosevelt Ave
Columbus, OH 43209
USA

Ship To:
Otha Gilyard
1380 South Roosevelt Ave
Columbus, OH 43209
USA

Customer

1-800-THE

professiona

PO Num:

Your order of Nov 10, 2014   **(Order No. 830702279)**

Loc: PM02
Box Size:

Qty	Description	Item #
1	**Bearing the Weight of Salvation: The Sot**	9780824524210

THANK

Page 1 of 1

Introduction

A T THE HEART of the Christian message lies the theme of transformation. Believers are called to a *metanoia*, a total conversion from a
previous way of life to a new one. The Scriptures portray this conversion in a vivid way. Consider the disciples' fearful hiding being transformed
into bold testimony after witnessing the risen Christ, or the figure of Paul,
the rabid persecutor of early Christianity, being thrown to the ground by "a
light from heaven," only to nurture and lead the fledgling movement he once
despised. Indeed, Christian history presents a litany of transformed lives that
witness to the power of Christianity's salvific message, from Antony of Egypt
and Martin of Tours in ancient times to Thomas Merton and Dorothy Day
in our own. They testify to the power of transformation in the Christian life.

Christians have often described this transformation in personal terms as
a movement away from sin. Be it the pull of pride, wealth, or promiscuity,
figures such as Augustine of Hippo, Francis and Clare of Assisi, and Ignatius
of Loyola have portrayed their acceptance of the Christian message as a
turning away from fleeting, deceitful, and even destructive temptations that
lay deep within the human person. In them one can see the transformation
called for by the Christian gospel as a complete change of a person's reality,
of her or his life and thought.

Yet just as the Christian message has effected the inner transformation
of many lives, it has also effected a transformation of the world in which
these believers lived. In living out the transformation at the heart of the
gospel, Christians have changed the face of their societies, through means
ordinary and heroic. These examples, such as Catherine of Siena's demands
on the papacy or Bartolomé de Las Casas's confrontation of the Spanish *en-
comenderos*, demonstrate how powerfully a lived Christianity can transform
the reality of the world.

In this study, I explore this gospel-inspired transformation in the life
and work of Ignacio Ellacuría, a Basque Jesuit theologian who became a
naturalized Salvadoran, and ultimately was killed because of his witness.
Though the world would come to know Ellacuría because of the violent
death he suffered at the hands of an assassin, his life story testifies to tireless
daily commitment to a profound vision of Christian discipleship.[1] During
the course of his life, he assumed various tasks. He collaborated with the

1

philosopher Xavier Zubiri, encouraging the reclusive thinker to write and subsequently publish his works. He edited the prominent journal *Estudios Centroamericanos*, which analyzed the sociopolitical reality of El Salvador and became a major voice in working to secure a negotiated settlement to El Salvador's civil war. He taught philosophy and theology at the Universidad Centroamericana José Simeón Cañas (UCA), eventually assuming the position of rector (president). Ellacuría participated in the formation and direction of the Central American Jesuits, becoming a much sought after source of advice for novices preparing for priesthood.

In all of these tasks, Ellacuría manifested a dogged commitment to living out the Christian calling to serve others. He brought theological reflection to all of these actions and, in turn, allowed his theological work to be affected by these many tasks. While his story speaks of great personal transformation, it also tells of the powerful effect that he, and the others at the UCA, had on the national reality of El Salvador. In doing so, Ellacuría leaves behind a legacy of fidelity and sacrifice worthy of any of the great martyrs in Christian memory.

Ironically, those who killed Ellacuría justified their action with epithets that question this martyr's witness: Marxist, atheist, and traitor.[2] This fact comes as no surprise in a climate in which hundreds of catechists, religious, priests, and an archbishop could be kidnapped, tortured, and even murdered.[3] Even the theological movement of which Ellacuría is a prominent example, Latin American liberation theology, has been cast under a shadow of suspicion. While hailed by some as innovative theological reflection on Christian faith lived out in the context of horrible suffering, liberation theology represents, to its critics, a compromise of the gospel message utilizing reductionist thought forms. Assessing Ellacuría's legacy, then, addresses both the growing body of knowledge on this extraordinary theologian and ongoing reflection on Latin American liberation theology, including evaluation not just of its past articulation, but its continuing relevance for future work as well.

While the debates concerning liberation theology have existed for several decades now, the assessment of Ignacio Ellacuría's work is only in its nascent form.[4] In English-language scholarship, though there are few sources, they represent a solid initiation to Ellacuría's work.[5] Each author recognizes in Ellacuría a fertile ground for future theological thought. While the present volume contributes to Ellacuría's assessment, it does so within the wider dialogue concerning the legacy of liberation theology, an end achieved by attention to the theme of soteriology.

This book concentrates on Ignacio Ellacuría's account of Christian salvation and discipleship. It claims that Ellacuría's description of discipleship must be understood as part of a larger account of Christian salvation that is philosophical, christological, and ecclesiological in nature. The motivation behind this thesis lies first in Ellacuría's remarkable biography. In Ellacuría, one possesses not just an intellectual account of Christian discipleship, but a martyrial performance, a lived testimony that connects intrinsically to his intellectual output.

The thesis also recognizes that the emphasis on the importance of praxis to theology and faith represents one of the outstanding contributions of Latin American liberation theologians.[6] Since Ellacuría wrote a good deal on Christian discipleship incorporating the language of praxis in multiple forms (e.g., personal, structural, ecclesial), exploration of his treatment of this theme could enrich what is already a significant body of work.[7] Moreover, in light of the manner that Karl Marx's interpretation of the term "praxis" has colored its subsequent connotation, analyzing Ellacuría's treatment of the term within the notion of Christian discipleship may assist in adjudicating the issue of Marxist influence, whether fruitful or deleterious, on liberation theologies.[8] This attention to discipleship cannot be limited to what Ellacuría wrote about the subject; it must also consider how his life informed and expressed what he thought about Christian salvation and the manner in which Christians should act in the world.

Bearing the Weight of Salvation

In the early hours of November 16, 1989, six Jesuit priests, their housekeeper, and her daughter were taken from their beds and murdered by soldiers of the elite Atlacatl unit of the Salvadoran military. This shocking event not only focused worldwide interest on El Salvador's civil war — interest that many credit with finally getting the warring parties to resolve their differences in a negotiated settlement — but also sparked growing curiosity about what the Jesuits at the UCA in San Salvador were doing that would draw such a violent response.[9] In particular, the figure of Ellacuría, philosopher, theologian, president of the university, and leading public intellectual of El Salvador, emerged as crucial to understanding the events at the UCA.

When one acknowledges that Ellacuría and the others at the UCA did not simply die, but in fact were assassinated, then logic demands an answer to the question, "Why were they killed?" Indeed, why would an assassin feel it necessary not just to kill Ellacuría, but to choose the symbolism of desecrating his brain on the lawn of the university? Clearly, Ellacuría's death stemmed from his way of life carried out at the UCA, primary to which was using his intellectual gifts. Thus, an explanation of why Ellacuría was killed involves not only an accounting of his actions but an investigation of the content of his vast corpus of writings. Though many studies are necessary to account for this multifaceted thinker, the present book explores the theological link between Ellacuría's life and his vision for how Christians, considered both individually and as *ecclesia*, should act in the world. It also suggests that the attempt to fulfill this vision prompted his martyrdom.

Crucial to Ellacuría's account of Christian behavior in the world, what I will call discipleship, is his profound theological understanding of Christianity's fundamental message, salvation in Jesus Christ, or what might be described theologically as soteriology. For in soteriology, one deals both with Christ's redemptive act and the believer's reception of that gracious offer — a reception that involves faith and action. Therefore, this study attempts to substantiate a claim concerning the intrinsic relationship between discipleship and soteriology: the manner one chooses to live as a follower of Christ in the world affects, and is in turn affected by, the way one articulates the Christian claim of salvation in Jesus Christ. In the case of Ellacuría, the manner of Christian life embodied at the UCA flowed from a particular vision of Christian salvation and powerfully affected that very vision. In exploring that vision, this study will touch upon several themes that radiate out of this martyr's life and death.

Ellacuría's work both illumines the tragic episode at the UCA and assists in understanding the story of the Catholic Church in El Salvador at that time. Certainly, Ellacuría's tenure at the UCA cannot be separated from the tumultuous period in El Salvador's history, particularly for members of a church that could justly call itself persecuted. Ellacuría's years at the UCA, coinciding with the deaths of thousands, were punctuated by tragic events. The best-known to U.S. observers include the 1977 assassination of the Jesuit Rutilio Grande, the assassination of Archbishop Oscar Romero in 1980, and the rapes and murders of four U.S. churchwomen later that same year.[10] The civil war of the 1980s brought Ellacuría into the national spotlight, particularly because of the UCA's attempts to analyze the national reality and to persuade the warring parties to negotiate. These efforts led to periods of exile, numerous bombings of the campus, and finally, the tragic martyrdom. Thus, Ellacuría's legacy represents a crucial link in the story of this persecuted church, whose testimony commands attention from all those wishing to be faithful to the Gospel's call.

Ellacuría's story also provides another strand in the tapestry that is the wider tale of liberation theology in Latin America at the end of the last century. Curiously, though some Latin American liberation theologians have attained a measure of recognition in academic and wider circles, this cannot be said about the social, political, and ecclesial contexts of their countries of work. Though critics might commonly name figures such as Gustavo Gutiérrez, Juan Luis Segundo, and Leonardo Boff, few are familiar with the events in Peru, Uruguay, and Brazil that profoundly shaped their theological reflection.[11] El Salvador occupies a unique place in the consciousness of many in the United States because of figures such as the Jesuits, the four U.S. churchwomen, Archbishop Romero, and the fierce debates over U.S. foreign policy in El Salvador that occurred during the 1980s. Yet these events have not prompted a corresponding familiarity with Ellacuría, who represents, along with Jon Sobrino, the foremost representative of liberation theology in that country.[12] Ellacuría's case provides a unique opportunity to appreciate liberation theology comprehensively as an intellectual task within an ecclesial context.

This book offers both a description of Ignacio Ellacuría's account of soteriology and discipleship, and a prescriptive claim about its importance for present and future theological work. The task will unfold (chapter 1) by locating Ellacuría's theology historically as part of the Latin American liberation theology movement. Its focus will be on liberation theologies as fundamentally soteriological, as a particular form of proclaiming Christian salvation that has profound implications for the behavior of believers. Indeed, it would not be an exaggeration to claim that much of the furor over liberation theology has centered principally on ecclesial discipleship, the theological implications for the nature of the church and its action in the world.

After analyzing the significant themes treated by major Latin American liberation theologians and the central criticisms levied in the Vatican documents on liberation theology as soteriological, the first chapter concludes by reviewing Ellacuría's responses to the Vatican critiques. These responses will serve to underscore the soteriological nature of the debate and to signal the important theological topics that permeate Ellacuría's entire theological enterprise. By organizing these topics as philosophical, christological, and ecclesiological in character, the chapter serves as a template for the subsequent body of the study.

Having located Ellacuría's thought historically and contextually, the study will turn to its central descriptive task: exploring Ellacuría's soteriology and account of discipleship (chapters 2–4). The methodological guide for considering Ellacuría's soteriology derives from his own proposal for Latin American theology: an integrated, threefold (noetic, ethical, praxis-oriented) method characterizing the human confrontation with reality (*enfrentarse con la realidad*).[13]

In this study, the questions posed by Ellacuría will be directed to his own soteriology and his critics' views. This allows us to grasp more fully the central components of his soteriology — its philosophical underpinnings, its account of Jesus Christ as principle of salvation, and its proposal for Christian action — and to recognize their interdependence. Thus, the central questions will be: How, philosophically and theologically, does Ellacuría account for or realize the weight of reality (*hacerse cargo de la realidad*) (chapter 2)? How does he locate, in Jesus Christ and in today's crucified people, the point from which to carry on or shoulder the weight of reality (*cargar con la realidad*) (chapter 3)? How does he advocate that Christians respond to and take responsibility for the weight of reality (*encargarse de la realidad*) (chapter 4)?[14]

Because this study contends that liberation theology, and specifically that of Ellacuría, still offers important resources for contemporary theological discourse, its final chapter will consider recent criticisms of liberation theology lodged by thinkers of the so-called "radical orthodoxy."[15] In particular, it focuses on their challenges to liberation theology's philosophical underpinnings and account of Christian ecclesial discipleship. Their work positions itself as an alternative to liberation theology in offering a critique of the modern capitalist order and advocating a distinctive form of Christian practice. While the debate concerns the nature of Christian discipleship in the world, the roots of the debate may also be viewed as intimately connected to the interpretation of Christianity's salvific message. Since it also represents some of the most provocative discussions of present theological discussion, recourse to radical orthodoxy offers a critical foil against which the continuing value of Ellacuría's thought might be construed.

Ultimately, by concentrating on soteriology and discipleship, this study highlights Ellacuría's theological preoccupation with articulating the divine-human relationship in a way that contributes to faithful action in the world. If the Second Vatican Council represents, in part, the culmination of mid-twentieth-century Roman Catholic debates on grace and nature, then Ellacuría's liberation theology marks a next generation's continuation of this debate, but with a deeper historical consciousness.[16] If an earlier generation fought to overcome the dualisms inherent in an extrinsic view of grace, then Ellacuría's soteriology carries forward the task by trying to overcome the dualisms inherent in a narrow view of historical reality.

This notion carries several implications. The first concerns Ellacuría's relationship to modern philosophy and theology. A central complaint against Latin American liberation theologies is that they are reductionist, trapped within modernity's "meta-narrative." A response to this critique may be found in Ellacuría's attempt to speak coherently of the transcendent in relation to the historical. By articulating reality as historical reality, Ellacuría stresses the dynamic and interrelated character of all existence. Moreover, by identifying all intramundane reality as rooted ultimately in the reality of God, Ellacuría provides a distinctive Christian view of creation that sees transcendence "in" and not "away from" the world. This ability indicates a critical stance toward modernity — one that, while wary of its excesses, avoids the categorical rejection advocated by others.

If Ellacuría attempts to overcome the philosophical separation of transcendence and history, then, second, he also tries to overcome a false "spiritualization" of Christology that separates Christ from historical reality. Not only does this mean understanding Jesus of Nazareth's death within the context of his confrontation of the powers of sin in his world, but it means understanding that death in connection with the deaths of the poor, the ones Ellacuría calls the "crucified people." If Jesus' death and resurrection call for conversion and faithful discipleship, then the ongoing crucifixion of the poor and oppressed is the historical presence of that call. Without replacing or lessening the distinctive character of the christological mysteries —

his incarnation, life, crucifixion, resurrection, and return — Ellacuría's view overcomes those Christologies, and concomitant modes of discipleship, that would diminish the historical implications of the mysteries.

Finally, this study reflects on a third theme: the manner in which Ellacuría's vision of Christian discipleship entails a creative and mutually transformative engagement with historical reality. Ellacuría's vision at once possesses the confrontational characteristics of prophetic theologies while retaining the participative character of more mystical theologies. This graced vision of the world does not fall into naïveté concerning the existence of radical evil; on the contrary, because it constantly engages the historical reality of Latin America, it continually calls for prophetic condemnation of sin in the world. Yet because it recognizes the universal presence of God, it possesses a humble openness to allow itself to be transformed. This mutually transforming view of Christian ecclesial praxis overcomes both a materialism that would dedicate discipleship exclusively to the work of justice, and a spiritualism that would devote itself merely to piety and cultic practices.

Ellacuría's hope and call for Christian engagement in historical reality also provides a sober, integrated vision of the church that seems lacking in the exalted ecclesiologies of other contemporary theologians. Though the church is called to be prophetic, it too is guilty of sin — in its members, in its complicity with sin. Furthermore, since the spheres of "world" and "church" often cannot be delineated clearly, the call to transformation always reflects back on the church. There is no room in this vision for a sectarianism that is naïve about Christians' place in the world and the fundamental sin of the world: those conditions that allow for the majority of the globe to spend lifetimes (often cut short) in the shadow of death. The openness of a transformative vision, however, should not be mistaken for conformity. For clearly, Ellacuría's thought and life demonstrate that the transformation called by discipleship may require the ultimate cost for nonconformity, a martyr's death.

In the end, all of Ellacuría's activity sealed his fate with the powers that ruled El Salvador. Though the assassinations at the UCA shocked most observers for their brutality, in many respects they came as no surprise. His tireless commitment to unmask the reality of El Salvador, to find a negotiated settlement to the civil war, to create a peace with justice for the poor, and to embody the church's preferential option for the poor, inevitably led to one fate for Ignacio Ellacuría: martyrdom. His martyrdom culminated a lifelong attempt to be a faithful disciple of Jesus Christ, and it did so intertwined with his tasks as a Christian philosopher and theologian. This biographical connection between Ellacuría's theology and life signals a corresponding link between Ellacuría's soteriology and his account of Christian discipleship.

Reflection on a martyr does not end with the reality of death, but the hope for new life. Ultimately, this project echoes those sentiments expressed by Joseph O'Hare, S.J., in his homily delivered days after the UCA martyrs' assassinations:

> With deep hope in the Resurrection of the Lord, we pray that the final word in the drama of El Salvador be one of life and hope rather than death and despair. We pray that the irony of that tiny tortured country's name, El Salvador, will be redeemed by the resurrection of its people.[17]

Chapter One

Liberation Theology:
A Soteriological Debate

S INCE CHRISTIANITY'S INCEPTION, believers have linked its message of
salvation to a corresponding form of living. They have appropriated
Jesus' invitation, "Come, follow me," in the particular circumstances
of their times. Whether it be the testimony of martyrs in Rome, or the flight
of hermits into the Egyptian desert; in separate oases of monastery walls,
or in the streets of large cities — Christians have adopted myriad forms of
life in response to the proclamation of the "good news," salvation in Jesus
Christ.

Of course, differing modes of discipleship sometimes come into conflict.
Over the centuries, the church has had to delineate between those forms
of life that are harmonious with the gospel message and those that are
not. Moreover, the judgment between accepted and rejected discipleship is
often adjudicated according to the dogmatic beliefs related to those behaviors. Witness the discernment between Franciscan and Albigensian poverty,
Carmelite mysticism and that of the *Alumbrados,* or the dogmatic issues
underlying Donatist sacramental practices or strict Arian moral codes.[1] Con-
flicting Christian practices often point to intellectual or dogmatic differences
in how to interpret Christian salvation. This indicates a dynamic relationship between the Christian understanding of salvation in Jesus Christ, or
soteriology, and the way of life following Christ, or discipleship.

To speak of soteriology in the sense above includes its traditional denotation, the doctrine of redemption through the atoning death of Christ; for
the sake of this study, however, it also connotes a broader account of the
gracious, creative, and salvific relationship of God to humanity and all creation.[2] How can one speak of salvation without discussing creation, grace,
or the church? As a fuller account of Christianity's hope of salvation, a
true *soterio-logos,* soteriology, which in the narrowest sense is a subset of
Christology, expands to take up themes found in fundamental theology, the
doctrine of creation, Christology, ecclesiology, and the doctrine of grace.
When seen in this broader sense, soteriology necessarily, if not always explicitly, dictates an account of Christian behavior in relation to the account

of God's gracious, salvific activity, and by bringing this relation to light, we can often uncover critical points of divergence among contemporary theologies.

The emergence of Latin American liberation theology toward the latter half of the twentieth century serves to illustrate the power and controversy engendered in this intersection of soteriology and discipleship.[3] Witnessing massive poverty on a continent that overwhelmingly professed Christianity, some believers came to analyze and address the structural causes and symptoms of this suffering. Theologically, this pastoral action led to reflection on its relation to Christianity's promise of salvation.[4] When the Second General Conference of Latin American Bishops (CELAM) convened in Medellín, Colombia, in 1968, it declared, "As Christians we believe that this historical stage of Latin America is intimately linked to the history of salvation."[5] Statements like these point to the hermeneutic possibility that evaluating the debates over liberation theology, both liberation theologians' central tenets and their critics' negative assessments, is carried out best with attention to the intersection between soteriology and discipleship.

Though some commentators have stressed the novelty of liberation theology, reference to soteriology as a broader account of God's gracious and salvific relationship with humanity helps locate Roman Catholic liberation theology within a tradition. Namely, it represents a second generation's wrestling with one of the twentieth century's most important theological problems: how to understand the relationship between nature and grace.[6] From the pioneering studies of authors such as Maurice Blondel and Joseph Maréchal, to the landmark work of Henri de Lubac and Karl Rahner, the century witnessed a profound shift in Roman Catholicism away from an extrinsicist view that reified and separated the realms of "nature" and "supernatural."[7] By trying to understand terms such as "liberation" and "salvation," Latin American liberation theologians take up the ongoing challenge of articulating the relationship between human nature and the gratuitous hope of union with God.[8]

This chapter begins by sketching out fundamental themes found in Latin American liberation theologians' *soterio-logos*. Specifically, the manner in which they articulate the connection between the terms "salvation" and "liberation," the notion of the preferential option for the poor, and the emphasis on praxis as integral to theology and faith indicate ways that these theologians attempt to announce the salvific message of Christianity in light of the multiple challenges of their context.

After identifying the soteriological core of liberation theologies, we move to analyzing liberation theology's critics in a similar manner. In particular, Vatican documents, which represent the most significant critiques of liberation theology in the 1970s and 1980s, focus their criticisms on fundamentally soteriological themes: the danger of reducing salvation to the sociohistorical, understanding Jesus Christ as merely a historical liberator, and viewing Christian discipleship in terms of Marxist class struggle.

Finally, the framing of the liberation theology debate as soteriological prepares us to consider the soteriology of Ignacio Ellacuría both within this broader context of soteriological concern and as the core concern that unites the various theological themes he treats. In his brief defense of liberation theology, Ellacuría intones the central theological themes that resonate throughout his entire written corpus. As a correlate to the triad of themes associated with liberation theology, this analysis will identify the central motifs that outline philosophical, christological, and ecclesiological dimensions of Ellacuría's soteriology and its powerful account of Christian discipleship in the world.

Liberation Theology as Soteriology

The intervening years since the historic Medellín CELAM conference have seen numerous developments in Latin American liberation theology. In academic circles, liberation theologians enjoyed a heyday of interest in the 1970s and 1980s for their ability to take up traditional theological themes and offer innovative interpretations from the perspective of the poor and marginalized. There was also great interest in the ecclesial counterparts to this theological reflection, the *comunidades eclesiales de base* (CEBs) in countries throughout Latin America. Moreover, liberationist voices emerged from other poor regions throughout the world, such as Southeast Asia and sub-Saharan Africa, and from marginalized groups who recognized the significance of race and gender for issues of oppression and liberation.[9]

Even at the height of its popularity, liberation theology was coming under intense criticism, both of its intellectual reflection and of the practices it advocated.[10] The criticism of the former centered primarily on theologians' use of theory and data from the social sciences and Marxist philosophy, while the latter concentrated on the challenges to traditional hierarchical notions of ecclesiology manifested in communities of the poor. Moreover, as the novelty of liberation theology in North American and European academic circles waned, and new Latin American episcopal appointments reflected strong opposition, many began to speak of the "death" of liberation theology.[11] While the reports of its demise may be exaggerated, liberation theology has in fact entered a new period of reflection and assessment.[12]

An understanding of Latin American liberation theology as soteriological provides a way to clarify its chief contributions and the forms of discipleship linked to this theology. Liberation theologians have explored a wide range of theological topics. For example, one may speak of liberation Christologies, ecclesiologies, Trinitarian theologies, and works of spirituality.[13] Yet three themes point to a soteriological core of all these topics. The first derives from the title given to this theology, "liberation," which refers to the manner in which its proponents relate the terms "salvation" and "liberation." Second, the "preferential option for the poor" represents their locus for theological reflection on Christian salvation. Finally, the call for Christian discipleship enfleshed as historical praxis emerges as a dimension of God's sanctifying transformation of the world.

By taking examples of how certain liberation theologians (in particular Gustavo Gutiérrez and Clodovis Boff) treat these themes, I hope to substantiate the claim that liberation theology attempts to retrieve the notion of salvation within a particular context of poverty and oppression, and by doing so, advocate a version of Christian discipleship that more adequately addresses that context.[14] Subsequent chapters will demonstrate how Ellacuría articulated these central themes of liberation theology in a distinctive way in light of his philosophy of historical reality. These themes fruitfully illustrate both the manner in which Ellacuría shared intellectually with other Latin American colleagues, and the directions in which he forged his own distinctive interpretation.

Thus, we now turn to three significant themes of Latin American liberation theology — liberation-salvation, the preferential option for the poor, and the importance of praxis — to illustrate the soteriological character of these theologies and to assist in mapping out and understanding the opposition that liberation theologians have engendered over time, particularly as those misgivings were articulated in Vatican documents.[15] After these analyses, the chapter will close by offering a preliminary glance at Ignacio Ellacuría's position in this debate and how it might clarify a reading of his vast theological corpus.

Salvation-Liberation

An obvious place to begin reflection on the theology of liberation is that central term in its title: liberation. As one commentator points out, the "of" does not signal a genitive, lest this be considered a "theology of" a particular topic.[16] Rather, these theologians find in the language of liberation a retrieval of the incarnational dimension of that which Christian theology has understood under the category of salvation. For example, many liberation theologians focus upon the biblical images of the Exodus and of the Reign of God to think through that portion of biblical testimony to God's salvific action in history.[17] It would be reductive to claim that these theologians imply a simple equation between socioeconomic liberation and Christian salvation. In fact, it is precisely in the complex manner that these theologians work through the relationship between these two terms that one discovers the creative dimension of this theology and a differentiation of voices.

Focusing on the relationship between the terms "liberation" and "salvation" provides an opportunity to clarify the method of these theologians.[18] Since the language of liberation also represents a significant theme from social scientific analyses of Latin American poverty, the way that liberation theologians use this language often indicates how they understand the relationship between theological reflection and their contemporary situation, between theology as a discipline and the social sciences. To the degree that the term "liberation" designates the salvific hope of oppressed peoples, its use reveals much about how liberation theologians articulate that theological notion contrary to salvation, the present reality of sin. Thus, the liberation-salvation relationship provides much of the ground for soteriological reflection because it names both the realities from which and toward which salvation moves. Given the foundational importance of this relationship and its widespread influence among liberation theologians, a brief summary of Gustavo Gutiérrez's treatment of the two terms illuminates this point.

From his earliest writings, Gutiérrez has reflected upon the language of liberation and salvation, a language that has remained key to his thinking ever since and has influenced theologians across geographical and generational boundaries. In *A Theology of Liberation*, Gutiérrez carefully differentiates three "reciprocally interpenetrating levels of meaning of the term *liberation*."[19] These levels of meaning cannot be understood in a linear fashion, but should be seen as possessing a mutuality, an inner dynamic such that no temporal order should be attached to them. Gutiérrez describes each of these levels of meaning as having a corresponding arena of activity and an intellectual discipline that most appropriately reflects on the realities of each dimension. Here too one should avoid reifying what is essentially a heuristic schema.

The first level of meaning for the term "liberation" refers to the hope of oppressed peoples to be free from those economic, social, and political conditions whose effect is summed up by one term, death.[20] Liberation at this level of meaning calls for the meeting of basic needs, but also for the transformation of social structures that create this situation of death for the poor.[21] This indicates the importance of the social sciences in coming to understand the reality of the poor. Following the Second Vatican Council's mandate to discern the signs of the times, Gutiérrez acknowledges the importance and *relative* autonomy of the social sciences in helping fulfill this directive.[22] Yet for Gutiérrez liberation's meaning is not limited to an economic connotation.

In the second level of meaning, the term "liberation" refers to human realization in history, indicating a qualitative nuance not readily indicated by the first level of meaning. Gutiérrez acknowledges those changes that must accompany the more material aspects of liberation.[23] Attention to this level of meaning underlies Gutiérrez's contrast between the European theological concern for the "non-believer" and the Latin American concern for the "non-person." Liberation in this sense takes up those intangible aspects, personal and interpersonal, of human fulfillment. It refers to the human struggle for self-realization, the creation of a new human being.[24] Thus, Gutiérrez acknowledges the importance of philosophy, particularly that with a utopian imagination, in providing a vision of liberation at this level.

The third level of meaning refers to that communion with God and with other human beings usually connoted by the term "salvation." The obstacle to this sense of liberation is encapsulated in the term "sin." It would be a mistake, however, to regard this level of meaning as abstract or ahistorical. Gutiérrez is careful to note that whatever its complexity, the process of human liberation is fundamentally one, a claim that stems from his assertion of history's unity. "There are not two histories, one profane and one sacred, 'juxtaposed' or 'closely linked.' Rather there is only one human destiny, irreversibly assumed by Christ, the Lord of history."[25] Gutiérrez stresses that liberation from sin and liberation for love do not occur outside of historical processes.

Thus for Gutiérrez, the term "liberation" does not indicate a concept alongside and distinct from that of *salvation,* but at a basic level, merely serves as useful translation of the biblical term *soteria.* As such, liberation must be understood as possessing the three interpenetrating levels of meaning. This complexity of meaning warrants against the reduction of salvation to socioeconomic liberation, but it also decries any understanding of salvation in purely abstract or ahistorical terms.

While Clodovis Boff acknowledges that the term "liberation" has various sociological and theological usages, his interpretation of its relationship to salvation becomes clear in his bifurcation of theology as a discipline. He understands liberation theology as a political theology, a "second" theology that is distinct from first theology. First theology "treats directly of specifically 'religious' realities — the classic themes of God, creation, Christ, grace, sin, eschatology, the virtues, the commandments, and so on. [Second theology] will have 'secular' realities for its subject matter: for example, culture, sexuality, or history."[26] Despite this distinction, Boff argues for a unity between these "two" theologies at the level of pertinence, the *theologizans.* First and second theology are both theology, not different disciplines; they share a *ratio formalis.*[27]

The distinction between first and second theology involves that upon which theologizing is to be done, the *theologizandum.* Furthermore, that which is *theologizandum* for second theology, concepts such as culture, sexuality, or liberation, requires certain mediations to be properly thought about theologically. Since Boff identifies "liberation" as a *theologizandum* for second theology, he cautions that the term cannot easily be equated with a term from first theology such as "salvation." Before asserting any sort of equivalence, more about the term "liberation" would need to be understood through three central mediations: socioanalytic, hermeneutic, and practical.[28]

For Boff, the distinctions between the various levels of meaning that Gutiérrez delineates in "liberation" lead to aporias concerning the process of liberation.[29] In identifying Gutiérrez's proposal with what he calls "the Chalcedonian model" of response to the question of liberation, Boff suggests that in Gutiérrez's schema concerning liberation and salvation, "the answer has been decided from the beginning of the debate in a determinative fashion."[30] To Boff, the "Chalcedonic method" properly attempts to articulate dualities, but fails because it remains at the level of first approximation.[31] For Boff, a better understanding of liberation and salvation comes through the three mediations than through use of the Chalcedonian model.

Boff restricts liberation to an object of historical materiality. To add any more would be mystification.[32] For the theologian, the real content of the term "salvation" has nothing in common with what the social scientist calls "liberation." Boff notes that the difference is not just of degree, but of order. Yet on the conceptual level he admits that there is an analogical relationship. Theologians make use of the idea of human liberation in order to reflect on the idea of God's salvation. Thus, liberation functions as a *theologizandum* for theology, but, in this task, Boff determines that first theology reveals its limits. "First theology is not endowed with such a nature as to be capable of setting up a possible relationship between the reality of salvation and the reality of liberation." For Boff, it is a "transcending gaze" that reflects on traditional theological *topoi* and arrives at a conclusion such as, "God's salvation is *like* human liberation."

Boff avoids using the language of identity between liberation and salvation in favor of what he calls the language of "topical realization," or "installation."[33] By this, he wishes to affirm that salvation or, using New Testament language, the Reign of God, is in some manner in the world. Rather than using a phrase such as "salvation is liberation," Boff prefers the expression "salvation is installed in liberation," such that society functions as a *topos* for the Reign (and one of many possibilities). Boff acknowledges that ultimately the relationship between salvation and liberation is mysterious. He even notes how the Christian tradition contains examples of both the language of topical identity and that of difference. Yet the distinction between theologies and the language of topical realization furnish Boff with a manner for speaking of the relationship between liberation and salvation that moves beyond the "simple reciprocal relationship" he sees engendered in the Chalcedonic model.

This sampling from two liberation authors indicates the general contours of their approach to the relationship between the terms "liberation" and "salvation." More than simple conflation, each author wrestles with the proper way to express the ultimately mysterious notion of God's relationship to humanity and the world. In doing so, they express a concern for fidelity to the Christian hope for salvation through Jesus Christ, while at the same time demonstrating a fidelity to the historical experience of the suffering peoples of Latin America and their hope for liberation. It is this twin striving for fidelity that leads to consideration of the role of the poor in theological reflection. Ultimately, relating the terms "liberation" and "salvation" drives liberation theologians to think through the poor as those whom the Bible portrays as receiving God's special care. Thus, they articulate the preferential option for the poor.

Preferential Option for the Poor

While one might describe liberation theologians' reflection on salvation and the poor as innovative and indeed revolutionary, one can also see how these themes resonate throughout the Christian tradition. For their part, Roman Catholic liberation theologians demonstrate the influence of the Second Vatican Council in considering salvation and the poor.[34] Consider how the opening lines of *Gaudium et spes* identify "the joys and the hopes, the griefs and the anxieties of the [people] of this age, *especially those who are poor*" with those of the followers of Christ, and then go on to proclaim "the news of salvation which is meant for every [person]."[35] Methodologically, *Gaudium et spes* influenced these liberation theologians by recognizing "the duty of scrutinizing the signs of the times and of interpreting them in the light of the gospel. Thus, in language intelligible to each generation, she [the church] can respond to the perennial questions which [people] ask about this present life and the life to come, *about the relationship of the one to the other.*"[36] In these lines, one can see those elements influential to the liberation theologians: an integrated view of the church in, not apart from, the world; an attention to the plight of the poor; and a directive to study the contemporary situation as significant — all intertwined with the language of salvation.

Gutiérrez believes that one of the most important historical processes in the contemporary period consists in the emergence of the poor as a theological problem for Christians. While the problem of poverty is not new, Gutiérrez sees the irruption of the poor as the most significant question facing the church in his context of Latin America. In light of Christians' participation in the process of liberation, the language of the "preferential option for the poor" develops.[37]

For Gutiérrez, the term "preferential" does not signify a sense of exclusivity. To the contrary, linking preference to those most rejected demonstrates the gratuitous nature of God's love. Gutiérrez's definition reflects the Bible's description of God's love as both universal and with a predilection for the "least ones."[38] The latter phrase indicates the centrality of biblical testimony to the option for the poor. Liberation theologians often articulate the option for the poor out of biblical examples, ranging from the parable of the great judgment (Matt. 25) to the parable of the rich man and Lazarus (Luke 16). Gutiérrez himself offers a powerful reading of the book of Job in which he demonstrates that the option for the poor stems not from social analysis, nor even from human compassion, but from a theo-centric, prophetic option.[39]

Gutiérrez's use of the term "option" refers not to an optional choice that Christians have the luxury of making or ignoring, but rather to the gospel's command to opt for the poor. The Christian preferential option for the poor indicates a location from which theological reflection grows and is shaped — and therefore, the hermeneutic importance of the poor within this theological approach. This does not belie liberation theology's status as *theo-logy*. Fond of quoting the sixteenth-century Dominican friar Bartolomé de las Casas — "Of the least and most forgotten people, God has a very fresh and vivid memory" — Gutiérrez views the preferential option for the poor as a crucial dimension of the Christian response to God's love in discipleship.[40] The response, the need to opt, to make a commitment, applies as well to those who are poor.

For Clodovis Boff, the "topical realization" of salvation in the liberation of the oppressed reveals the importance of the preferential option for the poor. This realization does not imply simple theological identifications, but reveals the place where abstract formulation achieves historical realization. Theology, then, must involve discernment as to the nature of this historical realization, as Boff illustrates with the following example:

> Only when I move closer to the oppressed do I move close to God, whose image and "children of predilection" they are, God's favorite sons and daughters. And only when I'm loyal to my oppressed comrades am I faithful to my alliance, our covenant, with God. And only when I follow the poor am I following Jesus — which makes them a universal, absolutely necessary sacrament of salvation.[41]

For Boff, while the plane of salvation represents the larger horizon of liberation theology, the secondary horizon consists of the liberation of the poor. In terms of its object, liberation theology reflects on faith, developing the liberative meaning of that faith; and it reflects on the process of liberation, interpreting it in the light of faith. Indeed, Boff asserts that, to the degree that every subsequent theology must address questions concerning those who are oppressed, liberation theology, and its preferential option for the poor, are an intrinsic dimension to all future theology.

The Centrality of Praxis

Liberation theology's insistence on the centrality of praxis finds many allies in contemporary theology.[42] Yet for their part liberation theologians have wed this insistence with the preferential option for the poor to argue that praxis both possesses hermeneutic implications for theology and represents a key dimension of the salvific process, as that sanctifying transformation that occurs in faithful discipleship.[43]

If some liberation theologians have identified the theory-praxis relationship as one that has often meant the subordination of praxis to theory, Clodovis Boff does not equate the two terms, but in fact argues for a reversal. "Any theory, hence also theology, is concretely subject to the influence of praxis."[44] Among the levels upon which this subordination is registered is that of the theologian's social involvement. Here praxis surfaces and illumines certain problems that can be taken up by theory in the form of questions. Therefore, Boff emphasizes the importance of the theologian's involvement in the life of the poor.

When Boff states that liberation theology's starting point resides with the oppressed, he assumes explicit engagement with the life of the poor on the part of the theologian. As he explains, "Concrete liberation theology supposes a practical relation with practice, and not merely a theoretical relation. It implies a living contact with the struggle of the poor. Today's 'liberation theologian' is someone concretely committed to the cause of the oppressed."[45] In fact, Boff identifies the radical originality of liberation theology precisely in the "insertion of the theologian in the real life of the poor." Using images such as Gramsci's "organic intellectual" or "theological activist," Boff notes the logical and temporal priority of faith praxis before the second act of theological theoretization.[46]

Gutiérrez identifies solidarity with the poor as an essential dimension of Christian discipleship. In his reading of Job, Gutiérrez identifies Job's innocence not in individual uprightness, but in behavior to the poor.[47] Job is confident that he has acted properly because he has performed works of mercy for the poor. Even the rejection of idolatry is tied to commitment to the poor. Once again, the theocentricity of this approach identifies God's uprightness (*sedeq*) and judgment (*mishpat*) as central components of faithful practice.

Gutiérrez develops these notions in his reading of the Beatitudes.[48] In developing a liberation spirituality, Gutiérrez might be expected to concentrate on the Beatitudes of the Gospel of Luke, with the directness of their "blessed are the poor," rather than those of Matthew that praise the "poor in spirit." Gutiérrez, however, moves against the reading of Matthew's Beatitudes as "spiritualized" in order to ground a spirituality of Christian practice. As he expresses it, "The Beatitudes of [Luke] underscore the *gratuity of the love of God,* who 'preferentially' loves the concrete poor. Those of Matthew flesh out this picture by indicating the *ethical requirement in order to be a follower of Jesus,* which flows from that loving initiative of God."[49]

To be poor in spirit is to be a disciple of Christ. Those who mourn are blessed because they refuse to resign themselves to injustice and oppression in the world. Those who thirst for justice are blessed. The single-hearted do not separate theory from practice. The peacemaker brings about not simply the absence of violence, but *shalom,* that powerful connection between justice and peace. Naturally, those who behave in this way will inevitably find resistance and persecution, but the kingdom is promised them.

For Gutiérrez, the promises of the kingdom, the promises of salvation are "the fruits of God's gratuitous love, and therefore call for a certain kind of behavior."[50] Theologically, Gutiérrez links the liberation-salvation dynamic to a theo-centric preferential option for the poor that demands a discipleship of solidarity and commitment to the "least ones."

Thus, in these authors of Latin American liberation theology, a profoundly soteriological sense becomes clear. They wrestle to articulate the divine-human relationship that Christianity claims as salvific. They do so primarily in their treatment of the related terms "liberation" and "salvation." The manner in which they adjudicate the proper relationship between these key terms varies widely. Despite these differences, however, liberation-salvation undergirds the preferential option for the poor and the importance of praxis. To the degree that liberation theologians perceive the theological task as intrinsically woven with these central themes, these theologians reveal the soteriological thrust of liberation theology. They demonstrate that any assessment of liberation theology — though it may take into account factors such as its novel understanding of theology's relationship to the social sciences, its distinctive biblical hermeneutics, and its relation to social theorists or philosophers — must account for this theology as soteriology, as an articulation of Christian salvation.

The Vatican's Caution: Reducing the Kingdom

As much as liberation theology caused excitement on the academic and ecclesial scenes, it also engendered fierce opposition. Viewed in retrospect, this opposition exhibits a complexity and history similar to that of liberation theologies themselves.[51] Many criticize liberation theologians' use of Marxist thought and categories particularly for its political and economic implications.[52] Others, while remaining in the realm of theology, fail to see the nuance of positions articulated by liberation theologians and so dismiss the project entirely.[53] Even those sympathetic to Latin American liberation theology, including feminist, black, and Latino/a theologians, have faulted the Latin Americans for not developing their critique on the questions of race and gender.[54]

The most significant and influential criticisms of liberation theology, however, have come from the Vatican.[55] Since the overwhelming majority of Latin American liberation theologians are Roman Catholic, their interaction with the Vatican has drawn the most attention from both those within the church and outside observers. However, this attention has not always implied a close reading of magisterial documents. Many Roman Catholics have accepted a simplistic vision of "liberation theology vs. the Vatican," lacking familiarity with the different Vatican figures and statements made in these debates.

Ultimately, the Vatican's differences with Latin American liberation theology become articulated in soteriological terms. For example, in the Congregation for the Doctrine of the Faith's instruction, the deep suspicion of liberation theologians' use of Marxist thought underlies the cardinal accusation of reductionism, specifically reducing salvation to a historical project.[56] The nature of this accusation bolsters the fundamental claim presented in the present work, namely, that the controversy surrounding liberation theology may be understood fundamentally as a soteriological one. If so, then charting the Vatican's concerns with liberation theology involves a parallel schema to the earlier exposition of liberation theology's central themes. Vatican criticism is best understood as focused on the manner in which liberation theologians have articulated: the connection between the concepts of liberation and salvation; the preferential option for the poor; and the importance of praxis (particularly for its ecclesiological implications).[57] These points are best demonstrated in the documents from the Vatican's International Theological Commission (ITC) and its CDF, headed by Cardinal Joseph Ratzinger (now Pope Benedict XVI), directly addressing Latin American liberation theology from 1977 to 1984.[58]

The International Theological Commission

One of the earliest Vatican documents concerning liberation theology comes from a dossier of reports composed by the ITC.[59] These reports were collected, synthesized, and published in 1977 under the title *Declaration on Human Development and Christian Salvation*. The ITC document presents a rather favorable acknowledgment of liberation theology's central soteriological themes. It recognizes the "profound unity that links the divine history of salvation accomplished through Jesus Christ to efforts undertaken for the welfare and rights of humankind."[60]

While rejecting the idea that salvation and secular history are identical, the declaration also rejects the dualistic separation of the two. In its account of the church's mission, the document declares that the church "should sharpen its conscience so as to make a critique of the social order under the guidance of faith," one that includes "a strong kinship with the poor."[61] The document also asserts that faith can be "fructified and perfected only by deeds," acknowledging that the Holy Spirit is "active even outside the visible church." Thus, at least in a general way, the ITC affirms a unity-in-distinction between liberation and salvation, solidarity with the poor, and the importance of Christian action on behalf of justice as an essential part of discipleship.

While the document remains generally sanguine about themes of liberation theology, it does sound a cautionary note concerning "some theological movements" that conceive the unity between salvation and liberation so as to "consolidate the gospel of Jesus Christ ... with secular history."[62] A philosophical and theological reductionism stands out as its primary concern. As the document avers, "We have to take special care not to fall into a uni-dimensional vision of Christianity that would adversely affect Christology and ecclesiology, our view of salvation and of Christian existence, even theology's proper function."[63] The document responds to this vision by positing a centrist approach that falls into neither monism nor dualism. While it affirms the "unyielding unity that links eschatological salvation and human effort," it also spells out the distinction between the two.

When extended to the sphere of human activity, the commission attempts to maintain a similar middle path between perceived (reductionist) extremes. While asserting that genuine faith does not condone inhuman living conditions, it also claims that "faith's praxis is not reducible to changing the conditions of human society." It must include items such as conscience for-mation, change in mental attitude, and adoration of God. The document shuns political controversy as the "onset of violence," and claims, "Although theology is oriented in part toward praxis, its more prominent function is to seek understanding of God's word." Therefore, human activity must be nei-ther utterly divorced from worldly suffering, nor seen as if "God's lordship and human progressive construction of the world were one and the same thing."[64]

The ITC's declaration cannot be understood as a condemnation of lib-eration theology. At most, it represents a cautionary note to those who might interpret its themes in an extreme fashion. Its most direct critique of a concept found in liberation theology lies in its disputing the legiti-macy of "institutional sin." While recognizing social implications of sin, the document prefers to assert that the "power of sin, injury and injustice can penetrate social and political institutions." Nowhere does there appear an explicit condemnation or association of liberation theology with Marxist thought, except in the document's caution that the church's unity is imperiled if difference in social classes is "taken up into a 'class struggle.'"[65]

Joseph Ratzinger and the Congregation for the Doctrine of the Faith (CDF)

In 1982, Joseph Ratzinger was made prefect of the CDF, an appoint-ment that marked a heightening of rhetoric against liberation theology. Shortly after Ratzinger's elevation to prefect, an Italian magazine pub-lished his "preliminary notes" concerning the theology of liberation in Latin America.[66] The notes revealed Ratzinger's mind-set as the congregation pre-pared its instruction on the theology of liberation that would appear the following year.

Though he acknowledges liberation theology as encompassing a wide spectrum of positions ranging from the CELAM documents of Medellín and Puebla to "radically Marxist positions," Ratzinger elects to restrict his notes to the latter.[67] This choice indicates a change in tone from the ITC's musings on a movement that it cautiously deems positive, to an ominous characterization of liberation theology as "a fundamental threat to the faith of the church."[68] Yet even in this marked change in tone toward libera-tion theology, Ratzinger's notes reaffirm the centrality of soteriology to the debate. As he avers, "The question of soteriology, that is, the problem of salvation, of redemption (or liberation, as they prefer to say), has become the central question of theology."[69] In order to understand this central ques-tion, Ratzinger reads liberation theology as symptomatic of the challenges faced by the Roman Catholic Church since the time of the Second Vatican Council.[70]

He characterizes this period as one in which humanity experiences a fun-damental alienation, a "lack of redemption," that calls for liberation. For Ratzinger, "secularist liberation programs are attempting to achieve this lib-eration exclusively in the immanent plane, in history, in this world. But it is precisely this limited view, restricted to history and lacking an opening to transcendence, that has brought man to his present state."[71] Thus, Ratzinger explicitly identifies reductionism, articulated as being closed to transcendence, as the central problem in liberation theology. According to Ratzinger, liberation theology's exclusive attention to immanence emerges from its reliance on a Marxist interpretation of history. This theological turn to Marxism represents a deterioration of the Second Vatican Council's turn to the world through a naïve acceptance of the sciences as authoritative. Marxist analysis of history and society implies an analysis of the world exclusively in terms of class struggle. Thus, important theological concepts are stripped of their transcendent significance.

For Ratzinger, reliance on Marxist thought means a deterioration of theological ideas. The Bible's view of history becomes the Marxist dialectic. Christian hope becomes a working for the future that is defined in terms of class conflict. In terms of soteriology, "The word redemption is largely replaced by liberation, which is seen against the background of history and the class struggle as a process of progressive liberation."[72] There can be no fruitful dialogue between Christians and Marxists. "Marxist ideology actually uses the Jewish-Christian tradition and turns it into a godless prophetic movement; man's religious energies are used as a tool for political ends and directed to a merely earthly hope, which is equivalent to standing on its head the Christian yearning for eternal life."[73]

Given the content of these notes, it is no surprise that the CDF's *Instruction* follows Ratzinger's criticisms, squarely identifying its differences with liberation theology in the area of soteriology. The document summarizes its central charge in this way, " 'Theologies of liberation' especially tend to misunderstand or to eliminate, namely: the transcendence and gratuity of liberation in Jesus Christ, true God and true man; the sovereignty of grace; and the true nature of the means of salvation, especially of the church and the sacraments."[74]

After acknowledging the aspiration for liberation in Latin America as a principal "sign of the times," the document notes that expressions of this aspiration must be discerned carefully. This discernment requires that the biblical and magisterial teachings on liberation and sin be understood correctly. In contrast to these, liberation theology is characterized as "tempted to emphasize, unilaterally, the liberation from servitude of an earthly and temporal kind... to put liberation from sin in second place."[75] This temptation is so great that, under the heading "A New Interpretation of Christianity," the document declares, "To some it even seems that the necessary struggle for human justice and freedom in the economic and political sense constitutes the whole essence of salvation."[76] Therefore, the document's critique of the liberation-salvation relationship warns of "the temptation to reduce the gospel to an earthly gospel."[77]

The document speaks much more favorably of the preferential option for the poor, noting its appearance in magisterial documents and its consistency with the biblical message. It even lauds theologies of liberation for restoring to a place of honor the texts of the prophets and of the Gospels in defense of the poor, although it then laments that they "go on to a disastrous confusion between the poor of Scripture and the proletariat of Marx. In this way they pervert the Christian meaning of the poor."[78] Ultimately, if the option for the poor leads to a hermeneutic priority on the political dimension of human liberation, then the document sees dire consequences for understanding salvation in Jesus Christ.

> One is led to deny the radical newness of the New Testament and above all to misunderstand the person of our Lord Jesus Christ, true God and true man, and thus the specific character of the salvation he gave us, that is above all liberation from sin. . . . An exclusively political interpretation is thus given to the death of Christ. In this way its value for salvation and the whole economy of redemption is denied.[79]

Finally, the emphasis on praxis also represents a serious impediment to the correct understanding of the nature of Christian salvation. While the document does affirm that traditional theology has always maintained a practical as well as speculative orientation, it condemns as Marxist the claim that "analysis is inseparable from the praxis and from the conception of history to which this praxis is linked." Class struggle means the implicit denial of "the transcendent character of the distinction between good and evil."[80]

Many observers incorrectly view the Vatican documents of the 1980s as a condemnation of liberation theology. This mistake is due in part to a nagging rhetorical device in the documents themselves. They consistently warn about the possible dangers and temptations of liberation theology without ever condemning a single author or text. So while they might represent a close of a chapter in liberation theology's history, the Vatican documents do not signal liberation theology's demise nor the end to consideration of the important themes it raises.

Our study thus far indicates that the Vatican's criticisms represent merely a first salvo in an ongoing conversation concerning how best to speak about the gracious, salvific relationship between God and humanity. The CDF's *Instruction* sums up the "first generation" of suspicion directed toward liberation theology: that concern for liberation "horizontalizes" Christian salvation, that one interpretation of the option for the poor reduces Christ's salvific activity and message to the "merely" historical, and that the emphasis on praxis reduces Christian discipleship to Marxist class struggle.

These admonitions would not just generate response from the first generation of liberation theologians, but would provide a point of entry for the second generation as well.[81] In the case of Ellacuría, the 1984 *Instruction* appears at the peak of his professional activity. The Salvadoran civil war was raging. Ellacuría was rector (president) of the Jesuit university and writing some of his most significant theological essays, essays that would define his historical soteriology. Yet before one can grapple with the period of Ellacuría's mature theological production, some attention to his background and development is necessary.

The Development of a Liberation Theologian

Early Formation: From the Basque Country to El Salvador

Biographical materials on Ellacuría are generally organized around the geographical shifts in Ellacuría's life and the mentors associated with those journeys.[82] Starting with his entrance into the Society of Jesus as a seventeen-year-old in the Basque country, Ellacuría left the heart of the Jesuit world in Loyola, the birthplace of St. Ignatius, as part of a small contingent sent to Central America. There Ellacuría encountered the first of his great mentors, the novice master Miguel Elizondo. Elizondo instilled an appreciation in the young novices for the native peoples of Central America, and a central lesson about inculturation: to bring the gospel, one must understand their living conditions, their suffering. As one novice was to comment years later, "Those who came here as [older] priests died as Spaniards — something it would be hard to say of those of us who came here as eighteen-year-olds."[83] Ellacuría would eventually immerse himself in El Salvador's reality, even adopting Salvadoran citizenship, but first he and the others had to complete their Jesuit formation.

After completing the novitiate, Ellacuría began his period as a "scholastic," studying the humanities and philosophy from 1950 to 1955 in Quito, Ecuador. Ellacuría's intellect began to surface there under the tutelage of an Oxford-trained classical scholar, Aurelio Espinosa Pólit. Espinosa, a specialist in Sophocles and Virgil, also had interests in early and contemporary Ecuadorian novelists and wrote on theology and philosophy. An occasional poet, he also advised the Ecuadorian government on cultural affairs. He modeled the sort of diversity of commitments, in multiple fields, that Ellacuría would eventually adopt. Espinosa enlivened history, science, literature, and philosophy, and Ellacuría had the sort of brilliance that could plunge into all of these fields and be successful.[84]

Ellacuría returned to El Salvador to complete his regency (the three-year period during which Jesuits in formation are assigned to work in an apostolate). After teaching in the seminary there for three years, he departed for Europe to complete his theological studies for ordination. In 1958, he traveled to Innsbruck, Austria, and met the third of his great mentors, Karl Rahner.[85] Though the subject of Rahner's influence on Ellacuría requires an extensive analysis of its own, it might best be summarized in two of Rahner's groundbreaking insights.[86] The first involves the notion of grace. Rahner belongs to that generation of theologians that was rethinking the neo-scholastic distinction and opposition between nature and grace, the natural and supernatural.[87] Developing the dynamic notion of grace as God's self-communication to humanity, Rahner refers to the notion of a "pure nature" without grace as a "remainder concept." Human beings, by the very fact that they were created, and created with an openness to receive God's self-revelation (as "hearers of the word"), are constituted by grace.[88] In a sense, Rahner reinforces Elizondo's lesson regarding inculturation, and Espinosa's concerning the openness to all the humanities, for these all flow from a wide perception of grace, of God's presence. It suggests that Rahner helped his fellow Jesuit, Ellacuría, adopt the old Ignatian axiom, "finding God in all things."

The other component of Ellacuría's studies with Rahner was the excitement of the time leading up to the Second Vatican Council. As one classmate later reported, "Rahner would give us a class one day, finish the class, and get on an airplane to Rome in order to repeat this same class to two thousand bishops. Afterward he'd come back to us and tell us what the bishops had asked him."[89] Rahner's experience of communing with the bishops of the world deepened his reflections on the Catholic Church as a world church and on the historical nature of God's self-revelation.[90] One can see this influence in the council's two great constitutions: *Lumen gentium* and *Gaudium et spes*. It was the latter document that had particular influence on Ellacuría and other Latin American theologians, with its declaration that the church must become aware of the profound suffering in the world, and must, in its efforts to spread the gospel, address the pressing social issues of the age, such as poverty and war.[91]

Though Ellacuría completed the long process of formation having been influenced by these great figures, he had not yet met his most significant intellectual mentor. After his ordination on July 26, 1961, while spending time in Bilbao, Ellacuría decided to pursue his doctorate under the great Basque philosopher Xavier Zubiri. This was no easy task. After Zubiri's departure from the University of Barcelona in 1942, occasioned in part because of conflicts with pro-Franco elements within the university, he elected to limit his teaching to private *cursos* he held in Madrid.[92] Though no longer formally associated with the university, Zubiri allowed Ellacuría to make special arrangements to complete his doctoral studies at the Universidad Complutense of Madrid, with Zubiri himself as his director. In Ellacuría, Zubiri discovered not just a student, but a collaborator. Their collaboration began during Ellacuría's studies, 1962–67, and ended only with Zubiri's death in 1983.[93]

Ellacuría's studies with Zubiri occurred not just at a formative time in Ellacuría's intellectual life, but also in Zubiri's. For 1962 saw the publication of one of Zubiri's major works, *Sobre la esencia*.[94] A significant moment in Zubiri's career-long attempt to develop a position critical of the excesses he identified in both idealism and realism, this work reconsidered the notion of essence, identifying it as a "structural moment" of the real.[95] While the development of the category of reality (*la realidad*) marked his significant philosophical contribution, Zubiri's thought also possessed an important theological moment. Humans, he claimed, are immersed in reality, but reality is also re-ligated, "tied back to," that which we call God.

Zubiri's insights had a profound and lasting effect on Ellacuría, whose own philosophy and theology turned to reality considered as historical reality.[96] This insight served both to coalesce the different influences on Ellacuría's thought and to drive him forward in shaping his distinctive contributions. Theologically, one can identify a notion of grace operative in Ellacuría's development: in Elizondo's respect for the peoples of Central America, in Espinosa's appreciation for all of the humanities, in Rahner's articulation of the human person and the self-communication of God, and in Zubiri's formulation of reality and *religación*. All of these strands found their way into Ellacuría's consideration of historical reality and the salvation offered in the gospel. Upon completing his doctorate in 1967, Ellacuría returned to El Salvador, the historical reality in which he would dedicate the remainder of his life to proclaiming and manifesting the good news.

Before turning to that most important period in Ellacuría's biography, one must note that Ellacuría had the opportunity to remain in Spain for the remainder of his career. Zubiri enthusiastically petitioned the Jesuit superior general, Pedro Arrupe, to allow this brilliant student to remain as his collaborator. Ellacuría's superiors determined, however, that his presence in Central America was too important. Therefore, they decided that Ellacuría would spend academic years in El Salvador, leaving summers to collaborate with Zubiri. Ellacuría enthusiastically received this assignment, which entailed sacrificing the peaceful intellectual pursuits of Europe for the difficult conditions and reality of life in El Salvador.

Immersion in El Salvador

Ellacuría's return to El Salvador coincided with a period of reflection on the Jesuit mission in Central America.[97] His intellectual reflection on historical reality fused with the discipleship of Ignatian spirituality in the 1969 meeting that Ellacuría co-directed, with his old novice master, Miguel Elizondo. Using the structure of Ignatius's *Spiritual Exercises,* Ellacuría pondered the mission of the Society in light of the *Exercises'* First Week meditation on sin. This meditation focused on sin not only because of its importance for any Christian reflection, but because "in it one finds a theological principle, and a practical principle of spirituality, in order to understand our mode of acting in a Christian way."[98] Coming on the heels of the landmark Latin American Bishops' Conference held in Medellín the previous year, Ellacuría's presentation mirrored CELAM's reflections on structural sin by tying the Jesuits' mission to a confrontation with the radical sin of injustice and poverty. This concept of sin inspired a distinctive understanding of salvation history and discipleship.[99]

The early 1970s brought dual responsibilities for Ellacuría — as an academic, publishing his first major book, and as a religious, serving as director of formation for Central American Jesuits. The latter work brought him into contact with yet another important figure, the Jesuit superior general (and fellow Basque) Pedro Arrupe.[100] Not without conflict, Ellacuría would learn much from his relationship with Arrupe. He recognized in Arrupe the attempt to have the Society of Jesus adopt the *aggiornamento* that John XXIII had called for the entire Roman Catholic Church in the Second Vatican Council. This attempt led to those changes made during the General Congregation XXXII of the Society of Jesus in 1975, which defined the focus of all Jesuit ministries as "the service of faith and the promotion of justice."[101]

Moreover, Arrupe incarnated Ignatian spirituality in a way that recognized the promotion of justice as an intrinsic part of living Christian faith, a crucial task particularly for those Jesuits living and ministering in the unjust conditions of Central America. Ellacuría's tenure as director of formation lasted only five years, with many in the province, above all its older members, hostile to the content and unrelenting force of Ellacuría's leadership. The principle of discipleship developed at that time, however, would last his entire career and inspire a particular vision of the Jesuit educational mission as fidelity to the national reality and plight of the poor.[102]

In the 1970s, Ellacuría realized his first significant work both in academic publishing and growing responsibilities at the university. The year 1973 saw the publication of Ellacuría's first major theological work, *Teología política,* a collection of essays that would prove controversial. Though the first part of the work contained noteworthy theological reflections on the notion of salvation history and salvation in history, it was the latter part, an investigation into the nature of violence, that drew the most attention. Following other liberation theologians' reflections on poverty and injustice as a "first violence," Ellacuría did not disqualify outright the attempt by some Christians to confront this violence with violence of their own.[103] The controversy over his work only intensified when, in 1976, he became editor of the journal *Estudios Centroamericanos* (ECA). When an early and rather timid attempt at agrarian reform was abandoned that year due to pressure from wealthy landowners, Ellacuría published, "A sus ordenes, mi capital" (At your service, my capital), a piece that shows the sometimes scathing manner with which he would treat perceived injustice.[104]

Ironically, while some of the young Jesuits criticized Ellacuría for emphasizing study at the university over direct activism, Salvadoran newspapers labeled him a communist. Ellacuría was profoundly committed to a form of discipleship that sought justice for the poor of El Salvador; this did not, however, imply a purely activist, much less revolutionary, mode. To those young Jesuits yearning to leave studies behind and be "with the people," Ellacuría often reminded them of the importance of doing theology "*at* desk, not *from* a desk."[105] For him, the work of UCA in shedding light on the national situation represented one of the most effective forms of service to the poor majority. His opponents apparently agreed with him, bombing the UCA several times in 1976.

Ellacuría's increasing criticism of the government and military reflected a corresponding deterioration in their respect for human rights, and even for the church. In March of 1977, the same year that the International Theological Commission published its *Declaration on Human Development and Christian Salvation,* assassins killed the Jesuit priest Rutilio Grande. The government did not allow Ellacuría, away on one of his periodic trips to Spain, to return to El Salvador until August of the following year. A campaign of intimidation and violence against the church continued in the following years. The end of the decade witnessed two significant moments that changed Ellacuría's life: in 1979, he assumed the role of rector at the UCA; and in 1980, the last of Ellacuría's great influences, Archbishop Oscar Romero, was assassinated. Though Ellacuría would spend the next decade thinking through Romero's powerful legacy, the immediate result of the assassination was Ellacuría's second exile to Spain, this time because his name was found on a list of targets for assassination. The exile did permit Ellacuría to assist Zubiri in completing his magnum opus, *Inteligencia sentiente.*

When appointed archbishop in February of 1977, Romero seemed an unlikely influence on Ellacuría. Years earlier, Romero, a conservative bishop and member of Opus Dei, denounced efforts at the Jesuit high school to educate its students about the plight of the poor.[106] He also played a key role in removing the Jesuits from the diocesan seminary. Yet the assassination of Rutilio Grande, occurring only three weeks after Romero's installation as archbishop, seemed to transform him. In a step of great humility, Romero asked for advice from the Jesuits as to how the church should respond to the assassination. Many of the Jesuits, including Jon Sobrino and Ellacuría, later cited this moment as the beginning of their reconciliation with Romero and a profound shift in Romero's own spiritual journey.[107]

Romero came to symbolize for Ellacuría the manner in which the church should carry out its mission. Romero, taking "Sentir con la Iglesia" (To be of one mind/heart with the church) as his episcopal motto, became consumed with discovering the reality of the country and asking the difficult questions: Why the suffering? Why the disappearances? Why the killing of demonstrators? Why so much violence?[108] To the people of Aguilares (where Rutilio Grande worked), he said, "We suffer with those who have suffered so much, we are truly with you, and we want to tell you, my brothers, that your pain is the pain of the church."[109] Romero called these poor the image of Christ crucified on the cross. In response, one of the Jesuits said, "To tell afflicted *campesinos* that they are Christ today in history, and to tell them that sincerely, is the most radical way a Christian has of restoring to them at least their dignity, and helping them maintain their hope."[110]

Sadly, an assassin silenced this voice of consolation. On March 24, 1980, a single bullet pierced the heart of Oscar Romero while he celebrated mass. In a homily delivered only a few days after the assassination, Ellacuría declared, "With Monsignor Romero, God passed through El Salvador."[111]

Negotiating a Peace

After Romero's assassination, Ellacuría plunged into the work of the UCA and its analysis of El Salvador's reality — a reality that by this time included civil war. Not only had groups like the FMLN (Frente Farabundo Martí para la Liberación Nacional) and the FDR (Frente Democrático Revolucionario) coalesced as a violent revolutionary movement, but with the election of Ronald Reagan as U.S. president, the Salvadoran national security forces received substantial increases of military aid.[112] Early on, Ellacuría concluded that neither side of this violent conflict represented the true interests of the poor majority, even though these poor paid the most in terms of suffering and lives lost. Ellacuría asserted a position he would continue to advocate until his death: he called for the emergence of a "third force" (besides the military and the guerrillas) made up of civil organizations, laborers, etc. — a force not only to call for a negotiated peace to the hostilities, but to arrive at a peace based on social justice.[113]

Though early on in his career Ellacuría had not condemned outright the concept of revolutionary violence, he devoted the remaining years of his life to working for a negotiated settlement of the civil war. A prime example of this negotiation came in the wake of the 1985 kidnapping of President Napoleón Duarte's daughter, Inés. Despite pressure from the U.S. not to negotiate with the guerrillas, Ellacuría and Archbishop Rivera y Damas facilitated her release in exchange for political prisoners, thereby averting a possible explosion of violence. As Phillip Berryman notes, "When the complex negotiations threatened to break down, it was Ellacuría who skillfully proposed alternatives and deserved a good deal of the credit for the eventual solution."[114]

In his final years, Ellacuría maintained a schedule that was daunting. His teaching and administrative work continued at the UCA. He welcomed visitors to the university and accepted many invitations to speak, even debating Roberto D'Aubisson, reputed mastermind behind much death squad activity and the assassination of Archbishop Romero. He did all this while continuing his prolific writing. As one Jesuit remembers, "When he was asked to rest, Ellacuría responded that the people did not get rest from the war, nor from poverty."[115] Indeed, it remains unclear how long Ellacuría and the other Jesuits, such as Ignacio Martín-Baró and Segundo Montes, could have physically sustained their work had they not been cut down by assassins' bullets.

These tireless efforts, the years of formation, the contact with great mentors and influences, the intensity of El Salvador's structural injustice, and the tragedy of its civil war are the context of Ellacuría's theology. They are the book in which Ellacuría attempted to articulate a word of good news, of salvation. They are the complex factors that constitute Ellacuría's distinct contribution to the soteriological debate over liberation theology.

Ellacuría Enters the Debate:
A Preliminary Defense of Liberation Theology

As Ellacuría became more enmeshed in the various activities of the university and developed his distinctive liberation theology, it was inevitable that he would weigh in on those critiques most voiced by his Salvadoran opponents — the criticism of liberation theology coming from Rome. Having examined the first exchange in the conversation between liberation theologians and the Vatican's reservations earlier, the chapter now concludes with Ignacio Ellacuría's response to the Vatican documents.[116] In his defense of liberation theology, Ellacuría not only echoes many of the concepts articulated by his Latin American confreres, but invokes the significant themes and categories that permeate his entire theological enterprise. Thus, Ellacuría's response to the Vatican properly situates Ellacuría's place as a liberation theologian, confirms the soteriological character of the debate, and serves to introduce the more detailed analysis of his soteriology that will be taken up in the remainder of this study.

On one level, determining Ellacuría's response to the Vatican documents involves nothing more than citing those articles in which he specifically mentions any of the documents and offers either support, criticism, or analysis of the points in question. However, this represents merely a preliminary move in assessing Ellacuría's place in the soteriological debate identified in the chapter thus far. Since the Vatican documents make serious wide-ranging challenges to liberation theologians, a more comprehensive response to these challenges emerges only from the wider corpus of Ellacuría's writings. In a sense, his life's work constitutes a "response" to the challenges laid out in the Vatican documents, and indeed made by all of liberation theology's critics.

This chapter concludes by examining Ellacuría's explicit responses to the Vatican's documents as a way to identify the central points of Ellacuría's broader theological project. These responses confirm that soteriology represents the proper lens with which to analyze this debate. Echoing the major themes of his Latin American confreres — namely, the relationship between liberation and salvation, the preferential option for the poor, and the importance of praxis — Ellacuría signals both his continuity with these other liberation theologians and the distinctive manner in which he shapes his "historical soteriology."[117] Moreover, Ellacuría's responses indicate the philosophical, christological, and ecclesiological themes that characterize his entire theological *oeuvre*. Thus, the central points found in Ellacuría's response to the Vatican critiques will serve as an introduction to the content of his thought explored in the subsequent chapters.

Salvation and the Church of the Poor

Although Ellacuría did not issue an official response to the ITC declaration of 1977, he did publish an article on soteriology and ecclesiology that explicitly takes up the ITC's central criticisms and replies with themes characteristic of his entire theological project.[118] While Ellacuría acknowledges the generally supportive tone of the ITC, he indicates the weaknesses of its analysis on philosophical, christological, and ecclesiological grounds. Of course, the ITC's document represents only part of the context behind Ellacuría's theology in 1977. In March of that very year, the assassination of fellow Jesuit Rutilio Grande, along with an elderly man and young boy, marked the beginning of an intense campaign against priests, catechists, and others involved in pastoral work in El Salvador.[119] Therefore, behind his comments lie not just a theological defense, but the weight of theology done in the midst of persecution.

If Ellacuría can be thought of as composing a defense of liberation theology, then this defense begins with a preliminary definition of liberation theology itself.

> The theology of liberation understands itself as a reflection from faith on the historical reality and action of the people of God who follow the work of Jesus in announcing and fulfilling the Kingdom. It understands itself as an action by the people of God in following the work of Jesus and, as Jesus did, it tries to establish a living connection between the world of God and the human world.[120]

In this definition lie the seeds of Ellacuría's theological vision. He underscores the secondary nature of theology as a reflection on the lived experience of the church, but twins this reflection with that on "historical reality" as well. How Ellacuría understands this historical reality, particularly as a key component in the connection between God and humanity, indicates the manner in which he will explicate the liberation-salvation connection. He links this connection to the christological understanding of Jesus' mission, a mission that is inherited by the body of believers. Ellacuría takes up these themes in relation to the ITC's criticisms.

Ellacuría lauds the ITC for recognizing the connection between Christian salvation and what it calls "human promotion." Indeed, he views it as a vindication of liberation theologians over against "theologians of reaction" who have labeled their work "a digression and sociologizing deformation."[121] Yet he cannot accept the dualistic nature of the formulation "Christian salvation and human promotion," but seeks an organic unity. Throughout this essay, and indeed his theological work, Ellacuría strives to formulate the copula "and" in such a way that "there are not two levels of problems (the profane level on one hand, the sacred level on the other), neither are there two histories (a profane history and a sacred history), but only one level and one history."[122] This unity does not indicate a simple uniformity, but requires viewing what Ellacuría calls a "structural unity."[123]

Certainly, the unity that Ellacuría proposes does not overlook the profound disjunct between the nature of the world and that of the Reign of God, but like a previous generation that sought to overcome a reified distinction between nature and the supernatural, he searches for a non-reductionist integration. Ellacuría, with reference to the historical Jesus, views the effects of sin within a larger unity. "There are not two worlds incommunicado (a world of God and a human world); what there is instead — and what the same historical Jesus shows us — is the fundamental distinction between grace and sin, between the history of salvation and the history of perdition. Yes, both in the same history."[124] Indeed, the nature of Jesus' mission and proclamation of the Reign of God serves as a kind of touchstone for the unity of salvation and liberation, and of the ecclesiological mission that issues forth because of this unity.

Ellacuría's attempt to articulate perceived dualities not as dualisms, but as items possessing a structural unity, extends to his ecclesiology as well. He wishes to differentiate the mission of the Christian church from any specific political action while still advocating a profoundly political role for the church in the world. "The mission of the church is not the immediate fulfillment of a political order, but the fulfillment of the Reign of God."[125] The phrasing Ellacuría most often turns to is that of the church as a leaven in the world, or the church as a fundamental sign or sacrament of salvation. If this might suggest a possible conflation of salvation and liberation, Ellacuría finds recourse to negative language as a possible solution. "The history of salvation is meaningless if it does not include the sociopolitical dimension, which is an essential part but not the whole of it."[126] Thus, while not equating salvation with the sociopolitical, Ellacuría asserts their necessary connection.

Ellacuría uses the same kind of negative formulation when working out the nature of Christian life in relation to justice, the seeking of which he calls "the historical form of active love." While Ellacuría does not wish simply to baptize any action that claims to be seeking justice, he also cannot countenance the formulation of Christian discipleship without reference to justice. Ellacuría claims, "Not all struggles for justice are the incarnation of Christian love, but there is no Christian love without a struggle for justice when the historical situation is defined in terms of injustice and oppression."[127] So while Ellacuría will provide a theoretical framework in which to establish a connection between those poles indicated by terms such as "transcendent" and "immanent" elsewhere, his use of negative language here signals his concern to establish a unity for perceived dualities without creating dualisms.

The caution with which Ellacuría approaches the question of salvation applies to the manner in which he describes the relationship of liberation theology to Marxist thought. He denies that liberation theologians merely repeat the ideas of Marxist theorists. Rather, he first asserts the reality of the oppression faced by the majority of Latin Americans and then notes that this oppression can be analyzed using a number of theoretical instruments. As for liberation theology and Marxism, Ellacuría avers, "The same historical facts which the oppressed perceive as unjust oppression, and which Marxism interprets as the exploitation of human labor and as the consequences of that exploitation, are interpreted by faith and theology as the reality of sin and as an injustice that cries out to heaven."[128] For Ellacuría, Marxist thought may be useful when describing the historical reality of Latin America, but he gives it no more value than as a theoretical tool.

The notion that provides Ellacuría the clearest lens on the situation of Latin America, particularly that of El Salvador given the events of that year, is not Marxist theory but the crucified Christ. In one of Ellacuría's most significant theological contributions, he identifies the oppression of the third world as a "renewed crucifixion of Jesus Christ, who is present in the oppressed."[129] While he develops the notion of the "crucified people" elsewhere, here it serves to note how the reality of the poor provides a *locus theologicus* for liberation theologians.[130] The preferential option for the poor stems from the christological insight that revelation occurs in the "least ones," in those crucified today. The duality of oppression and liberation seen through the eyes of faith renders an understanding of the Christian message of salvation that involves liberation from the historical situation of oppression.

In short, Ellacuría's response to the ITC involves the attempt to correlate salvation and liberation by avoiding dualisms that would see them as distinct moments or levels of human experience. Ellacuría's use of negative language indicates that he does not wish to reduce salvation merely to a historical liberation, but conversely, he cannot posit the fullness of salvation without historical liberation. This understanding of salvation draws from a particular understanding of Jesus Christ and his mission. In the "historical" Jesus' mission, passion, and resurrection, which involve a confronting of injustice, a death, and hope mirrored in the poor of Latin America, Ellacuría links his understanding of salvation-liberation to the preferential option for the poor and directs them to Christian discipleship. If these reflections coincide with the beginning of a phase of persecution in El Salvador, then his subsequent responses to the Vatican not only show a development in his thought, but run concurrently to heightened persecution in the midst of El Salvador's civil war.

A Theological-Pastoral Response

Seven years after his response to the ITC's *Declaration,* a response nested within the argument of an article, Ellacuría responded to the CDF's *Instruction* not only adopting this method once again, but responding directly as well.[131] In tone and content, these responses echo much of Ellacuría's reaction to the earlier *Declaration.* Just as the CDF had increased the negative rhetoric against liberation theology, however, Ellacuría responds with a sharpened criticism of his detractors' assessments. While acknowledging that the CDF has pointed out salutary and even necessary theological themes in the writings of liberation theologians, Ellacuría goes on to identify the rhetorical and interpretive errors he sees in the CDF's *Instruction*. In particular, he takes aim at a methodology that signals no specific authors or written works, but rather refers to "some" liberation theologies that might have certain dangers associated with them. To address his concerns, Ellacuría conducts what he calls a "theological-pastoral" study, a study that once again, while referring especially to soteriological themes, lines up important philosophical, christological, and ecclesiological rejoinders to the critics.

Ellacuría addresses concerns about the Latin Americans' attention to "liberation" by focusing on how the term must be understood in a truly *theo*-logical manner, within an understanding of God's salvific activity in the world. Indeed, in perusing Roman Catholic ecclesial documents, Ellacuría identifies Paul VI's *Evangelii nuntiandi* as considering liberation in this truly theological manner.[132] So as the CDF *Instruction* defines liberation theology as "theological reflection centered on the biblical theme of liberation and liberty and over the urgency of its incidental practices,"[133] Ellacuría clarifies the nature of this "centering." While centering may mean "concentrating on," in the case of liberation theology it also means:

> to study all of the usual themes of theology, not even excluding the strictly Trinitarian, from a central perspective, which would be freedom-liberation. In this case, not even the freedom-from, that is, liberation, would be reduced to an exclusively sociohistoric liberation, and much less would a freedom-for or freedom-toward be reduced to obtaining an ordering of humanity in which social injustice could disappear.[134]

Ellacuría makes a case for centering on liberation as a manner to re-examine theological formulation without it necessarily being a reduction of theology. Indeed, the necessity lies in the positive contribution that such reflection makes.

In what emerges as a common trope for Ellacuría's other theological works, liberation theology accounts for poverty and social injustice in theological terms as a deformation of the Trinitarian presence in history. In underscoring the importance and necessity of liberation theology, Ellacuría defines as necessary "a theology that takes absolutely seriously this reality [of poverty] that negates divine paternity, supernatural filiation, and the animation of the Spirit."[135] Now the substance of his argument with the CDF concerns whether there are liberation theologies that understand liberation in a way that approaches theological reflection, and even Trinitarian reflection, in a reductionist manner.

Ellacuría takes the CDF *Instruction* as an important assertion that all theological reflection must be balanced, that Christian reflection on the mystery of salvation cannot exclusively focus on either the temporal or abstract. So while he agrees with the litanies of caution elaborated in the

Instruction, he does not view these as license "to dismiss the necessary connection between the Reign of God and human liberation."[136] In fact, since the *Instruction* insists on this necessary connection, Ellacuría briefly examines the dual deviations possible when considering Christology, ecclesiology, sacraments, the theological virtues, and Christian praxis. What troubles Ellacuría about the *Instruction* is that it appears to condemn only the temporal temptation and not the abstract. Moreover, it remains an open question to Ellacuría whether there are in fact any liberation theologians guilty of the dangers named in the document.

Since the CDF *Instruction* spends much of its time criticizing liberation theologians' use of Marxist thought, Ellacuría addresses this concern at length. Ellacuría disputes the attribution to Marxism of several necessary characteristics such as atheism, the denial of human rights, and an overly simplistic relation between praxis and theory. He disputes these not on theological grounds, but on basic methodological and factual ones. In his opinion, the CDF does not demonstrate a "scientific sobriety" in its analyses, analyses that do not differentiate different periods in Marx's development as a thinker, much less acknowledge the extraordinary diversity in the ways that Marxist thought has been appropriated in subsequent generations. In short, Ellacuría once again finds a limited usefulness in Marxist theory that makes it a helpful tool when appropriated critically.

Ellacuría identifies recent ecclesial reactions to Marxist thought by placing them on a spectrum that ranges from the CDF's unqualified rejection, and Paul VI's cautious reading, to John XXIII's openness to any elements of non-Christian thought that may be fruitful for Christian reflection. While Ellacuría appears most sympathetic to the open-reformist mode of the last position, he emphasizes that the demands of each historical moment indicate that at the very least one cannot decide on the value of Marxist analysis *a priori*. Each specific instance will determine the value (if any) of its use.[137] In the case of Latin American liberation theology, Ellacuría argues that the use of Marx peaked in the late 1960s and, referencing Clodovis Boff, even then represented a tool, not a *Weltanschauung*. So while Ellacuría acknowledges that the probable targets of the CDF's accusations are Gustavo Gutiérrez, Leonardo Boff, and Jon Sobrino, he unequivocally asserts that they are not guilty of said accusations.[138] In fact, noting the role of Latin American theologians' development and self-criticism, he concludes that the *Instruction* simply appears ten years too late.

Having addressed the accusations against liberation theology, a task negative in nature, Ellacuría discerns a way forward for the theology of liberation in a number of positive aspects that even the CDF acknowledges in its formulations. He lauds the CDF for recognizing that the poor should take their preferential place in theological reflection. This indicates an understanding of sin not only as interior, but as material and sociohistorical as well. For Ellacuría, cautious use of Marxist thought might aid in this process, a use that Ellacuría notes might also create points of crisis for Marxist thinkers as well. The preferential option for the poor indicates ways in which theological concepts should be historically realized, but it also indicates for Ellacuría the importance of maintaining a strong notion of transcendence. Ellacuría finds consolation in the fact that John Paul II himself has, in his address in Santo Domingo, supported some of the significant ideas of liberation theologians, such as the "preferential option for the poor" and the notion of "social liberation."[139]

If Ellacuría's "theological-pastoral" response to the CDF represents a more vehement defense of liberation theology, it corresponds to the more barbed criticisms found in the *Instruction*. Yet Ellacuría remains on familiar ground by indicating in his defense the importance of the salvation-liberation connection, the preferential option for the poor, and the way these two are related to Christian praxis. If these themes receive a defensive treatment in this response, his positive development of these ideas will not just indicate the ways in which Ellacuría's thought corresponds to that of other Latin American liberation theologians, but it will also signal the broader philosophical, christological, and ecclesiological themes of Ellacuría's soteriology. Thus, a sketch of this "positive" analysis will provide a thematic blueprint for the remainder of this study's exploration of his thought.

A Way Forward for Liberation Theology

Though Ellacuría's essay on the historicity of Christian salvation will receive attention in subsequent chapters, here it serves to link Ellacuría's explicit response to Vatican criticisms to his wider theological work. As such, this essay takes up the arguments made in previous responses to the Vatican challenges and places them in a soteriological context. Ellacuría emphasizes the difficult, but necessary, task of articulating both the historical and transcendent dimensions of Christian salvation without falling into dualisms. Of course, in the person of Jesus Christ, Ellacuría acknowledges the supreme form of the historical-transcendent connection for Christians. Yet he emphasizes not just the manner in which Jesus Christ's ministry, death, and resurrection indicate the manifestation of the divine life as the removal of sin, but also the importance of this divine option for the poor to Christian discipleship.

Ellacuría frames his argument as the attempt to understand the relationship of Christian salvation to historical liberation, a task that he believes will "clarify a fundamental point for the understanding of the faith and for the effectiveness of Christian praxis."[140] As in previous articles, Ellacuría finds in the Vatican documents an explicit recognition of liberation theology's achievements in this area, mentioning Hans Urs von Balthasar and Joseph Ratzinger as specifically offering words of approval.[141] After noting their recognition of liberation theology's significance, Ellacuría turns to address their concerns by positively formulating the fundamental ideas in his soteriology.

The Latin American liberation theologians focus on articulating the salvation-liberation connection in different ways; Ellacuría does so by drawing on a distinct notion of transcendence. For Ellacuría, transcendence "calls attention to a contextual structural difference without implying a duality; something that enables us to speak of an intrinsic unity without implying a strict identity."[142] If Ellacuría's earlier defense of liberation theology demonstrated concern for dualisms, then here he indicates that the way he will overcome that danger involves not just negative formulations, e.g., "salvation is not...," but a concept of transcendence that may coherently speak of the divine-human connection.[143]

Ellacuría's formulation of transcendence both indicates a defense of liberation theology and signals important differences among the liberation theologians. In particular, Ellacuría expresses concern that Clodovis Boff's formulation of theology "might cause a distorted image of the theology of liberation" because his distinctions could be reified as dualisms.

> The theology of liberation should not be understood as a political theology, but as a theology of the Kingdom of God, so that the material distinction between a T1 that deals with the classical themes of God, Christ, the church, and a T2 that deals with more specifically human and/or political themes, is not acceptable in itself.[144]

Ultimately, Ellacuría views this kind of formulation as leading to conceptual separations when speaking of the divine and human, salvation and liberation, faith and praxis. For Ellacuría, a careful notion of transcendence, particularly understood as a "transcendence in" rather than a "transcendence away from" provides a more fruitful path than Boff's distinction of subdisciplines.

Ellacuría's notion of transcendence represents a key to understanding the salvation-liberation connection in his thought, and indicates a philosophical approach reliant on more than Karl Marx. Indeed, in an essay that considers the fundamental themes of his soteriology, Ellacuría never alludes to Marx or Marxist thinkers nor employs Marxist categories. His notion of transcendence here derives explicitly from a "historical" reading of the Bible and cannot be understood without recourse to the phenomenology of Xavier Zubiri. In Zubiri's language about reality, and specifically that mode of Trinitarian presence in reality, one can see the roots of Ellacuría's understanding of salvation-liberation, transcendence, historical reality, and indeed the philosophical frame of his soteriology.

Ellacuría takes great care to understand the duality of central theological motifs as possessing a unity, and this approach affects the manner with which he understands Jesus Christ. Ellacuría suggests, "The New Testament clearly and specifically demonstrates the problem of historical transcendence by showing the what and the how of the relationship between God and humanity, between Christian salvation and human fulfillment."[145] Demonstrating this insight is a central problem for any soteriology. In its christological dimension, Ellacuría's soteriology views Jesus as "the supreme form of historical transcendence."[146] This form of transcendence in history undergirds a profoundly theo-logical understanding of the preferential option for the poor. Rather than simply indicating a human preference, the preferential option for the poor flows from an understanding of God's salvific acts in history. "Whoever makes contact with that people [the poor] and their state of prostration makes contact with the God who acts in history; ... theopraxy is the starting point of the process of salvation."[147]

Even Christian praxis or discipleship gets conditioned by Ellacuría's understanding of transcendence, his attempt to express the divine-human duality as indicating a fundamental unity.

> The total unity of a single history, of God in humanity and of humanity in God, does not permit the evasion of focusing on either extreme: only God or only humanity. But neither does it leave us with the duality of God and humanity; rather it affirms the dual unity of God *in* humanity and humanity *in* God.... Therefore it is not merely a political, or merely historical, or merely ethical praxis, but a transcendent historical praxis, which makes manifest the God who becomes present in the acts of history.[148]

Ellacuría formulates praxis as a contemplation-in-action that possesses a profoundly transcendent dimension. As a concept, it emerges from both his philosophical and christological convictions and indicates a strong ecclesiological sense of mission.

Conclusion

In the Gospel of Mark, a rich man asks Jesus the question, "What must I do to inherit eternal life?"[149] After summarizing the commandments, Jesus responds with a simple directive, "Go, sell what you have and give to the poor, and you will have treasure in heaven; and come, follow me."[150] A question concerning salvation prompts a response involving discipleship.

In this book, I claim that Ignacio Ellacuría's work represents a novel approach that draws out the essential connection between soteriology and discipleship. As a prelude to this claim, the details of Ellacuría's life portray a link between theological reflection on salvation and embodied practice of discipleship. Though Ellacuría left behind a vast and significant corpus of writings, his legacy involves more than scholarly output. His martyrdom culminates a priest's life, a life dedicated to following Jesus Christ in service of the poor majority of his country. That life of Christian discipleship, intimately related to his theological convictions, must be seen as soteriological action, a lived participation in the salvation offered by God through Jesus Christ. His martyrial performance prompts a further analysis of his theology's context and theoretical components.

This chapter has attempted to show that Ellacuría's theology belongs to that larger theological approach with which he self-identified, Latin American liberation theology. On the surface, this is an unremarkable claim. Ellacuría's status as a liberation theologian could be verified by his inclusion in many conferences, publications, and subsequent studies of the movement.[151] Though liberation theology's breadth justifies analysis from a multitude of perspectives, this study of Ellacuría contends that three theological emphases, central to liberation theology's articulation, form a constellation of ideas that revolve around a fundamentally soteriological core. These are the use of the terms "liberation" and "salvation," the preferential option for the poor, and the importance of praxis. These themes emerge from the attempt to proclaim the gospel of salvation to the poor, and they demand a way of life that participates in that process of salvation.

If the three themes indicate liberation theology's soteriological character, then the counterclaims found in the Vatican documents on liberation theology validate the claim that what is at stake in the debate is a rethinking of Christian salvation and its relationship to Christian discipleship. Whether it be attacks on its philosophical foundations, theological categories, or ecclesiological manifestations, the vigorous debates over liberation theology represent some of the most vital in contemporary theology. They demonstrate that vitality, I would maintain, because they go to the root of the Christian message: salvation in Jesus Christ and the manner in which to follow him.

The remainder of this study will build on the ideas present in Ignacio Ellacuría's defense of liberation theology. Though articulated in a seminal form, the central categories of his soteriology and account of Christian discipleship appear in Ellacuría's response to the Vatican's cautions. In each case, whether it be developing the philosophical view of transcendence that would undergird a coherent notion of liberation-salvation, articulating an understanding of Jesus Christ's salvific role and its relationship to the ones he calls the "crucified people," or emphasizing the necessary and sacramental function of historical Christian discipleship, Ellacuría's soteriology takes great pains to articulate the divine-human relationship inherent in these theological notions without conflation or separation.

While a previous generation of Catholic theologians wrestled with integrating the notions of nature and supernatural to produce a richer and more biblically faithful notion of divine grace, Ellacuría advances that project by trying to articulate Christian salvation in conjunction with his rich and dynamic understanding of historical reality. If God's grace means salvation for humanity, then Ellacuría's theology was devoted to understanding that salvation in its philosophical, christological, and ecclesiological dimensions in order to proclaim it as good news and to move others to shape a historical reality that more clearly reflected the Trinitarian presence of God.

Chapter Two

Principle and Foundation of
Ellacuría's Soteriology

J OHN O'MALLEY ASSESSES the beginning of Ignatius of Loyola's *Spiritual Exercises* in a way that sheds light on how to approach the theology of the Jesuit martyr Ignacio Ellacuría. He states:

The "Principle and Foundation" before that [First] Week presents considerations about the ultimate purpose of life and about the created universe as ordered to the praise, reverence, and service of God. The First Week follows with considerations about the heinousness of sin and the havoc it wreaks in the individual and in society.[1]

Commentators and critics often rush to assess Latin American liberation theology in terms of social structures, massive poverty, the struggle for justice, and other themes that point to the context of heinous sin from which this theology originates. Yet for all their merits such approaches tend to overlook the profoundly grace-centered theological view latent in the writings of many of these theologians. In the case of Ellacuría, any attention to questions of injustice and the affliction of the ones he called the "crucified people," occurs within a wider view of historical reality as graciously tied to the creating and saving Trinitarian God.

This chapter attempts to sketch what might be considered the "principle and foundation" for Ellacuría's soteriology. If the previous chapter suggested a view of soteriology that goes beyond the doctrine of redemption, then an accounting for this principle and foundation here assists in exploring Ellacuría's answers, whether explicit or implicit, to certain fundamental questions: Who or what is being saved? Who or what is the agent of salvation? From what is there need for salvation? How is liberation relevant? In what manner may one speak about the assumed "subjects" of these questions and their possible relation?

These questions suggest that for soteriology there exists a kind of frame, a basic understanding upon which a theologian relies in order to explore the relationships within the triad of human, God, and world. Within this frame, the Christian theologian attempts to articulate God's salvific relationship to

40

humanity in the world. Therefore, an exploration of Ellacuría's soteriology begins by identifying this frame and investigating the sources upon which Ellacuría draws to sketch and fill out this frame.

Analysis of this frame first involves a summary of Ellacuría's dynamic view of human existence installed in historical reality.[2] To accomplish this, one needs recourse to the influence of Ellacuría's mentor, Xavier Zubiri. In Zubiri's description of human intelligence as a "sentient intelligence," Ellacuría discovers a way to speak of human existence in a dynamic and profoundly interrelated sense. Where Zubiri strives to overcome a perceived separation of sense and intellect, particularly in modern idealism, Ellacuría seeks to portray human existence in a manner that does not pit the "individual" over against other persons, society, the world, or history. By understanding the human person within historical reality and its demands, Ellacuría offers a way out of the dilemma left in the wake of some versions of modern thought: either a reductionist view of an individual closed within history, or a reactionary escapist view of human transcendence that avoids the consequences and demands of life in this world.

Though these key elements bolster the assertion that Zubiri's influence on Ellacuría is properly identified as philosophical, there also exists a theological trajectory in Zubiri's thought that, though not as well-documented, represents a significant influence on Ellacuría's soteriology and its intellectual frame.[3] While Zubiri's philosophical realism concentrates on intra-mundane reality, his description of reality includes what he describes as a "theologal" dimension. This idea offers Ellacuría a way to talk about reality as created, as having a basic dimension that is "tied back" (re-ligated) to God without conceiving of God in reductionist terms.[4] This view of God's relation to humanity permits Ellacuría's soteriology to handle notions of transcendence and history without either conflation or opposition, and to speak coherently of a God who is both transcendent and intimately involved with the world.[5] Ultimately, it means a view of Christian discipleship understood as a participation in the Trinitarian life.

The manner in which Ellacuría describes human reality and God's transcendence constitutes, therefore, a principle and foundation of his soteriology, a way to speak of the created and graced universe ordered to the praise of God. So just as Ignatius of Loyola turns to consider sin in the first week of the *Exercises* after the principle and foundation, Ellacuría also assesses the sinful reality of his world and the need for salvation.[6] In his consideration of sin, Ellacuría transforms an essentially meditative, if not mystical, understanding of God's presence in graced creation into a prophetic acknowledgment of a world in dire need of God's salvific action.[7] Ellacuría's acknowledgment of El Salvador's, indeed the world's, reality as riven with sin animates his insights on the need for salvation and the form of Christian discipleship in the world. For him, this salvation cannot reach its fullness without human liberation.

With these critical pieces in place, the underlying thrust of Ellacuría's soteriology comes into view. Ellacuría attempts to articulate Christian salvation by overcoming dualisms latent in Western thought that threaten its true evangelical character. For salvation is not good news if humanity is separate from reality, God apart from the world, and liberation not part of the struggle against sin. Ellacuría treats the historical and transcendent in a way that neither conflates them nor separates them completely. In doing so, he takes up the challenge of describing God's gracious self-offer to a humanity thoroughly and constitutively immersed in historical reality. This reality lays bare humanity's profound need for salvation, and its call to, or even demand for, a form of discipleship that participates in that salvation. Understanding human existence within reality and its demands, viewing this reality as ultimately tied to God's presence, and discerning proper fidelity to reality — these three movements represent the principle and foundation of Ellacuría's theological vision and soteriology.

The Human Person — Reality Animal

In his reflections on salvation, Ellacuría continues along a trajectory mapped out by his teacher Karl Rahner and others of the previous generation: a move away from the extrinsic view of grace found in the reified neo-scholasticism of the late nineteenth and early twentieth centuries. However, for Ellacuría, overcoming the dualism inherent to a "pure nature" divorced from the supernatural represents only a first step. A coherent soteriology must overcome two other dualisms: a divide within the human being itself between sense and intellect, and the separation of the human person from reality.[8] Talk of salvation gets distorted if the one who receives salvation is merely a detached "thinking" subject, and if salvation is privatized or removed from historical reality. So while Ellacuría owes a great theological debt to Rahner, he moves away from the philosophical moorings of this mentor in German idealism to a philosophy that emphasizes that humans possess a basic and constitutive embeddedness or installation in reality in order to speak properly about the salvation offered them by God.

Ellacuría's perspective on the human person reflects the substantial influence of Zubiri's philosophy. Indeed, even though several figures must be counted as influences upon Ellacuría, his thought owes its greatest debt to this Basque philosopher.[9] While it is difficult to document this influence in its entirety, Ellacuría himself identifies its heart well when he notes:

> One should not forget that Zubiri's intellectual mission was not to correct the past, but to approach intellectually the reality of things as closely as possible. In his view, it was not sufficient to return to things if that return were to mean a reduction of those things to "being" or "meaning." One must return to the reality of things because anchored

in that reality, held by it, and also impelled by it one can reach the being and meaning, but as the being and meaning *of reality.*[10]

These lines signal the two important implications of Zubiri's thought that will help us examine Ellacuría's critical anthropology: the diagnosis of Western philosophy's central flaw as the separation of sense and intellect, and the ethical demands that emerge from the fact of human installation in reality. Moreover, by identifying humanity's relationship to reality as "anchored," "held," and "impelled," Ellacuría not only indicates the general demands placed on human beings, but gestures to the crucial elements that will characterize his method for Latin American theology.[11]

Ellacuría's philosophical-theological anthropology opposes the weaknesses latent in the construal of the "modern" subject: its hyper-individualism, its removal from history, its inner cleaving of sense and intellect.[12] One cannot divorce Ellacuría's human person from its constitutive dynamic interaction/immersion in reality. In discerning who the Christian disciple is, who it is that is being saved by Christ, Ellacuría considers the human being within the complex dynamism and web of relationships that constitute reality. For Ellacuría, human reality is personal and essentially open; it possesses individual and social dimensions. This human person finds itself in historical reality that is material, spatial, temporal, and biological, and because of this, talk of human salvation must also be rooted with this physico-biological orientation.[13] Though Ellacuría will talk of the fullness of salvation as metahistorical, he stresses that it must take root in history.

Though a complete study of Ellacuría's anthropology goes beyond the scope of this study, analysis of Zubiri's proposal of humans as possessing sentient intelligence in reality, and Ellacuría's contextualizing this human sentient intelligence in historical reality, illuminates the anthropological frame in which Ellacuría considers Christian salvation and discipleship. Because the basic tenets that undergird Zubiri's magnum opus, *Inteligencia sentiente,* offer an interpretive lens through which Ellacuría considers humanity, its existence, and the existence of the world theologically, it might be most helpful to begin this study with a description of Zubiri's great intellectual task: the attempt to surmount what he perceived as the separation of sense and intellect in the modern concept of human intelligence.[14]

Sentient Intelligence: Humanity Immersed in Reality

Zubiri's thought emerges from that period in the early twentieth century which held a profound dissatisfaction with the assumptions of modern science and philosophy. A restless and exacting mind, Zubiri took a leave of absence from his chair in the history of philosophy at the Universidad Complutense of Madrid to travel the various centers of learning in Europe and explore the many disciplines he deemed necessary components to a new and creative philosophical view.[15] These studies put Zubiri in contact with the most advanced work in mathematics and the sciences at the time, the insights from which were breaking down the reified assumptions of modern science.[16] Philosophically, it is no coincidence, then, that Zubiri turns a critical eye to what he takes to be the dominant mode of modern Western philosophy: idealism.

In the preface to *Inteligencia sentiente*,[17] Zubiri himself notes that this massive work on human intelligence arrives nearly twenty years after his previous significant text, *Sobre la esencia,* a work in which Zubiri explored the concept of reality.[18] The modern critic might see this as the correcting of a logical blunder, for one must account for the possibilities of human knowing itself before one can speak about knowing reality. While Zubiri acknowledges that an investigation of reality might require some concept of knowing, he refuses the idea that this concept of knowledge must necessarily precede. Rather than accepting the Kantian starting point of critique, Zubiri counters that no investigation of knowledge could be completed without a concept of reality either. In this rhetorical reversal lies the heart of Zubiri's philosophical project: to overcome the dangerous effects he sees stemming from the separation of sense and intellect in the Western philosophical tradition.

Zubiri attempts to forge a middle road between a realism that prioritizes reality over reason, and an idealism that prioritizes knowledge over reality. For Zubiri, "knowledge and reality are congeneric at their root."[19] This assertion counters a move that Zubiri traces as far back as Parmenides: namely, "that to know something intellectively is to know intellectively that it 'is.' "[20] In its modern form, this separation of sense and intellect, and the concomitant prioritizing of one over the other, appears in the Kantian legacy of separating the problems of metaphysics and epistemology. For Zubiri, philosophy as a task must address both of these problems simultaneously. Before any critique of knowledge or epistemology, Zubiri carries out an analysis of intelligence itself that attempts this balance without separation.

Instead of conceiving of human intellection as posterior to sensing, a process in which sensory perception of confused content is delivered to the intelligence that then sorts it out, Zubiri unifies the process under the name "sentient intelligence." When Zubiri refers to intelligence as "sentient," he does not mean the non-rational, or feeling (*sentimiento*), but more radically the senses or sensing (*sentidos/sensibilidad*). So the phrase "sentient intelligence" counters the idea of "sensible intelligence," Zubiri's designation of that earlier concept in which the senses merely offered material to intelligence. Zubiri avers, "Human sensing [*sentir*] and the act of intelligence [*inteligir*] are not only not opposed, but indeed, in their intrinsic and formal unity, constitute a single and unitary act of apprehension."[21] By this statement, Zubiri does not annul the differences between sensing and intellection, but merely highlights them as possessing a unity.

In the key summary statement of this philosophical vision, Zubiri says, "Human intellection is formally the mere actualization of the real in the sentient intelligence."[22] This definition consists of three key terms that best summarize Zubiri's attempt to account for human knowing as an integrated process of sensible-intelligible apprehension of reality. First, "intellection" signifies the attempt by Zubiri to overcome the "logification of intelligence," which identifies the task of intelligence primarily as predicating about data received from the senses. Second, "real" indicates his effort to counter the "entification of reality," which reduces reality to a mere subset of being. Finally, "mere actualization" signals the priority that Zubiri places on the dynamic encounter with reality that should lie at the heart of the philosophical task, with a reality not dependent on humans to make it real.[23]

When Zubiri considers intellection, his primary objective is to overcome what he describes as the logification of intelligence. This phrase indicates the tendency that Zubiri sees latent in Western philosophy to identify human intelligence primarily with what the mind as logos predicates about an object. It creates a separation between reality as sensed and reality as ideas, between human intellection and reality itself.

Zubiri traces this tendency back to Parmenides and Plato's *Sophist,* and states that it "culminated in the work of Aristotle, for whom the logos itself is the *apophanesis* of what a thing is."[24] While not denying the importance of logos (understood here as the mind's capacity to judge, affirm, conceive, etc.), Zubiri places priority on the "primordial apprehension" of reality as part of, not prior to, human intelligence, which would also include the functions of logos and reason.[25] What Zubiri terms "logification" should not be equated to what Jacques Derrida calls "logocentrism," the prioritization of the spoken word over the written word that grounds a metaphysics of absolute presence and origins.[26] Though there are similarities — for example, Zubiri's desire to overcome modern "dualisms" and Derrida's attempt to deconstruct the "binary oppositions" of structuralism — ultimately, they differ regarding the human access to reality. Zubiri's "sentient intelligence" is more than the semiological access to reality proposed by Derrida. For Zubiri, reality cannot be dependent on human knowing or the construal of meaning because it always possesses a character of what he terms *de suyo,* meaning a sense of "of itself," "its own-ness."[27]

For Zubiri and Ellacuría, human intelligence does not create reality, but finds itself in direct contact with, even confronted by, reality in sensible apprehension. The senses not only give us content but make reality formally present for us.[28] This does not imply a realism in which human knowing simply mirrors an exterior reality, because reality itself is not considered a "thing," but a formality.[29] Zubiri describes this apprehension as *de suyo.*[30] He associates with the human perception of reality what Thomas Fowler describes as "an overwhelming impression of its veracity, a type of 'guarantee' which accompanies it, that says to us, 'What you apprehend is reality, not a cinema, not a dream.' "[31] So human perception of reality has two aspects: what the apprehension is of, and its self-guaranteeing characteristic. For Zubiri, this corresponds to the *content* and *formality of reality,* respectively.

Primordial apprehension of reality represents the first of a three-part structure, not process, of knowing. Zubiri emphasizes the direct and immediate nature of this apprehension while affirming its complexity.[32] Apprehension has a variety of features, and these can be variable. Zubiri uses the example of a landscape that may consist of a variety of features but may still be apprehended unitarily. Even if one turns attention to a specific part of the landscape, it does not destroy or nullify the unitary apprehension. So one may distinguish two manners in which human beings can have this apprehension without nullifying the sentient primordial apprehension. Humans may use this apprehension as the basis of other intellections, or simply apprehend the real as real "in and by itself." "The intellection of the real in and by itself ... has its own 'modal' character, a primordial modality; the apprehension of something in and by itself is, modally, the primordial apprehension of reality."[33] This primary mode of intellection then implies humanity's basic and direct embeddedness in reality.

While Zubiri emphasizes primordial apprehension as the primary mode of human intellection in order to overcome the "logification" of intelligence, logos and reason emerge as ulterior modes of intellection that consist in a "stepping back" from direct embeddedness in reality. Though ultimately dependent on primordial apprehension, logos does allow for a fuller content in which reality is actualized more richly. Logos offers explanations of things vis-à-vis other things. Zubiri even terms logos a "re-actualization" within a field of what has already been actualized in primordial apprehension, as the discerning of real things within their reality field (*realidad campal*).[34] "Logos is a sentient intellection in which one declares dynamically, in the medium of reality within a field, what one thing is *in reality,* based on another."[35]

Reason involves the actualization of real things in worldly reality (*realidad mundanal*). While reason includes that which humans understand through further study and methodological explanation, it need not exclusively connote rational explanation. A number of activities and disciplines assist humans in apprehending reality as worldly reality, such as music, art, poetry, literature, and theology. A significant undercurrent to Zubiri's study is the modesty with which he describes human understanding. There is a strong sense in which reality goes beyond (*más allá*) what can be apprehended directly, immediately, and in a unitary fashion.[36] Certainly, this version of reason lies a great distance from a reductionist vision of reason as omnipotent in the face of mystery.

Zubiri uses the example of our perception of color to summarize sentient intellection.[37] In the primordial impression of reality, we apprehend that a color is real, that the color is its own reality. As logos, we also apprehend that this color is in reality with respect to other colors or other qualities. For example, we know a color as "red." Finally, as reason, we also apprehend that this red color is real with respect to pure and simple reality itself; for example, that it is a photon or an electromagnetic wave.[38] Zubiri's conception of sentient intelligence valorizes human sensing as part of the structure of intellection. No bridge between human thought and reality is necessary because human intellection, as sentient intelligence, is already installed in reality. As Ellacuría avers, "It remains clear that true reality is not reached by escaping the senses, annulling the sensorial life; on the contrary, it is reached by putting the senses into full and fecund use."[39]

As a Roman Catholic theologian, Ellacuría will explicate discipleship as a full and fecund manifestation of human existence in historical reality. Building on Zubiri's notion of sentient intelligence, Ellacuría conceives of human intelligence as a fundamentally biological activity. While he acknowledges that intelligence possesses a structure proper to it, Ellacuría views it as being in primary unity with humanity's other biological features. "The human being's total physical reality is the primary reality from which the human apprehends intelligently (*intelige*), knows (*conoce*), and understands (*entiende*)."[40] Whatever heights the exercise of intelligence may reach, it never loses its sentient and biological orientation. This indicates the way that human beings, as real, are intrinsically related to other real things, but not at the expense of multiplicity and difference. Just as Ellacuría proposes that intelligence itself possesses a primary unity with a differentiation of features, so he identifies a unity-in-difference to reality itself.[41]

With Zubiri's notion of sentient intelligence, Ellacuría avoids the distortions to Christian discipleship that emanate from a prioritization of either sensing or thought. The human being is no longer internally dual, but possesses a unified faculty of sentient intelligence. Moreover, because the function of this unified faculty of sentient intelligence is the actualization of the real, Ellacuría emphasizes that philosophical and theological reflection on Christian salvation and discipleship must be tied to historical reality.

By grounding human intelligence in reality, Ellacuría hopes to evade those dangers inherent in idealist views without succumbing to a closed materialism.[42] In this, Ellacuría demonstrates awareness of what Zubiri identified as the second grave error of reductionist idealism, the "entification of reality."[43] If the "logification of intelligence" refers to a reduction of human intelligence to the function of *logos*, then the "entification of reality" identifies how entity (*ente*) and being (*ser*) have displaced reality in philosophy.[44] This entification follows from "logification" because if intellection is subsumed under logos, then that which is understood is termed "being," not reality. In Zubiri's work, this displaces reality as simply a mode of being. For Ellacuría, "entification" leads to escapism. "Humans are led astray from the exigencies of reality to the possible illusions of being, where being is not rooted in reality."[45] Overcoming the entification of reality involves a fidelity to reality that counteracts deceptive ideology and clearly discerns the ethical demands inherent in human existence.

Ellacuría inscribes this insight into a theological method that takes seriously the demands of reality. Just as Zubiri described sentient intelligence as a unified action of interrelated moments, so Ellacuría articulates the human encounter with reality as possessing a threefold, interdependent character.

Ultimately, Ellacuría employs this theological method to envision human participation in salvation as active and dynamic while maintaining the transcendent and divine nature of that salvation.

Apprehending and Engaging Reality

The notion of intelligence as related to physical reality, a direct legacy of Zubiri's view of sentient intelligence, leads Ellacuría to a key definition of intelligence and human existence:

> The formal structure and differentiating function of intelligence, within the structural context of human features and the permanent biological character of the human's unity, is not one of comprehending being or capturing meaning, but rather that of apprehending reality and confronting oneself with it [*enfrentarse con ella*].[46]

In order to illustrate the implications of this apprehension and confrontation with reality, Ellacuría employs the Spanish noun *cargo* and its verbal forms whose range of meaning includes carrying a duty, burden, or load. In doing so, he explicates the significance of the emphasis on reality. If Zubiri's work represents a philosophical overcoming of the "logification of intelligence" and the "entification of reality," then Ellacuría generates an understanding of humanity-in-reality that undergirds his theological attempt to describe human salvation (soteriology) and human participation (discipleship) in that salvation. For Ellacuría, the encounter with real things in reality possesses three dimensions: noetic, ethical, and praxis-oriented.[47]

Ellacuría describes the noetic dimension of the confrontation with reality as "realizing the weight of reality" (*el hacerse cargo de la realidad*).[48] The phrase connotes a full accounting of reality, a knowing of reality that goes beyond an idealistic picture of a detached subject accumulating objective data. Ellacuría utilizes the Zubirian notion of sentient intelligence to assert that humans must be willing to exert the effort (scientific, philosophical, etc.) to know reality as it really is.[49] Realizing the weight of reality, as an active and engaged *noesis*, performs the task that Ellacuría calls "historicization." Namely, it establishes the relationship of a concept to historical reality. The process of historicization often unmasks ideologies that hide or disfigure reality. In his soteriology, Ellacuría will often refer to prophecy as that proper realizing of the weight of reality.

As a moment of theological method, realizing the weight of reality indicates a theological discernment of both the graced and sinful character of reality. It involves elaborating the revealed truths of the Christian faith in, and not opposed to, historical reality. This does not imply a reduction of those truths, but a view of transcendence in history. As such, it not only identifies reality as created, but also as hoping for salvation. Naming the sin of the world, accounting for its pernicious effects, and discerning the steps toward a liberation from this sin in its removal from reality represent the other side of realizing the weight of reality.

A second dimension of human engaging of reality consists in "shouldering the weight of reality" (*el cargar con la realidad*), an ethical correlative to the noetic realizing of its weight. If human beings, in sentient intelligence, have the ability to apprehend what reality is and what it demands, then this indicates a fundamental ethical demand of intelligence. This demand would not exist if historical reality were somehow extrinsic to human beings. In particular, reality offers humans the opportunity to make genuine commitments by where they locate themselves within reality and respond to its demands. The human engagement with real things in reality occurs in a specific location, a location that both influences and is influenced by the noetic dimension.

Theologically, shouldering the weight of reality indicates the importance of the preferential option for the poor in terms of locating oneself in the place that affords the greatest access to the real. For Ellacuría, the primary instantiation of the option for the poor rests in the incarnation, ministry, preaching, and passion of Jesus Christ. Yet too often this option has been "spiritualized" so that its historical character either diminishes or disappears. Therefore, Ellacuría's Christology focuses on the historical character of Jesus' ministry and death that serves as the principle and model for disciples' shouldering of the weight of reality. Moreover, he recognizes a historical continuation of that definitive moment — the crucifixion of Jesus — in the contemporary crucifixion of the world's poor. They function, in part, as that location where God chooses to reveal Godself in weakness. Their shouldering of reality's weight, of the sins of the world, calls others to shoulder that weight in the hope of resurrection.

A third dimension of the confrontation with reality, "taking charge of the weight of reality" (*el encargarse de la realidad*), makes explicit Ellacuría's understanding of intelligence as praxical. Ellacuría speaks about assuming the responsibility to transform reality through action. The human confrontation with reality involves the responsibility to ensure that reality is as it should be.[50] This action, or praxis, transforms reality and correlatively transforms the human being as well.

Theologically, conversion, prophecy, and discipleship correspond to this taking charge of the weight of the reality. Of course, given his understanding of reality as dynamic and interrelated, Ellacuría does not advocate a mere activism, but a personal and ecclesial participation in transformation of historical reality. Far from being a contemporary Pelagian, Ellacuría views the taking charge of reality's weight as a sacramental participation in the life-giving Trinitarian presence in the world.[51]

In explicating the three dimensions of the confrontation with reality, Ellacuría provides a dynamic view of human existence that relies upon the philosophical insights of Zubiri. Ellacuría underscores the importance of Zubiri's work as a response to a philosophical tradition that seems able neither to confront (*enfrentarse*) reality, nor to realize its weight (*hacerse cargo*).[52]

This invocation of the terminology that Ellacuría has coined for Latin American theological method demonstrates how Zubiri's philosophy is inscribed in Ellacuría's own theology. Where Zubiri develops the theory of sentient intelligence to overcome the problems that he identifies as logification and entification, Ellacuría brings out the demands of the confrontation with reality to map his theological method, grounding soteriology and discipleship in reality. In supporting Zubiri's diagnosis of the twin problems in modern idealistic thought, Ellacuría reveals his own critical relationship to the tradition of thought stemming from the Enlightenment.

In order to contrast Zubiri with Enlightenment thinkers, Ellacuría identifies the thought of Descartes and Kant as insufficiently critical precisely in neglecting to consider the unitary act of intellection before distinguishing between sensing and intellect. Yet Ellacuría does not see in Zubiri a nostalgic attempt to do philosophy in premodern terms.[53] Knowing how influential Kant's thought was to Zubiri, Ellacuría reformulates the three famous questions attributed to Kant in terms of reality to demonstrate Zubiri's critical difference. So "What can I know? What should I do? In what can I hope?" become "What is reality? In what does the act of intelligence (*inteligir*) consist? What access to God might there be?"[54]

These questions are meant to indicate the manner in which Zubiri's philosophy leads to something deeper than the "anthropological subjectivism" of much modern thought. For Ellacuría, it leads to a view of human existence immersed in reality that makes profound ethical demands. Far from a reified modern subject, Ellacuría's historical human being lives, moves, and breathes within the dynamic web of relationships that constitute reality (and thus, the human being as well). Ellacuría forges a new anthropology that overcomes dangerous dualisms and opens to the importance of history. Understood theologically, this view of humanity indicates that human salvation and the human practice of discipleship must be seen in their most *real* sense.

There exists a type of hermeneutic circle at work in the human engagement with reality. This circle, however, is not one merely of meaning or understanding, but of reality itself. Activity (the praxis-oriented moment) transforms reality, implying both a new reality to realize (noetic) and a new place to shoulder its weight (ethical). Of course, mention of *praxis,* a term so important in the Marxist lexicon, signals the critiques levied against Latin American liberation theology regarding materialist reductionist views of human activity. Yet these accusations ignore the fact that Ellacuría's framework includes both a dynamic view of intramundane reality and a view in which reality possesses a "theologal" dimension in which the transcendent God, who cannot be described as another thing in reality, remains thoroughly involved with the world. If that is the case, then human activity does not necessarily collapse into a strictly historical, intramundane project. Therefore, to make good on these claims, attention now turns from Ellacuría's view of humanity in reality to how he speaks about the God who creates, sustains, and ultimately saves reality.

God Transcendent "in" History

In a tribute written shortly after Zubiri's death, Ellacuría dubs him a theologal philosopher.[55] Ellacuría concludes his elegiac piece by praising Zubiri for knowing that

> neither the question of humanity, the question of history, nor the question of humanity's salvation and history can be considered adequately without keeping the theologal dimension in mind; that dimension in which the human being is more than himself or herself in a religated way, simultaneously, in each moment a pilgrim overwhelmed by the power of the real.[56]

These lines both underscore Zubiri's important philosophical influence on Ellacuría and intimate an important aspect of this influence generally overlooked by commentators.[57] For Zubiri provides Ellacuría with not just a fundamental vocabulary and set of concepts in his account of reality, an influence one might describe as philosophical, but also a way to speak about God in relation to the world — to use his term, a theologal influence — that deepens Ellacuría's historical soteriology.

Identifying this theologal influence provides insight into Ellacuría's hermeneutic for biblical texts that vividly portray God's salvific activity on behalf of humanity. Zubiri's concept of the theologal suggests a manner for speaking of God's salvific activity without diminishing the sense of divine transcendence crucial to the Christian tradition as well.[58] If Zubiri's notion of transcendence represents an important influence, it is because this notion allows for "non-contrastive" theological discourse, discourse that avoids either collapsing the divine into history or setting up an opposition.[59]

The implications for Ellacuría's soteriology are twofold. First, since critics have attacked liberation theologies precisely for their alleged reduction of transcendence, Ellacuría's use of Zubiri's work indicates one possible manner in which liberation theologians may maintain a strong sense of God's immanence without surrendering to an immanentism. By initiating theological reflection in a reading of reality's "fundament," Ellacuría takes advantage of the ways that Zubiri's thought overcomes dualisms pervasive in modernism's oppositions and speaks of God's "transcendence-in" history. Second, Zubiri's language helps Ellacuría speak about salvation — positively as presence of the Trinitarian God, who is the source of life and fulfillment, and negatively as liberation from sin that is social and historical as well as personal.

The Theologal Dimension of Reality

Zubiri's reflections on God commenced rather early in his writings and continued until the end of his life.[60] The three most significant writings came from the three major periods of his career. The most important of the essays from his earliest period as a scholar (prior to 1945) entitled "In Regard to the Problem of God"[61] and "Supernatural Being: God and Deification in Pauline Theology" appeared in his publication *Nature, History, God*. The second crucial text resulted from a 1973 seminar given at the Gregorian University in Rome. This essay represents the culmination of a series of *cursos* on God subsequent to the 1963 publication of *On Essence*.[62] Finally, Zubiri's last reflections on the theme of God appeared in his posthumously published *El hombre y Dios*, the first of what was meant to be a theological trilogy.[63] This text is of considerable importance for our study not just because it represents Zubiri's final and most thorough exploration of the topic, but because Ellacuría himself served as its editor. Ellacuría performed this task during the years just prior to his own assassination, a period that saw publication of some of his most significant theological essays.[64] While Zubiri's philosophy permeates Ellacuría's own work, it is his writings on God that are particularly influential on Ellacuría's soteriology.[65]

Zubiri begins his earliest reflections on "the philosophical possibility of the problem of God" by indicating that he wishes to discuss both the content of this problem and the assumptions.[66] In doing so, Zubiri carefully notes that, rather than engaging in a "proof" for the existence of God, he wishes to examine the presuppositions behind the demonstrations of this type. He identifies the debate regarding the "existence of an external world" as analogous to the problem of God.[67] This rhetorical move allows him to correlate to the problem of God a pitfall of the former debate: the positions taken in the debate over the existence of an external world involve a presumption of the external world as some sort of fact. This "fact" is viewed as having an existence that is "added to" the existence of the subject, and it is this very assumption that Zubiri draws into his reflection on the problem of God.[68]

In what would be the template for his analysis of sentient intelligence, Zubiri opposes both a naïve realism that assumes the exteriority of reality as something that presents itself flatly to humans from the outside, and a subjective idealism that refers to this exteriority simply as a position of the subject. Yet he does not make his opposition in terms of a middle position; on the contrary, he wishes to show how the very opposition implied in both positions encloses the discussion in an assumption that itself must be overcome. Thus Zubiri proposes a portrait of human existence in which the exteriority of the world functions not in opposition, as *factum* (given) or as "added to," but as a formal ontological structure of the human subject. Zubiri's position requires one to shift from viewing the exteriority of the world as something in contrast to personal existence, to viewing it as an empowering ontological structure, a formal and constitutive element of personal self-realization.[69]

In turning to the question of God, Zubiri relies on a constellation of concepts that, though they often seem to overlap, form the basic structure for how he approaches the problem. A brief explanation of these concepts — reality as a "fundament," the "power of the real," and *religación* — assists in sketching Zubiri's position and indicating the significant ideas adopted by Ellacuría.

Zubiri's view of reality as fundament negotiates a seeming polarity between human alterity to and identity with reality by suggesting that humans are simultaneously immersed in reality and are relatively absolute realities constantly realizing themselves. Human persons are constituted not merely by their features (*notas*), but by the peculiar character of their reality as "their own" (*suya*). As we have seen in the explication of sentient intelligence, human beings apprehend other things as *de suyo* as well. In this sense, Zubiri suggests that the person is "ab-solute" (*absoluto*), but stresses that this really is only a relative absolute because it is an acquired character.[70] This relatively absolute reality experiences an ongoing dynamic of self-realization with each action. Zubiri claims that "with each action the human configures a form of reality."[71] This self-realization occurs not of an isolated, autonomous self that acts in a world that is other, but in a dynamic reality "within" reality and moved by its power. It is in articulating this power of the real that Zubiri attempts to account for alterity without implying dualism.

The differentiation between real things and the power of the real signals the location of the fundament of human existence. Zubiri suggests that although humans realize themselves through things that possess for them the power of the real, this power of the real is not identical with the things themselves. He describes other things as merely "intrinsic vectors" of the power, and they are so by the fact that they are real. So Zubiri's problematic, which he describes as the "enigmatic" character of reality, consists in this: humans realize themselves in a form of reality that things themselves do not impose on them, but they cannot do it without things. Things open possibilities for adopting a form of reality. Zubiri believes that humans do have to choose (*optar*), not simply as mental preference but to "ad-opt" a form of reality in action that they have chosen.[72] Yet because real things and the power of the real are not equated, it becomes apparent that there is a precise internal structure, which Zubiri describes as fundament. "The power of the real in things is nothing other than the occurrence [*acontecimiento*] of the fundament in them."[73]

In his description of the power of the real, Zubiri underscores that the "force" (*fuerza*) of reality is something beyond its formal character as *de suyo*.[74] If reality as fundament indicates a sense of reality as *more* (*más*) without the distantial sense of *beyond*, then Zubiri may introduce an idea of transcendence as alterity without dualism, what Ellacuría will call a "transcendence-in." The notion of reality as fundament, as that "more" that is "in," leads to a portrait of human existence under the power of the real as "thrown (*arrojada*) among things."[75] If "lying open," gestures to Zubiri's notion of human existence as constitutively structured by the sentient apprehension of reality as formality, then being "thrown among things" signals fundamentality. So the human realizes self not just "with" things, but

"in" reality. Things hold for humans the power of the real because they are
not just their real properties, but for persons they also, as real, have a power
through which humans realize themselves. "The force with which the power
of the real dominates me and moves me to realize myself as a person is what
I call empowerment (*apoderamiento*). Humans may realize themselves only
empowered by the power of the real. This empowerment is what I have
termed religation (*religación*)."[76]

Zubiri utilizes the neologism "religation," from the Latin *religare*, to indicate the manner in which humans are "tied-back" or "re-connected" to the
power of the real.[77] It is important to Zubiri to note the physical character
of religation. Having stated that humans discover a non-identity between
real things and the power of the real, Zubiri carefully sketches the transcendental character of this power, but a transcendence that binds the human to
reality in terms of depth.

> Reality is a "more," but not one that is in addition to a thing, but rather
> a "more" *in the thing itself.* That is why in being with "this reality,"
> where I am is in "reality." Likewise, it is because of that which "this
> reality" can impose on me that it adopts a form in "reality." It is not
> a question of concepts, but of a physical character of the power of the
> real.[78]

Zubiri locates religation precisely in this power of the real. "Religation
is a manifesting experience of the power of the real and of the real itself.
It is an experience that is a physical verification (*probación*) of reality."[79]
Yet he also notes the experience of the power of the real as possessing an
enigmatic character. Using Heraclitus's description of the oracle at Delphi as
not proving nor denying, but merely signifying, Zubiri views the enigmatic
character of religation as a directional pointing in which the human both
apprehends things as formally real and is impelled to adopt a form of reality.[80] Ultimately, this enigmatic character points the human to the problem
of God because human beings, as relatively absolute, must decide whether
the power of the real is leading them to the absolutely absolute as fundament
of that power and of themselves.[81]

Thus, Zubiri describes the theologal as "a dimension of human reality
that involves, constitutively and formally, an inexorable confrontation (*en-
frentamiento*) with the ultimacy (*ultimidad*) of the real, provisionally and
nominally, that which we call God."[82] For Zubiri, "God" is not a concrete
idea, "being," or a "divine reality." As theologal, the term "God" signifies
the scope of the ultimacy of the real. Thus, Zubiri weds discussion of the theologal to analysis of human reality and sentient intelligence. His reflections
on the problem of God are not arbitrary, but arise as a constitutive question of human reality.[83] However, just as sentient intelligence overcomes the
"entification" of reality that would make reality dependent on human perception or understanding, here Zubiri's analysis avoids problems associated
with a modern subjectivist approach.

A return to the debate on the exteriority of the world provides Zubiri an analogy to undermine two erroneous assumptions he observes in most discourse on God.[84] First, one must not begin with the supposition that there exists a God, which one either proves rationally or clings to sentimentally, as one entity "beside" human subjects and subsisting things. One cannot speak of God as a thing, a fact, or something "in addition to" humans and things. Second, even the attempt to restrict discourse to God *quoad nos* raises serious suspicions. Though it correctly asserts human limitation regarding knowledge of God *quoad se,* the idea that humans have a faculty of access to God *quoad nos* reduces God's existence to *factum.* "Is knowledge, feeling (*sentimiento*), or any other 'faculty' the *organon* for entering into 'relation' with God? Might it not be that this latter is not the task of any '*organon,*' because the very being of the human is constitutively a being in God?"[85]

By indicating that the relation humans have with God reaches to the very being of humans, Zubiri directs the problem of God away from proofs or oppositional claims concerning divinity to an investigation of human existence, and even of the coming into existence of humanity itself. As in the debate on the exteriority of the world, Zubiri believes that the path out of restrictive assumptions of God as "beside" or "in addition to" involves a shift in perspective to the ontological structuring of human beings. This move does not imply a theological projection of the divine from human existence, but merely a way to articulate the alterity of human existence from the divine without divorcing it from God. This attempt will correspond with Ellacuría's theological attempt to overcome extrinsicist notions of human nature and divine grace, of salvation and history.

Religation makes the fundamentality of human existence real and evident to us.[86] What religates existence religates the world, but in humans religation is actualized formally. Religation is a dimension formally constitutive of existence. Recalling how "lying open" we discover that there are things, being religated we discover that "there is" that which religates.[87] Furthermore, Zubiri finally admits that we may designate that which religates by the word "God."

The human being finds God in her or his religated self-realization as a person. Therefore, the power of the real consists then exactly in that real things, without being God, are nonetheless real "in" God, that is, their reality is God *ad extra.* Therefore, to say that God is transcendent does not signify that God is transcendent "to" things, but that God is transcendent "in" things.[88]

Yet what does it mean to say that "there is" God? Zubiri plays with two verbs, the infinitive *ser* (to be) and *haber* (defective in English, it is rendered "there is"). A key contribution that Zubiri leaves to Ellacuría is the manner in which he works out how "there is" (*haber*) God without saying that God is (*ser*) in a reductionist sense.

Rather than "perfect" or "infinite," Zubiri uses the phrase *ens fundamentale* as a name for God. "That which religates us does so under this special form which consists in grounding us through making us to be. Hence, our existence has a fundament. . . . The primary attribute *quoad nos* of divinity is fundamentality."[89] So in some sense the parallels from the discussion on the exteriority of the world continue. Just as the exteriority of things pertains to the being of humans, religation pertains to the being of humans as well. In both cases, Zubiri emphasizes their similarity as constitutive dimensions of human existence; however, he notes how exteriority and religation are also contrary. For humans are open to things and find themselves among them and with them, but that is not the case with God. In religation, humans are not with God, but rather in God. They do not simply "go toward" God but "come from" (every "going to" is a "being carried" by God).

Thus, Zubiri's characterizations of God's involvement in human existence cannot be read as univocal assertions about divinity in the realm of being. "Neither is there properly an experience of God, as if He were a thing, a fact, or something similar. . . . God is not something which is in humans as a part of them, nor is God something which is added to them, from outside. . . . What of God there may be in the human is only the religation through which we are open to God, and in this religation God becomes patent to us."[90] As Zubiri identifies the tendency to enclose thinking in the circle of being, he not only opens a path to discourse about a truly transcendent God, but he also undermines talk of this transcendence that is oppositional.

Recalling the *ser/haber* distinction, Zubiri cautions against thinking that the "is" (*ser*) serves as the primary form in which humans enter into contact with things. Human understanding finds itself with things that "are," but also finds that "there is" that which religates and founds existence: God. So as consideration of things led to the radical understanding of human existence, Zubiri avers, "We are carried to an understanding not of what 'there is,' but of what 'makes that there be.'"[91] The problem for Zubiri of course consists in how to understand this "there is" that is attributed to God. If God is not "what there is," but rather what "makes something to be," then the primary mode by which "there is" God, for humans, is rootedness itself:

> That God has something to do with being is a consequence of the fact that the things that there are, are. But the problem is precisely that of determining in what this making-there-to-be consists. There is no identification of the being of metaphysics with God. In God the "there is" surpasses infinitely with respect to the "is." God is beyond being.[92]

The understanding of God in religation does not render a detached mode of human existence. Zubiri has a vision of the future when humans "will encounter [themselves] religated to God, not so as to flee from the world, and others, and themselves; but the other way around, in order to sustain and maintain themselves in being."[93] Rather than serve as an escape, religation reaffirms the imperative to encounter reality.

Zubiri sees all human beings, as relatively absolute, thrown down a route that leads one to the Absolutely Absolute. "Humans find God in realizing themselves 'religatedly' as persons. Therefore, the power of the real consists then exactly in that real things, without being God, are nonetheless real 'in' God, that is, their reality is God *ad extra*. Therefore, to say that God is transcendent does not signify that God is transcendent 'to' things, but that God is transcendent 'in' things."[94] Thus, for Zubiri, the domination or "being-seized" (*apoderamiento*) of the human by the power of the real is truly the empowerment of the human by God, and the intellection of God is the optative moment of the human's self-realization as person.

Zubiri's description of the human experience of God does not equate God with ordinary human experience of things, nor does it set up an opposition. While God is not the human person, the human person is in some manner God. The "and" of the phrase "human and God" is not copulative. "God" does not include the human, but "human" does include God. The mode of this inclusion is experience. "Because God does not transcend away from things, but in them; things are not simply non-God, but in some mode are a configuration of God *ad extra*. . . . The human is formally and constitutively the experience of God."[95] Therefore, the three essential moments of the human person's realization are: religation, *marcha intelectiva,* and experience, moments which are not seen as successive, but in which each one is founded in the other. Zubiri views them as constituting an intrinsic and formal unity, and this unity describes the ultimate structure of the human's theologal dimension.

Zubiri's account of the theologal represents an attempt to articulate the transcendence of God, but not in oppositional terms. It is a profoundly graced vision that sees reality imbued with God's presence at its very depths. As theologal, Zubiri's reflections do not utilize or reinterpret the theological language of a particular religious tradition, but remain within the realm of the human experience of reality.[96] Religation indicates the rooted dimension of reality in its very coming into existence. The human encounter with reality is one "in" a God that makes it to be. By differentiating the "there is" God from God "being," Zubiri coherently speaks of the radical involvement of God with the world without compromising God's transcendence. Zubiri's account does not jeopardize the human imperative to encounter and act in reality; on the contrary, the directional thrust "from God" to things makes the human encounter with reality paramount.

Since the theologal dimension is seen as individual, social, and historical, Zubiri acknowledges that it takes a concrete form, what he calls *plasmación*.[97] "*Plasmación* signifies the concrete form in which individually, socially, and historically the power of the real empowers the human being. . . . Religion is the *plasmación* of religation, the concrete form of the empowerment of the power of the real in religation."[98] Zubiri eschews the notion that religion is an attitude before the sacred. While the religious may be sacred, it is sacred because it is first religious. As *plasmación* of religation, religion provides a "concrete vision of God, humanity, and the world." Thus, Zubiri refers to Christianity as religion, a *plasmación* of religation, a form in which the power of the real, and thus God, empowers (in the individual, social, and historical) the human experientially. He views its main function as "deformation" because he sees the human as the formal projection of the proper divine reality — a finite manner of being God.

With its intricate structure and idiosyncratic vocabulary, Zubiri's approach to the question of God may seem far removed from the liberation theology of Ellacuría. However, Zubiri had a profound impact on his pupil, in both content and rhetoric. The way Zubiri addresses latent suppositions in discourse about God and his penchant for unmasking hidden dualisms provide a rhetorical model for Ellacuría. In his notion of God's transcendence "in" and not "away from" the world, and in his vision of life as the *plasmación ad extra* of God, Zubiri provides Ellacuría an imaginative way to construe that transcendent, yet intimate, relationship between God and humanity.

Participating in the Trinitarian Life of God

Ellacuría utilizes Zubiri's creative attempt to overcome the weaknesses of idealism, particularly its pernicious dualisms, not just in analyzing the human being, but in guiding his theological discourse. The "non-contrastive" manner with which Zubiri deals with the notion of transcendence colors Ellacuría's portrayal of God's salvific relation to humanity. Zubiri's thought allows Ellacuría to frame a soteriology that remains faithful to the biblical testimony of God's salvific activity while offering a post-idealist manner of articulating this truth that continues the rich legacy of liberation theology. Critical components of this lie in presenting transcendence as something "in," not "away," adopting the concept of *plasmación,* and describing human existence as participation in the Trinitarian life of God *ad extra.*

Ellacuría identifies a proper notion of transcendence as the key element in appropriately interpreting the nature of Christian salvation.[99] He claims that transcendence understood as separation, as movement "away from," does not correspond to that fundamental interaction of divine and human at the heart of the Christian faith articulated in its Scriptures. He notes that a glance at some of the basic mysteries of the faith (such as the nature of Jesus as human and divine, the church as historical entity and mystery, and even the sacred books as composed by humans and authored by God) indicates the importance of coherently handling the concept of transcendence. Moreover, the disjunct caused by this defective notion of transcendence applies directly to the problem of "the 'relation' between the different moments of a single praxis of salvation."[100]

Of course, by the time of Ellacuría's mature work, liberation theology had seen its flourishing and was sustaining intense criticism, particularly within Roman Catholic circles. As I argued in the first chapter, these criticisms centered on an alleged reductionism and a naïve application of Marxist political and social theory on the part of liberation theologians. Ellacuría notes that despite their criticisms, figures such as Hans Urs von Balthasar and Joseph Ratzinger actually support liberation theologians' fundamental attempts at understanding salvation and liberation.[101] Just as Zubiri viewed his work as trying to overcome the separation of sense and intellect latent in the Western philosophical tradition, Ellacuría identifies his own constructive liberation theology as trying to overcome a long tradition of dualism in dealing with the relationship between the divine and human.[102] He views this as "not primarily a conceptual issue, but a real issue. . . . It is not primarily a theoretical problem of the conjoining of two abstract concepts, one referring to the word of God and the other to human work."[103]

Ellacuría articulates Zubiri's notion of transcendence as the way to overcome the separation between the proclamation of the Reign of God and human efforts toward liberation. Ellacuría recognizes that the difficulty in speaking about transcendence increases dramatically as one tries to account for the historical nature of the Christian faith. The theologian must attempt to speak of these two poles without thereby creating polarity. In an attempt to maintain this balance, Ellacuría considers that transcendence indicates "a contextual structural difference without implying a duality, something that enables us to speak of an intrinsic unity without implying a strict identity."[104] He attacks the notion of transcendence as separation with words that could have been taken directly from Zubiri.

> There is a radically different way of understanding transcendence, more in line with the way reality and God's action are presented in biblical thinking. This is to see transcendence as something that transcends *in* and not as something that transcends *away from*; as something that physically impels to *more* but not by taking *out of*; as something that pushes *forward*, but at the same time *retains*. In this conception, when one reaches God historically — which is the same as saying when one reaches God personally — one does not abandon the human, does not abandon real history, but rather deepens one's roots, making more present and effective what was already effectively present. God can be separated from history, but history cannot be separated from God.[105]

Many of the elements of Zubiri's thought emerge as Ellacuría defines transcendence as "in," and not "away from."[106] The language of "more" indicates the sense of fundamentality and the notion of religation, even noting its physical nature. The sense of religation both as something that "ties back" and yet pushes humans forward in a *marcha* are also conveyed. Ellacuría draws out the importance of Zubiri's insights as encouraging an engagement in history, not denying or escaping it. Finally, Ellacuría recognizes that this does not collapse the divine into history. Just as Zubiri refused to handle the "and" of "God and human" as copulative, so Ellacuría affirms the unity/non-identity between God and history. Indeed, this understanding circumscribes Ellacuría's understanding of his task as showing "the fundamental unity of the divine and human in history," a task that involves applying this understanding of transcendence to a reading of the Hebrew and Christian Scriptures.[107]

In order to explore more fully his historical reading of the Bible, Ellacuría makes a seemingly tangential argument, but one that takes on significance when understood within Zubiri's conceptual framework. Ellacuría claims that in order to posit a Christian historical transcendence, "everything depends on how we understand creation."[108] He reminds us that creation conceived simply as one object (God) creating another object (creation) by efficient causality creates a duality between creator and creature that can lead to an extrinsic view of grace. So here the unity of the concept of transcendence mirrors his assertion in the unity of divine and human histories. As an alternative to a dualistic view of creation, Ellacuría speaks of creation as the "*plasmación ad extra* of the Trinitarian life, a freely chosen *plasmación,* but of the very Trinitarian life itself. This would not mean an idealistic causality, but a self-communicating and self-giving of the divine life itself."[109]

Here Ellacuría has taken Zubiri's formulation of creation as the presence of God *ad extra* while fusing it with the terminology of *plasmación.*[110] As he elaborates the meaning of this *plasmación,* Ellacuría clearly draws upon Zubiri's notion of human existence as a way of "being God." Ellacuría claims, "this *plasmación* and self-communication has grades and limits in which each thing, according to its limits, is a limited form of being God."[111] If one recalls that Zubiri described religion as the *plasmación* of religation, then one recognizes Ellacuría's attempts to move away from a dualistic view of the creator-creation relation as between two objects. Yet since it is based on Zubiri's view of divine transcendence "in" reality, Ellacuría's notion does not surrender the theological distinction between God the Creator and humanity as created.[112] Ellacuría utilizes an ambiguity in the term, which connotes either a physical manifestation of a non-physical concept or reality (a sense of identity), or a molding or grafting — much like the clay as a result of the potter's work (a sense of alterity).

Ellacuría identifies the notion of creation as the *plasmación* of the Trinitarian life as the "theologal character" of creation. Here the flood of Zubirian concepts continues. Ellacuría identifies human existence and history as possessing an essential openness in which the *plasmación* of the Trinitarian life is given more and more. "It is not only that God is in all things...but that all things would be formed (*plasmadas*) according to the Trinitarian life and would refer essentially to it."[113] This not only refers to creation — it indicates the manner in which believers may consider discipleship as an approach to God. "In this theologal dimension there is an experience, strictly speaking, and through it, a strict personal, social, and historical experience of God."[114] "There are grades and modes of this experience, but when it is truly an experience of the real theologal dimension of the human.... It is a physical tasting [*probación*] of the Trinitarian life itself, mediated, incarnated, and historicized."[115]

Ellacuría links this language of the Trinitarian life to the historical dimension of lived faith. In articulating a notion of human history as graced, Ellacuría does not want to echo the extrinsicist view of history's elevation by God; nevertheless, he wants to acknowledge that this grace is more than history as given. He states, "history is *de suyo* transcendentally open, and in that transcendentality there is already the presence, albeit inchoate, of God."[116] While demonstrating the influence of Rahner's notion of the supernatural existential on his thought, Ellacuría is quick to clarify that this transcendentality occurs not just in the individual, nor even in the sum of individuals that make up society.[117] Ellacuría views history and humanity in its entirety as possessing this presence of God. This must include all of humanity's historical works as the objectivization of a "yes" or "no" to God's self-communication, and the objectivization of grace in which either the divine self-giving and human action agree, or human action rejects the offer of grace.

Ellacuría emphasizes history as the location of revelation and salvation:

> As much as for the metaphysical density of historical reality as its essential openness, history, biographical and social, becomes the best place (metaphysical density) and the only place (openness) where a revelation and a doubly gratuitous salvation is possible, which allow human beings and all of humanity to partake of the Trinitarian life of God itself.... It can be maintained that in each creative act there is a manifestation *ad extra* of the Trinitarian life of God itself.[118]

Ellacuría quickly qualifies this assertion with the reminder that this is possible only for human beings, and human beings considered in an integral, historical way. For this salvation is not apparent simply as part of human nature as such. Rather, Ellacuría recognizes that this grace has manifested itself most clearly, enriching humanity the most, in "the strictly historical communication to specific persons, prophets of all types, and to entire peoples with whom different covenants have been established."[119]

Though the tone of much of Ellacuría's writing carries the analytical style of establishing or proving facts, in reality, he opens his theological reflections in an apophatic direction. To speak of the communication of the absolute mystery of God involves a "fundamental incomprehensibility."[120] So Ellacuría situates his theology within a fundamental acknowledgment of God as infinite mystery and possessing a "divine freedom" in communicating this mystery. In terms of Christian discipleship, this humility recognizes that no determined historical moment may capture the mystery in its fullness. Rather than placing all hope in the historical present, Ellacuría acknowledges that the mystery of God and complexity of history do not allow one to "univocally valorize events."[121] This hesitancy increases as one acknowledges that history, in its dynamism and those agents participating in it, often reflects the deformities of sin.

In framing his soteriology — that is, in his basic understanding of humanity and God's relation to humanity — Ellacuría demonstrates a creative adaptation of Zubiri's philosophy, particularly in its emphasis on overcoming separations or dualisms. Ellacuría's outlook appears to be a positive, generous, and even mystical reading of the universal presence of grace in the world. Whether in the language of the theologal dimension of reality or that of salvation history, Ellacuría's view conforms to that Ignatian phrase of "finding God in all things." Moreover, since it is built on Zubiri's ideas on sentient intelligence and transcendence "in" things, Ellacuría's reflections on human existence and God's transcendence demonstrate a non-dualistic character that helps overcome disastrous separations and extrinsic notions of grace. As much as his view is generally positive, it would be mistaken to end the analysis here without examining Ellacuría's reflections on the existence and nature of sin. For though he characterizes human existence as the *plasmación* of the Trinitarian life of God, Ellacuría also acknowledges that this *plasmación* is often masked or disfigured in the world.

The Historical Reality of Sin and Evil Needing Salvation

In analyzing Ellacuría's reflections concerning the human being in reality, and God's transcendence, much of his soteriological "frame" has come into focus. What remains includes that final concept of the triad: human, God, world. In Ellacuría's thought, the best way to analyze his understanding of world is under the category of history. Indeed, Ellacuría makes the case theologically for an understanding of salvation history as a salvation in history. As he indicates, "The human being is a historical reality, a historical essence; history is a reality of extraordinary metaphysical density, and the relations of the human with God, founded in freedom, are constitutively historical."[122] Yet just as the Gospel of John displays a profound ambiguity toward the world, Ellacuría speaks of history as the locus of salvation, but also of sin. Because of the pervasive reality of sin in the world, which is personal, social, and structural, Christians must speak of salvation in terms of liberation. With these final pieces of Ellacuría's soteriological frame in place, the subsequent chapters can explore the form of soteriology and discipleship that appear on his theological canvas.

Reality and Grace in History

Frequently, Ellacuría utilizes a certain rhetorical device in his essays on soteriology: he diagnoses a conceptual error that requires remedying. Consistently, he claims that a separation of concepts causes the conceptual error, a theme reminiscent of Zubiri's work, but often modulated for the particular argument that Ellacuría wishes to make. Ellacuría views the tendency to separate concepts and create dualisms as a pernicious and widespread tendency when considering the salvific relationship between the divine and human.[123] For Ellacuría, as a liberation theologian, a central question involves the relationship between the establishment of the Reign of God that Jesus preached and human efforts toward historical liberation. This question cannot be considered adequately by thinking of it as the bringing together of two abstract concepts. Doing so perpetuates what Ellacuría describes as:

> the long, intellectual elaboration, carried out over centuries, [which] has led to the conceptual separation of what appears in biographical and historical experience to be united. That conceptual separation is increasingly taken for granted.... The problem not only is not resolved, but is concealed, by separating the concept from real historical praxis and placing it ideologically and uncritically at the service of institutionalized interests. The problem is concealed, not mainly because the concept is abstract, but rather because it is not historical.[124]

In this diagnosis, several of Ellacuría's characteristic moves, and his debt to Zubiri, appear. First, Ellacuría situates the separation of concepts within a longer intellectual tradition. Like Zubiri, while this tradition is most often identified with modern idealism, it also includes the entire Western philosophical tradition reaching back to its roots in the Greeks. Second, Ellacuría discerns in the separation of concepts not merely an intellectual error, but an element of deception that has wider implications. The error springing from the separation of concepts often deceives, masks, or ideologically legitimates unjust principles or structures that create the suffering of others. Third, Ellacuría suggests a remedy for the separation of concepts that is based on a dynamic understanding of the human, history (as historical reality), and God's involvement in history.

Ellacuría's emphasis on history or historical reality represents a departure of sorts from Zubiri's treatment of reality; however, it does not constitute a complete break. As Antonio González points out, while Ellacuría belongs in that generation influenced by Zubiri's *Sobre la esencia,* his work also assumes the insights from a later series of Zubiri's *cursos* on the dynamic structure of reality.[125] In these *cursos,* Zubiri's analysis of the dynamisms in material things, life, the person, and society culminates with a study of the dynamism of history.[126] In history, all of these other dynamisms are made present, but they are also affected by history. González cites the following text as having a decisive influence on Ellacuría:

> The world, or reality as the world, is constitutively historical. The dynamism of history affects reality, constituting it as reality. History is not simply an event that happens to some passive realities, as gravity occurs to material realities. No: it is something that affects precisely the character of reality as such.[127]

Understood as dynamic structure, reality has dynamism inscribed within itself. As Ellacuría elaborates, "Reality is neither the subject-of dynamism, nor subject-to a dynamism, but rather is something constitutively dynamic. ... The world, as the respectivity of reality *qua* reality, does not have a dynamism, nor is it in dynamism, but rather is itself dynamic."[128] In the realization of reality as reality, history appears as the superior form of reality, as the place of fulfillment and revelation of reality.

For González, Zubiri's thought indicates that "the place of the overlap (*imbricación*) between reality and intelligence, between human and world, is precisely history."[129] Seen in Ellacuría's work, history defines the third horizon of philosophical reflection, which follows the Hellenistic emphasis on nature, and the modern concern with subjectivity. While these prior emphases are not abandoned, the perspective of history signals how nature and subjectivity should be properly understood to focus adequately on the fullness of reality. For Ellacuría, "the fullness (*lo último*) of reality, the metaphysical, is not accessible by the path of maximum abstraction, but by the turn to what is the maximum of "concretion" (*concreción*).... This total concretion is not just in process — and in that sense, evolutionary — but formally historical."[130] History, as the total and ultimate concrete realization of reality, becomes the true object of philosophy.[131]

While much more could be said concerning the importance of history in Ellacuría's philosophical writings, Ellacuría's theological consideration of history once again appears as an extension of the nature-grace debates of the previous generation of Catholic theologians. Rather than focusing on categories such as "nature" and "supernatural," however, Ellacuría turns his attention to the separation of two histories, the divine and human. Frequently, Ellacuría emphasizes the language of the "history of God" and "human history" not as two separate histories, but as "a single historical reality in which both God and human beings intervene."[132]

This linking of histories signals a significant theological task for Ellacuría: to demonstrate how " 'salvation history' is a 'salvation in history.' "[133] These terms indicate how Ellacuría favors a historical lens to speak of the unity between divine and human over what he terms the earlier "Hellenistic" language of natural and supernatural. These latter terms, "due to a Greek philosophical mentality that is quite alien to the orientation of the Bible," formulate the divine-human relation such that the "supernatural" refers to the Trinitarian God revealed by grace, and the "natural" signifies the human being as it appears to be *in se*. Ellacuría views this distinction as having "an incalculable impact on theology ... so that by our own day it has deformed Christian praxis."[134] Thus, the natural-supernatural split, like the separation of human and divine histories, represents a dualism fraught with theological danger, even extending to Christian praxis.

In identifying and overcoming the natural-supernatural dualism, Ellacuría evinces the impact of studies with Karl Rahner.[135] For in his definition and usage of the terms "natural" and "supernatural" as dualistic, Ellacuría explicitly identifies the extrinsic view of grace, characteristic of preconciliar neo-scholasticism, away from which Rahner and those of his generation wished to move. Ellacuría even (cautiously, but favorably) acknowledges the impact of Vatican II in spurring more theologians to speak of salvation history — much more useful nomenclature in Ellacuría's eyes. He admits, for instance, that one measure of clarity and depth is reached by substituting the term "salvation history" for "supernatural," and "salvation in history" for "natural."[136] Yet Ellacuría will try to advance this theological insight so that the implications of salvation's historical character may be realized.

In making a case for the historical nature of salvation, Ellacuría follows a similar analysis as Zubiri does when proposing his theory of sentient intelligence. Ellacuría cites the prejudice that salvation is ahistorical as rooted in a "Parmenidean and Platonic interpretation of Aristotle."

> This leads to a natural-substantial interpretation of the human and social realities. It views the human as part of the cosmos, as a natural being (*ente*), only with an elevated nature, or if one prefers, it pertains to nature more freely. Being is nature, and nature is being itself, despite its accidental and transitory mutations. In the end, nothing occurs, and if something occurs, it is always the same. Thus, a double reduction occurs: a static interpretation of nature and a naturalist interpretation of the human.
>
> At best, the unity of human-world-history is dislocated in the abstract notion of humanity in the world, understood as transpiring temporally. That is to say the world and history are made to be extrinsic additions to the human, who already is what she or he is and only needs to exercise that which he or she already is. Thus, both the structural implication of the historical human in a historical world and the essential dynamism of that structural implication are lost.[137]

These lines signal that dynamic notion of human embeddedness in reality characteristic of Zubiri's view of sentient intelligence, and the importance of history. If one takes seriously Zubiri's emphasis on the constitutive nature of the human's primordial apprehension of reality, then Ellacuría's emphasis here on the *intrinsic* unity of human-world-history naturally follows.

As a parallel to this understanding of humans and history, Ellacuría also notes a pernicious Hellenistic influence on Christian soteriology that leaves it "de-historicized with grave consequences for historical praxis and for the interpretation and efficacy of the Christian faith."[138] Here he follows a similar analysis to that of the natural-supernatural dualism, but phrases it in terms of the difference between a "naturalist" and "historical" understanding of salvation. The former is characterized by a view of salvation as "given (accidentally) in history, but not (essentially) historical."[139] While Ellacuría acknowledges the positive sense in which this theological approach takes seriously the revealed acts and words of God, he also detects a twofold limitation rooted in its ahistorical method. Namely, the acts and words are "reduced to objective intellectual formulations that are fundamentally closed and, through discursive mediations and deductive reason, converted into rational formulations of absolute validity that can abandon the principle from which they emerged."[140]

The danger of theological reflection that does not take seriously the historical nature of human existence and of Christian salvation lies in a tendency to remove itself from reality and leave that reality vulnerable to ideological and institutional forces that could distort it. Ellacuría illustrates this point by indicating how the "de-historicizing of Jesus" represents one of the most dangerous aspects of the "naturalist" ahistorical theological approach. By this, he means that even though the key moments of Jesus' life are accepted — birth, life, death, resurrection — their metaphysical and theological significance *as historical* are not treated. The emphasis instead goes to the metaphysical constitution of Jesus Christ or the hypostatic union. While the hypostatic union is an important concept, undue emphasis on it indicates a problem:

> What occurs is that the historical is converted to the natural, the existential to the essential. Followers leave behind the historical and existential as decisive elements for them to historicize the life of Jesus, whether in their personal lives or in the communal life of the Church. Instead, they are confident that what is important is some sort of ontological transformation whose proof is doubtful and whose historical efficacy is entirely accidental.[141]

After describing history as "the privileged place of revelation and salvation, as it has been chosen freely by God," he defines the historical as "that which comes to be actually real, in virtue of an option, whether it is made by an individual subject for herself or himself or for others, or by a social subject. There is always history when there is actualization of possibilities — and not just acting of potentiality — by means of an option (Zubiri)."[142] Ellacuría clearly puts forth a vision of history that relies on the Zubirian notion of reality, and the significance of his threefold method for Latin American theology emerges again in this emphasis on option in reality. Ellacuría situates discipleship as historical, not just as human action, but within the grace of the created order, which is itself historical.[143]

Because he views human existence as apprehending and opting, Ellacuría posits history as transcendentally open because it encompasses within itself this human openness to reality.[144] Of course, given reality's theologal dimension, the transcendental openness of history indicates, however inchoately, the presence of God, a presence that humans come to know through history:

> The distinct transcendence that in fact appears in history is an elevated and doubly gratuitous transcendence, which we know as such in a reflective and thematic way, only when there appears a series of historical occurrences, persons, words, and works, that come together in that primary transcendence. This does not occur only in this or that

separate individual, nor even in the totality of individuals, but also in that peculiar type that is history. The subject of this history is humanity in its entirety. . . . That historical subject, not just collective, but unitary, is the carrier of transcendentally open historicity. Yet it is so not leaving historical works behind because these will be the objectivization of a yes or no to God's communication. All historical acts, although in different grades, are an objectivization of grace, in which the divine gift and human action are in harmony, or an objectivization of sin in which human action is dominated by evil, rejecting the offer of grace.[145]

Though Ellacuría considers history as the graced location of salvation, so that salvation history must be understood as a salvation in history, he clearly indicates that profound ambiguities exist in this history.[146] Though he confidently posits the self-revelation of God in history, Ellacuría also displays a humility about the human capability to apprehend it. Even with a fundamental trust in Jesus as the "definitive criteria" of God's salvific self-revelation, Ellacuría describes God as absolute mystery. Though he claims that historical acts represent an objectivized response to grace, Ellacuría concedes that history's complexity prevents their univocal valorization. It demands evaluation of the many dynamisms at work. For Ellacuría, sin represents not just the great ambiguity of history, but that which cries for salvation in history. Thus, in his elaboration of sin, Ellacuría pieces together the final elements of the soteriological frame.

Sin: Personal and Social Disfiguring of God's Presence in History

The claim that salvation history is a salvation in history includes a parallel acknowledgment that sin has a historical dimension. While few contemporary theologians fail to accord any historical dimension to sin, the proper way to do this gives rise to fierce debate. Ellacuría challenges those who would relegate sin to a strictly private or "spiritual" sphere divorced from history, or who would view larger social evils, such as poverty, as merely an extension of personal sin. These views of sin dictate a corresponding view of salvation that also truncates any substantive link to history and the alleviation of human suffering in history. Thus, Ellacuría attempts to deepen the analysis of sin by situating it historically, and in doing so, he offers a view of liberation as the necessary, but not sufficient, condition for the fullness of salvation.

Ellacuría's treatment of sin mirrors that of other liberation theologians in its emphasis on sin not just as personal but as social.[147] Yet one ought not mistake this emphasis for an abandonment of the notion of personal sin. It merely signals the implications of Ellacuría's view of human existence in historical reality. Persons, not animals, things, or social structures, always commit sins, but the sin cannot be limited to the individual. Personal sin, as well as all personal activity, has implications as real, as historical. Thus, Ellacuría continues the language of the "objectivization" of sin.[148] As Sols notes, "[For Ellacuría] 'objectivization' signifies a *plasmación* in reality of an interior disposition."[149] Though Sols correctly understands the connotation of *plasmación* as the making physically manifest of something abstract, it is possible to look at his assertion as indicating a deeper relationship between personal and social sin that relates back to Zubiri's philosophical ideas. It may be seen, once again, as signaling a difference, without separation, of these concepts of sin.

Ellacuría situates his reflections on sin theologically in his questioning of the extrinsicist supernatural-natural distinction of earlier theologies. Arguing for it as a Latin American theological inclination, Ellacuría prefers to talk not of supernatural-natural divisions, but of grace and sin, and those categories historicized. "There are actions that kill (divine) life, and there are actions that give (divine) life. The former are the reign of sin, the latter are the reign of grace. There are social and historical structures that are the objectivization of the power of sin, and moreover, carry that power against human beings. . . . These constitute structural sin."[150] This assertion does not negate the concept of personal sin, but rather argues against a view, exemplified in von Balthasar's critique of CELAM's Medellín documents, that restricts sin solely to the realm of the personal. Collective sin indicates not a negation of personal sin, but an intrinsic dimension of its depth. In the same pattern of Zubiri's view of sentient intelligence and of transcendence, Ellacuría considers collective sin as beyond (*más allá*) individual sin, but with the sense of depth, not separation.[151]

The Zubirian-Ellacurían view of historical reality takes seriously the manner that human existence in reality is conditioned. Though human existence may be characterized by freedom, that freedom is conditioned by a myriad set of factors. These factors may be biological and physical, but they are also praxical. That is, the history of effects of all human behavior may have lasting effects such that the subsequent range of possibilities for "realizing" human freedom is greatly affected. As structures, these conditioning effects can, and in Ellacuría's eyes must, be evaluated theologically as sin if they lead to that which opposes God's will for human life. The Salvadoran campesino who cannot rise out of poverty feels the effects of this sin. Even the good-hearted coffee plantation owner who cannot change the system, yet benefits from it, is caught in this web of sin.

On Ellacuría's reading, liberation theology encourages people to change structures because it understands those structures as a negation of God's will. To those who might see in his de-emphasis of the natural-supernatural question a new version of Pelagianism, Ellacuría notes:

> The first question should be what there is of grace and of sin in humanity and history, but grace and sin seen not primarily from a moral perspective, much less from a perspective of fulfilling laws and

obligations, but rather seen primarily from what *makes present the life of God* among human beings. This is what makes the fulfillment of laws and obligations possible, rather than the latter bringing about the presence of God. It is not the law that saves, but faith and grace, although faith and grace that are operative, and at the same time, objectivized historically.[152]

Thus, Ellacuría not only shifts the emphasis away from the extrinsicist views of grace that have their origins in a sharp distinction between the natural and supernatural, but he advocates an alternative view of grace with a historical dimension that recognizes human existence as the presence of the life of God.[153] This historical dimension, with the Zubirian emphasis on history as the actualization of possibilities, means a clear identification of sin as death, as that which brings death to the poor. As Ellacuría notes succinctly, "The death of the poor is the death of God, the ongoing crucifixion of the Son of God."[154]

Building on the framework provided by Zubiri's language, Ellacuría identifies a twofold sense of sin as the negation of the inherent dynamism of divine presence in human existence. If he has already asserted that human existence possesses a dynamic openness to the divine presence, then sin means a negation of that dynamism in a privative and active sense. The negation as privative implies that it "impedes the 'more' of God being made present," and the active sense means an "absolutizing and divinizing of a limited creature."[155] Lest one believe that Ellacuría remains at the level of abstraction, he cites Oscar Romero's pastoral letters that identify the idolatry present in making wealth, power, private property, and national security absolute.[156]

Ellacuría views unjust poverty as the great negation of God's presence in, and will for, the world.

> The poor and their unjustly inflicted poverty, the social, economic, and political structures on which their reality is based, and their complex ramifications of hunger, illness, imprisonment, torture, assassinations, etc. . . . are all negations of the Reign of God, and one cannot think about the sincere proclamation of the Reign of God while turning one's back to these realities, or while throwing a cloak over them to cover their shame.[157]

In this assertion, Ellacuría focuses on God as the God of life. He takes seriously the ancient Irenaean motto, *Gloria Dei, homo vivens,* and historicizes it.

Ellacuría notes that the forces and dynamism of history and the agents who participate in them can darken or disfigure the communication of God. If the Reign of God can be obscured by the reign of sin in ideologizations and absolutizations, then one indication of salvation in history consists in the unmasking of idolatries, the structures that reify them, and the propaganda that disguises them. Since Ellacuría understands Jesus' mission as the proclamation of the Reign of God, his description of authentic discipleship involves historical participation in the overcoming of sin, including its structural forms. Ellacuría notes, "The life and action of Jesus would not be carried forward if there were no efforts to overcome these sins objectivized in institutional structures, in collective behaviors, and in the manner in which processes are constituted that determine the configuration of history in which human beings live their existence."[158]

Ultimately, Ellacuría's soteriology and view of Christian discipleship are geared toward the transformation of reality and the removal of sin.

> Objective sin should be redeemed. The sin is there, one can touch it with the hands, and it is not enough to have an extrinsic judicial pardon, but rather a real transformation is necessary.... The Christian's mission is to remove sin and build the world. There is a synthesis of secular and Christian action.... All sin leaves a mark and it is not enough to say, "I repent." It is a mark and it should be erased, and what erases the marks of sin is Christian action.[159]

Of course, to the degree that he has already indicated the source of grace and human existence as the Trinitarian life of God, Ellacuría's emphasis on human action for liberation must be seen as response to divine initiative and not a form of Pelagianism. Ellacuría's emphasis on transformative action entails both a strong view of Christian discipleship and a positive reflection on the fundamental goodness of the world. In his view of the dynamic immersion of human beings in a worldly reality that is religated to the presence of God, Ellacuría distinguishes between the world itself and the evil present in the world. For him, the world may be disfigured, but it is the location of humanity's encounter with God. "There is no access to God beyond the world."[160]

Conclusion

To understand what Ellacuría means when he speaks of Christian praxis or discipleship, one must understand how that praxis or discipleship functions within the larger framework of his soteriology. Yet Ellacuría's soteriology, in turn, relies on a framework, a depth structure, that provides significant concepts and overall coherence. I have described this framework under the title "principle and foundation" to invoke in a general way the analogous moment in Ignatius of Loyola's *Spiritual Exercises,* a work that thoroughly informs Ellacuría's spirituality.[161] Ignatius's "Principle and Foundation" provides a vision of all things as the graced creation of the saving God whom humanity is called to serve and praise. This chapter has attempted to describe how Ellacuría's principle and foundation resides in a philosophical-theological vision, indebted to Zubiri, of humanity, God, and

world in which humans find themselves in a dynamically interrelated historical reality imbued with the gracious presence of the creator and savior God
who transcends in history.

Ellacuría depicts the human person, the one who receives salvation, in
a manner quite different from the "subjectivity" of modern philosophical
thought. Drawing from Zubiri's monumental work on sentient intelligence,
Ellacuría views human existence as embedded in reality in a constitutive
manner. One cannot separate this human person or her or his intellection
from the complex web of relationships that constitute her or his existence.
Indeed, Ellacuría's resistance to speaking of a detached human subject finds
resonance in those recent streams of thought wary of modernity's tendency
to hyperindividualism. Yet rather than proceeding through a route of thorough deconstruction, Ellacuría pursues an "open material realism" that
identifies the demands that reality makes on the person. That the human
engagement/confrontation with reality involves not just a noetic, but also
ethical and praxical dimensions, will be taken up theologically in Ellacuría's
discussion of the preferential option for the poor and ecclesial praxis.

The reality that Ellacuría describes possesses a "theologal" dimension,
a dimension that allows Ellacuría to speak of divine transcendence "in"
reality, and not as separation. With this notion, Ellacuría incorporates the
biblical testimony of the God who saves in history in a way that does not reduce God or that salvation to exclusively historical objects. By deploying the
concept of the "theologal," Ellacuría may speak about traditional themes of
creation and salvation, of God's transcendence and immanence, coherently
and without reduction. Furthermore, Ellacuría's insights represent the next
step for the earlier Roman Catholic reflection on the nature-grace debates,
as he deepens the notion of grace as God's self-communication within historical reality. Thus, Ellacuría comes to understand salvation history as a
salvation in history.

In emphasizing that salvation possesses a historical character, Ellacuría
includes sin and liberation as essential themes. Sin problematizes positivistic
language about God and grace; it interrupts God language and reminds us
that the notion of creation as graced must include a dialectic of the reality
of sin in the world. Viewed in history, if grace signifies "the configuration
of humanity as the visible incarnation of the Trinity within it," then sin involves "the visible disfiguring of humanity that impedes the visible presence
of the Triune God."[162] Restoring this disfigured humanity involves a process
of liberation that is personal, social, and structural. Thus, in this framework, salvation means overcoming the disfigurement of sin and enabling
the *plasmación* of the Trinitarian life to be revealed explicitly in history.

Ultimately, Ellacuría's diagnosis of sin demands an account of salvation
and its concomitant discipleship. Reflection on sin helps to counter what
Ellacuría identifies as one of the greatest problems in contemporary spirituality: "that we do not see the Christian sense of our temporal actions, of
our protests against injustice, of the social struggle, etc.... Focused on the

problem of sin, it appears to me that one really finds a theological principle and practical principle of spirituality to understand, in a Christian way, our mode of acting."[163] The way Ellacuría advocates a Christian mode of acting cannot be understood apart from the manner in which he articulates the Christian mode of salvation.

Therefore, the following chapter will take up Ellacuría's soteriology proper. That is, it will explore how Ellacuría, rooted in the philosophical-theological framework described above, articulates the Christian belief in salvation wrought through the person of Jesus Christ. Just as his soteriological framework seeks to overcome dualisms, so will Ellacuría's christological reflection. It will build on the insights covered here: the human being's dynamic embeddedness in reality, creation as the *plasmación ad extra* of the divine life, divine transcendence in history, salvation history as a salvation in history, and sin as the personal, social, and structural disfiguring of the divine presence. Foremost in this description will be Ellacuría's handling of the figure of Jesus Christ and the notion of the Reign of God. As a liberation theologian, Ellacuría appropriates the Christian tradition through the preferential option for the poor. He understands the poor as a "crucified people" who continue Jesus' own bearing of the sins of the world. Ellacuría's soteriology will then revolve around a constellation of christological reflection that emerges from his philosophical framework and informs his distinctive view of Christian mission in the world — the participation in the struggle for liberation and life.

> Liberation from death will come to pass in its total and definitive form only by traveling through death to the enjoyment of eternal life, where what is substantive is once again life and not so much eternity; a life in which there will no longer be oppression, weeping, sickness, division, but rather fullness in the communication of God, who is life and love. Yet this definitive liberation should be anticipated, and it is empirically evident that if the sin of the world and the causes of sin are made to disappear, human life from its biological roots to its fullest culmination would occur for the large part of humanity in a much richer form.[164]

Chapter Three

Locus Salvificus:
Jesus Crucified and the Crucified People

A visitor to the UCA's chapel in San Salvador is confronted by images of the suffering the church endured throughout the civil war, particularly the assassinations of Ellacuría and the other UCA martyrs.[1] Behind the chapel's altar, crosses made by Salvadoran artisans are flanked by mementos of the martyrs on each side wall. To the right hangs a brightly colored painting of the martyrs.[2] To the left, bronze plaques mark the resting place of each of the martyrs. Perhaps the most moving testimony to the suffering of Salvadorans is not seen until the visitor reaches the front of the chapel and turns around. There, on the back wall, hang fourteen black-and-white sketches of bodies that have endured horrible deaths. The hands, faces, torsos, and legs all betray the marks of torture.

These drawings, which predate the assassinations of the UCA martyrs, function as a contemporary way of the cross. When asked where they should be placed, Ellacuría explained that they should be on the back wall so that when the presider of the Eucharist looks out onto the congregation, he would be confronted with the suffering of the people, with their reality.[3] Thus, Ellacuría links the celebration of the Eucharist — that remembrance of Jesus' Last Supper, the crucifixion, and resurrection through which the world's salvation comes — to the ongoing crucifixion of the poor today. In making this link between those who suffer today and the Jesus who suffered centuries ago, the Jesuit Ellacuría follows a central insight of Ignatius of Loyola.

In the First Week of the *Spiritual Exercises,* Ignatius's colloquy at the foot of the cross invites one to kneel before the crucified Jesus and ask, "What have I done for Christ? What am I doing for Christ? What ought I do for Christ?"[4] In his contemporary adaptation of this moment, Ellacuría suggests that believers must

set your eyes and hearts upon these peoples who are suffering so much, some from misery and hunger, others from oppression and repression, and then, before this people thus crucified, to make the colloquy . . . by asking, What have I done to crucify them? What am I doing in order to un-crucify them? What ought I do so that this people be raised?[5]

The connection between soteriology and discipleship drove Ellacuría's theological reflection. Ellacuría knew from experience that many prominent figures in El Salvador would publicly confess their fidelity to Christ and the church, while privately advocating (or tacitly accepting) the use of violence, torture, and murder to protect their own economic and political interests. To Ellacuría, this dualism, this propensity to separate a transcendent, "spiritual" faith from earthly, material discipleship, stemmed in part from a sinful wrenching of salvation from history. If Ellacuría recognized divine transcendence as "in," not "away from" the world, then he expressed salvation in a similar way. Furthermore, this salvation in history required a discipleship in history — one that sought to transform history.

As a Christian theologian, Ellacuría naturally placed Christ at the center of divine salvific activity. Yet he moved away from the type of abstract reflection that focuses on things such as metaphysical questions about Jesus Christ's nature. Working instead from a philosophical framework that emphasized the human dynamically embedded in historical reality, a reality that possesses a theologal dimension, Ellacuría developed a Christology focused on "the historical Jesus." In so doing, he did not ignore traditional christological titles and reflection, much less deny the divinity of Christ; rather, he focused on the life and ministry of Jesus of Nazareth, as portrayed in the Gospels, in order to understand the historical density of that life and to ground subsequent soteriological reflection and discipleship. In Ellacuría's mind, grasping the historical significance of Jesus' life, ministry, and death would translate into a more faithful, historical discipleship that carries on the mission of Jesus in the world today.

Though he wrote on a wide range of theological topics, Ellacuría focused on articulating the Christian claim of salvation, or Christian soteriology.[6] He carried out this task in a traditional manner, reflecting on the Bible as a primary referent, along with dogmatic, liturgical, and theological assertions of the Christian tradition. However, Ellacuría also paid explicit attention to the context from which he wrote: the poverty of El Salvador, whose majority population experienced extraordinary violence and repression in response to any attempt to improve its lot. This context of oppression and suffering drove Ellacuría to consider a central set of theological problems: how to speak about the salvation brought about by Jesus Christ, how to announce the good news of salvation to the poor who experience premature death, and how to proclaim the Reign of God in a country whose reality seemed entirely opposed to it.

This chapter will describe Ellacuría's response to these problems, and in doing so will set forth the christological dimension of a soteriology that demands historical discipleship. The analysis will be organized around three crucial, and related, constellations of concepts: the historical character of

Jesus' ministry and death, the continuing historical significance of crucifixion in the reality of the poor, and finally the historical demands of proclaiming and manifesting the Reign of God. In these three concepts, Ellacuría gives theological flesh to the claim that salvation history is a salvation in history. As a mediation of his central philosophical principles, Ellacuría's historical soteriology takes those insights and grounds them, revealing the transcendent-historical character of Jesus' ministry, the redemption that comes from his crucifixion, and the Christian hope for salvation.

The previous chapter focused on Ellacuría's "principle and foundation," that philosophical framework in which he understood the human being's dynamic embeddedness in reality, divine transcendence as a transcendence "in" history, and revealed salvation history as a salvation in history. In the nomenclature of Ellacuría's method, that framework represents a noetic "realizing of the weight" of reality. The present chapter explores the ethical demands brought to light by a historical understanding of Jesus Christ's crucifixion. Christians, who stand at the foot of the cross, precisely because it is the site of the definitive revelation of God, are confronted by God's preferential option for the poor. They are called to make that same option, which signals the "shouldering" of reality's weight. Of course, this soteriology will also demand expression in historical discipleship, a "taking charge" of the weight of reality in history.[7]

This chapter begins by examining Ellacuría's understanding of Jesus Christ — specifically, the hermeneutic complexity of his emphasis on "the historical Jesus." While the phrase connotes the several "quests" that have occupied biblical scholars for more than two hundred years, it functions quite differently in the writings of Ellacuría.[8] He does not focus exclusively on extrabiblical historical data and different historical-critical methods to ascertain what biblical statements can be attributed to Jesus of Nazareth. Instead, Ellacuría examines the Gospel portraits of Jesus from a faith perspective that accounts for the sociopolitical nature of the Gospels themselves. In essence, Ellacuría introduces a hermeneutic focused on the "historical" dimensions of Jesus' portrait in the Gospels, a hermeneutic that functions as a critical theory to overcome the spiritualization of Jesus' crucifixion. Ellacuría's view of the historical Jesus insists that Jesus' crucifixion cannot be separated from the life and ministry that led to that execution. In order to understand the salvific consequences of Jesus' assassination, Ellacuría stresses that rather than asking why Jesus died, we must ask why Jesus was killed.

The chapter then turns its attention to Ellacuría's reflections on the poor of Latin America as a critical element of his soteriology. While his historical reading of Jesus already yields much fruit for deepening soteriological reflection, Ellacuría takes seriously the claim that the contemporary poor represent a special locus of God's presence. By offering a complex reading of the poor, which includes social, christological, and soteriological dimensions, Ellacuría renders a powerful symbol of salvation in history, the image of a "crucified people." He correlates the suffering of the poor with the suffering of Christ in order to claim that if Christians confess that Jesus Christ died bearing the weight of the sins of the world, then that salvific process continues in the crucified people who also bear the sins of the world. In this notion, Ellacuría utilizes the preferential option for the poor as a way to employ the kenotic and incarnational trajectories of Christian theology while directing personal and ecclesial discipleship toward participation in the removal of sin and its structures in the world.

Ultimately, Ellacuría's account of Christian salvation relies on that image central to the preaching of Jesus: the Reign of God. In his understanding of Christ's life, death, and resurrection, and in his correlating that understanding with the reality of the poor of his time, Ellacuría ultimately views salvation as that utopic Reign that breaks into history in an incipient, but real, way with prophetic and apocalyptic force. This inbreaking, occurring definitively in the ministry and cross of Jesus, is continued by a prophetic church that attempts to follow him and carry forward his mission, even if it must pay the price of the cross. Thus, by combining his historical reading of Jesus with the notion of the poor as a crucified people, Ellacuría renders a soteriological vision faithful to the biblical vision of the Reign of God, one that calls for a real, prophetic discipleship that participates in the historical manifestation of the Reign, a salvation in history.

The Historical Jesus of the Gospels

While much of his early academic career consisted in writing philosophical works, principally related to the thought of Xavier Zubiri, Ignacio Ellacuría also published theological work, including the collection of essays entitled *Teología política.*[9] At the time, the third part of the book generated the most attention and controversy because it dealt with the notion of violence and did not unconditionally condemn the use of revolutionary violence as an option for victims of oppression. Decades after its publication, the first and second parts of this book emerge as more significant because they represent crucial building blocks of Ellacuría's thought. They signal what would be the theological preoccupation of his entire career: namely, trying to articulate a notion of Christian salvation and discipleship from his understanding of historical reality. In particular, these essays generate soteriological reflection from the most obvious starting point for a Christian theologian: the figure of Jesus Christ.

Ellacuría never produced a full-length Christology; nevertheless, his reflections on Jesus Christ constitute a major portion of his soteriological thought.[10] These reflections build upon many of the assumptions of his philosophical work, and so articulate Christian salvation inheriting the strengths of that framework. Moreover, that philosophical framework determines certain emphases in Ellacuría's christological work. For example, we have seen that Ellacuría adopted Zubiri's perception that the legacy of

Greek thought contains problematic consequences in modern thought — what Ellacuría termed "idealistic reductionism."[11] This basic understanding in Ellacuría's thought illumines why he focused his christological thought not on the speculative question regarding the nature of Jesus as divine and human, but on the historical dimensions and significance of Jesus' ministry as portrayed in the Gospels.

In analyzing the Gospels and later christological reflections, Ellacuría notes that they include certain logical assumptions, a *logos* that reflects the historical character and challenges of the Christologies themselves. Without relativizing or negating classical christological assertions, Ellacuría argues that the Greek logos that underlies much classical Christology, while contributing much, also possesses certain limitations. He asserts that this logos, exemplified in the Chalcedonian claim that Jesus is one *ousia* and two *hypostases,* represents a "rather adequate response to a particular historical situation," that "embodied certain permanent, but not definitive, achievements."[12] To the degree that he believes that the Greek influence on Western thought leads it to separate sense and intellect, Ellacuría claims that classical Christologies tend to focus entirely on Jesus' nature to the neglect of the historical character of Jesus' mission. This Greek logos, though providing useful insights, particularly in the context of the classical thought world, often lies behind a contemporary escapist theology that cannot, or will not, grapple with the current challenges of history.

This insight leads Ellacuría to propose a historical logos, in contrast to a (Greek) natural logos, for contemporary christological reflection:

> This historical logos should start from the fact, indisputable to the eyes of faith, that the historical life of Jesus is the fullest revelation of the Christian God. This logos should also be exercised methodologically as a logos of history that subsumes and moves beyond the logos of nature, a natural logos that has frequently bypassed the logos of being (*ser*) and of reality (*realidad*). Only a logos that takes into account the historical reality of Jesus can open the way to a total Christology and a Christology corresponding to the complexity of history; only with it could we discover that at the root of salvation history there is salvation in history.[13]

Ellacuría understands an intrinsic connection between "salvation history" and "salvation in history," and he views the figure of Jesus Christ as the clearest and most definitive example of this link. Thus, Ellacuría's early soteriological reflections center on what he describes as the "historical Jesus." In focusing attention there, Ellacuría, with several other liberation theologians, invites the suspicion of many historical-critical biblical exegetes.[14] Yet careful consideration of Ellacuría's terminology and claims reveals that his project differs from the "quest for the historical Jesus," or the "Jesus research" that occupies their attention.[15]

Ellacuría's focus on Jesus' historical reality has less to do with the attempts of German biblical scholarship to secure the *geschichtlich* or *wirklich* Jesus, and more to do with *la realidad histórica* of Jesus as portrayed in the Gospels, understanding the weight that this term carries in Ellacuría's philosophy of historical reality.[16] It represents a hermeneutic perspective that, acknowledging that human existence is intrinsically constituted by historical, social, and political factors, claims that interpretation of the Gospel portrayal of Jesus cannot be complete without taking these into account.

Ellacuría's examination of the historical Jesus takes into account the complexity of the Gospels as the product of early Christian christological reflection. He acknowledges that distinct Christologies exist in the Gospels, but this plurality does not call into question the inspired character of the Gospels; on the contrary, it demonstrates an important theological model. "The different [Christologies] are important because they indicate that distinct christological readings of the same historical Jesus are due, in good measure, to the situation and needs of those who have faith in Jesus."[17] Rather than performing a simplistic reading of the Gospels' Christologies or conflating them into one reading, Ellacuría recognizes the differentiated christological portraits, their relationship to specific ecclesial contexts and demands, and, finally, the theological imperative to perform the same christological task: a faith-inspired reading of Jesus Christ that reflects the situation and needs of a particular faith community.

Ellacuría's investigation of the "real" or "historical" Jesus does not seek what John P. Meier defines as the "total reality" or even the "reasonably complete portrait" of Jesus of Nazareth as he lived in the first century.[18] Rather, Ellacuría seeks the social, economic, and political dimensions of the Gospel portrait of Jesus that contextualize the reason why he was executed. His position represents a confessional-soteriological approach that plunges into what other interpretations of Jesus' crucifixion omit. It seeks to uncover the sociopolitical dimension of the scriptural portrayal of Jesus in the Gospel texts so that the soteriological question "Why did Jesus die?" may be answered only after answering the question, "Why was Jesus killed?" In doing this, Ellacuría historicizes the former question, grounding the soteriological interpretation of the cross and the discipleship that follows from that cross.

The Sociopolitical Dimension of Jesus' Messianic Ministry

Ellacuría believes that other Christologies, with the soteriologies they entail, base themselves on an *a priori* assumption of Jesus' nature as divine (and his self-conscious realization of that divinity), a continuing legacy of the Greek or natural logos. In contrast, Ellacuría proposes a historical logos that ties christological and soteriological assertions to an *a posteriori* understanding of the life and ministry of Jesus. Of course, this assertion stems from an *a priori* in Ellacuría's own thought: the defining character of the human immersion in reality, and the view of transcendence that acknowledges salvation history as a salvation in history. While these notions comfortably accommodate the Chalcedonian claim, they also indicate the importance of Jesus' historical life and ministry, which culminate in his crucifixion and resurrection, as a *real* starting point that illumines Jesus Christ's soteriological significance.

The turn to the sociopolitical dimension of Jesus' ministry indicates not just a hermeneutic imperative for reading the Scriptures, but a dimension of discipleship tied to that reading. "We would affirm not just that the way of the Father's revelation passes through the life of Jesus, but that only by taking the life of Jesus, by following [*siguiendo*] his life can one reach the revelation of the Father."[19] This position does not deny the truth or validity of subsequent traditional or magisterial understandings of Jesus Christ, but it affirms that these understandings should be rooted in the scriptural presentation of Jesus' life and ministry, a presentation with social, political, and economic dimensions that becomes manifested in the lives of Jesus' followers.

In describing the "sociopublic" dimension of Jesus' ministry, Ellacuría identifies Jesus as part of the prophetic tradition, an identification Jesus' contemporaries ascribe to him in the Gospels as well.[20] Like the prophets of the Old Testament, Jesus as prophet engages a religious and social critique attacking hypocrisy, ritualism, legalism, and oppression.[21] In the case of Jesus, no less than with other prophetic figures such as Amos and Isaiah, this critique, though religious in its language, cannot be separated from its sociopolitical implications. Ellacuría recognizes that the Christian interpretation of Jesus as a prophet exists in the oldest strata of the tradition, and he fleshes out this interpretation by identifying its sociopolitical dimensions.

Ellacuría perceives that the Gospels portray Jesus' prophetic ministry as possessing a religious and social character that puts him into conflict with leaders whose authority also has a religious and social character. By admitting that the religious leaders at the time of Jesus also wielded social influence, Ellacuría understands Gospel episodes, such as the execution of John the Baptist and Jesus' cleansing of the Temple, as socioreligious in character as well. For him, Jesus' prophetic behavior as religious critic and social critic necessarily reflect an undeniably political character. One of the central themes of Jesus' prophetic career consists in the dialectical opposition of poverty and wealth, not simply as ascetic, but as related in a decidedly sociopolitical manner. In the Gospels, Jesus condemns wealth as unjust by virtue of its relationship to poverty. Furthermore, Jesus ties this social dimension of wealth to a religious notion of wealth as idolatrous, in its tendency to become an absolute value.

Though Ellacuría draws upon a number of biblical passages to support his arguments, his interpretation of the incident between Jesus and the rich young man exemplifies how Ellacuría arrives at a notion of discipleship tied profoundly to soteriology.[22] Rather than interpreting this passage as "spiritualistic," in which the eternal life about which the rich young man asks Jesus is seen exclusively as the life beyond, or as "ascetic," in which the query pertains to a perfection attained by only a few individuals, Ellacuría claims that the passage deals with a historical following of Christ, a discipleship that, like Jesus' own ministry, has sociopolitical implications. Not allowing the Matthean phrase "if you wish to be perfect" to cloud the thrust of the passage, Ellacuría stresses how, particularly in Mark and Luke, the young man lacks not just perfection but salvation itself. Thus, Jesus' response indicates that "the Christian is not merely an ethical being who follows laws, but rather is a person who follows Christ's life in faith and attempts to live it as their own as much as possible.... Only those who are free from wealth are fit to follow Jesus and to continue his mission."[23]

Thus, the first step of Ellacuría's historical logos involves an examination of the sociopublic dimension of Jesus' prophetic ministry. This analysis yields a portrait of a Jesus who emphasizes lived faith as the key to salvific contact with God. Jesus' condemnation of wealth, because of its intrinsic relation to the existence of poverty, follows from the centuries-old connection that prophets established between religious adherence to the God of Israel and just social relations. This condemnation also signals why the social and religious leaders perceived Jesus as a threat. However, the full discussion of this threat and how it led to Jesus' execution comes in Ellacuría's next step in the historical logos: accounting for the messianic character of Jesus' ministry.

In adjudicating the political nature of Jesus' ministry, particularly in its relation to messianism, Ellacuría appears to be addressing not just religious and political questions of the past, but characteristics of his Salvadoran context as well. In a country in which catechists and religious workers could easily be branded guerrillas or communists to legitimize their kidnapping, torture, and execution, Ellacuría sees a parallel in the relationship between Jesus and the zealots.

Relying on historical-critical scholarship, Ellacuría does not hesitate to declare that Jesus was condemned for political reasons, as a political threat to Roman authorities.[24] However, Ellacuría also acknowledges that Jesus' ministry had a primarily religious character. Though he may have been mistaken for a zealot and even killed as one, Jesus was not a purely political rebel. Yet because his religious ministry and preaching had such an enormous social and political impact, Jesus was perceived by the authorities as a threat that needed to be eliminated.[25] Ellacuría's insight into this portrayal of Jesus carries a double significance: clearly, while this portrayal of Jesus calls for a discipleship engaged in serious sociopolitical questions, Jesus' difference from the zealots also negates a reduction of discipleship exclusively to the sociopolitical.

Ellacuría articulates an understanding of Jesus' messianism that includes, but is not limited to, its contemporary sociopolitical connotations. Jesus veers away from a purely political view of messianism, but he does not exclude it completely. He was mistaken for a zealot precisely because of the sociopolitical dimension of his ministry, even though that dimension does not fully account for the entirety of his ministry.[26] This interpretation is influenced by Ellacuría's non-dualistic approach to Christian salvation. "Salvation history has a direct relationship with salvation in history; as a mediation of full salvation, it has an ineluctable sociopolitical dimension. Going through it, one may pass beyond it as well, but one cannot move beyond without it, if that movement is to be effectively real."[27] Thus, Jesus' messianism, which includes social and political dimensions but is not limited to them, models a discipleship that though religious in origin and character has intrinsic connection to the social and political.

As a summary, Ellacuría states:

Jesus works to transform a politicized religion into a political faith. He does not abandon the idea of humanity's salvation, but he includes all dimensions of human salvation; from salvation in history, one must pass to a metahistorical salvation, and it is the announcing of the metahistorical salvation that is going to help what should be an authentic salvation in history, just as reciprocally, this authentic salvation in history is going to be the uniquely valid sign of what humans can understand as metahistorical salvation.[28]

Just as Ellacuría employed his philosophical framework to speak about God's transcendence and immanence coherently without conflation, he articulates a notion of salvation that emphasizes its historical dimension without dismissing its metahistorical character as well. In particular, the sociopolitical dimension of Jesus' ministry serves as a sign of what the historical character of salvation, and the subsequent character of Christian discipleship, looks like. More than a surface reading of the Gospels, Ellacuría's analysis strives to see Jesus within the complexity of the social, political, and historical reality of his portrayal. This "political faith" takes into account not only humanity-in-reality, but reality as theologal — a reality in which God transcends. So proper Christian discipleship consists in the living out of this political faith as fully engaged in history, but also possessing a dimension of the metahistorical.

For Ellacuría, the sociopolitical character of Jesus' ministry demands operative faith. Following his theological imperative to identify the following of Jesus as the mode of access to the Father's revelation, Ellacuría views in Jesus' ministry an intrinsic and inseparable connection between faith and discipleship. "There is in his [Jesus'] way of life and his mission a pronounced shift from a religious emphasis to one of operative faith.... On the personal manner in which discipleship [*seguimiento*] and faith are intertwined and mutually conditioned depends Christian holiness, that is, the salvific presence of God in humanity and humanity's access to God."[29] Ellacuría finds in the appeal to lived faith, particularly as an imitation of Jesus, an account of Christian living superior to the abstract notion of supernatural grace elevating a deficient human nature. In other words, he finds in it a superiority of the historical logos over the natural logos. This account, though articulated in religious terminology, involves sociopolitical action on the part of the adherent.

The earliest of Ellacuría's soteriological reflections center on the figure of Jesus and the sociopolitical dimensions of his preaching and ministry. These elements, the results of the application of a historical logos or hermeneutic to the Gospels' portrayal of Jesus, provide Ellacuría insights into his own situation and illuminate the character of discipleship in that situation. For Ellacuría, Jesus' political execution signals a kind of parallel equation: just as the sociopolitical dimension of Jesus' ministry was mistaken for the revolutionary ends of the zealots, so has the work of committed Christians, which naturally entails a sociopolitical dimension, been mistaken for the ends of revolutionary guerrillas. While the connections of this discipleship to soteriology reflect Ellacuría's insights into the relationship between salvation history and salvation in history, the fullest soteriological import of his analysis of Jesus and his ministry comes in considering the salvific character of Jesus' death and resurrection.

Why Did Jesus Die? vs. Why Was Jesus Killed?

A few years after the publication of *Teología política,* Ellacuría wrote an article whose title reveals contrasting approaches to the salvific import of Jesus' passion: "Why Did Jesus Die? and Why Was Jesus Killed?"[30] For Ellacuría, the former question comes from a view of Jesus' death as expiatory in an abstract or ahistorical manner, a death whose inevitability has little to do with Jesus' public ministry and way of life. The latter question, however, indicates a further step in the historical logos he had been developing. It takes seriously the life of Jesus and his proclamation of the Reign of God as that which put him in conflict with social, religious, and political powers that would strike against him.[31]

By identifying and differentiating the two significant questions about Jesus' death, Ellacuría does not wish to deny the validity or importance of the first question. He affirms the salvific importance of Jesus' death; however, he takes issue with those who would articulate that importance without reference to the life, preaching, and ministry of Jesus.[32] While personal or psychological interpretations of Jesus' death may be interesting, they too easily fall prey to an abstract or escapist theology that ignores historical reality.[33] For Ellacuría, attention to why Jesus was killed recognizes Jesus' crucifixion as the culmination of his ministry, while at the same time articulating the salvific importance of the crucifixion in a manner that an abstract atonement theory does not.

Ellacuría's opposition to an abstract atonement theory stems from the importance of history in his philosophical framework. For Ellacuría, an interpretation of atonement that expresses Jesus' death as a "natural" necessity eliminates the responsibility of those who killed Jesus. Moreover, it does not call for any action on the part of the believer to destroy injustice or build love to counter sin in the world. To realize the theological importance of the cross in salvation history, Ellacuría returns to his historical logos, one that emphasizes the dynamic sense of God as creator who transcends "in" the world.[34] Within this framework, God raises the crucified one from the dead because he proclaimed the Reign, a Reign that does not transcend "away" from history. Jesus' death is necessary, but not as a design of abstract creation. The necessity stems from the reality of what happens in history.

Ellacuría recognizes the necessity of Jesus' death as prefigured in the prophets; however, this prefiguration occurs not simply in their words, but in what occurred to them. "This [historic] necessity is grounded in the opposition between the proclamation of the Reign and the historical verification of sin. Resisting oppressive powers and struggling for liberation in history brought [the prophets] persecution and death, but that resistance and struggle were simply the historical consequence of a life that responds to God's word."[35] The logic of the prophets that carries through to Jesus consists in death's necessity, but a necessity that stems from the opposition of the Reign of God and the reign of sin.[36] If death is necessary because of sin, then this "historical" necessity demands a look at the causes of death, the larger sin of the world.

In focusing on a larger sense of sin, Ellacuría does not wish to eliminate consideration of personal sin. Yet to the degree he believes that the "natural" logos tends to overemphasize this, Ellacuría counters with an understanding of that sin as "a 'collective reality' that grounds [*fundamenta*] individual sins and makes them possible. It is this theologal and collective sin that destroys history and impedes the future that God wanted for it."[37] The description of sin as theologal depicts sin in its wider aperture as the obstacle to God's will for the world. It recognizes that just as the will of God takes form in history, preeminently in the life and ministry of Jesus Christ, so does this anti-will. As objectivized in historical powers that oppose the proclamation and manifestation of God's will for the world, this sin necessarily kills those like the prophets, Jesus, and even those today who proclaim, and live according to, God's will.

Ellacuría seeks a way to affirm the traditional phrase "Jesus died for our sins," while simultaneously affirming the insights that come from his historical logos into Jesus' execution. The claims about Jesus' self-consciousness are adjudicated with a wisdom that comes from practical experience. Ellacuría draws on the model of Archbishop Oscar Romero to demonstrate how Jesus could possess a sense of his imminent death and the reasons for that death without resorting to exaggerated claims about Jesus' self-knowledge based more on a theological notion of his omniscience.[38] Moreover, this type of knowledge of his imminent death would not contradict those moments of fear and abandonment portrayed in the Gospels, as the claim of omniscience does. Archbishop Romero and many other martyrs illuminate a continuity with Jesus' death that reveals the hallmarks of Christian discipleship.[39]

So Ellacuría's detailed examination of the scriptural texts leads him to conclude that they portray Jesus' death as the result of his ministry, as a result of the growing opposition to him from social, religious, and political leaders. He asserts that none of the evangelists' accounts of Jesus' crucifixion — not even those of Luke and John, who provide in Jesus' final words some self-conscious understanding of a wider meaning to his death — can be described as an abstract expiation. "Jesus dies on the cross accused by his enemies, abandoned by his disciples. All of this comes as a result of what he did during his life, as the result of his radical opposition to those who had just defeated him by crucifying him."[40] For Ellacuría, the Gospels do not communicate an ahistorical or extrinsic expiation; on the contrary, what occurred in his death came as a consequence of his life: the announcement and realization of the Reign of God among human beings.[41]

Ultimately, Ellacuría's reflections on Jesus Christ rest on an understanding of the Reign of God as that to which Jesus dedicated his life, that which would lead to his death, and finally, that which gives content to the notion of salvation from sin. To the question, "Why would you die?" Ellacuría would have Jesus respond, "To bring about the Reign of God." This response corresponds with the importance of the Reign in Jesus' preaching, and it illuminates the faith required of Jesus that he would ultimately be vindicated.[42]

Before turning to analyze Ellacuría's understanding of the Reign, it would be helpful to assess the results of the analysis so far. Ellacuría focuses attention on the "historical Jesus" because he believes it to be the best way to ensure a faithful, historical Christian discipleship. His "historical logos" involves rethinking the significance of Jesus' death by placing it within the sociopolitical-economic situation portrayed in the Gospels. According to this "historicization" of Jesus' death, Jesus was killed because of his confrontation with the reigning powers of his day. Theologically, then, reflection on the salvific import of Jesus' death, whether in the language of redemption, expiation, or other categories, must include the implications of the fact that Jesus was killed. When Christians "stand at the foot of the cross," they must do so acknowledging that the cross is a political form of execution. Thus, if Christians are moved to discipleship in that gaze upon the cross, that discipleship should possess the social-political-economic marks that characterized Jesus' life: a historical way of the cross.

He summarizes the significance of that life in this manner:

> They kill Jesus for living a historical life, one that includes a concrete proclamation of the Reign of God. Then, that life, taken away, is converted into a life for all human beings in a permanent and transcendent manner that elevates that historical life. Furthermore, this elevation, I believe, should extend to the lives of human beings and the life of society in order to enrich them, because in reality society's life and humanity's life is full of sin....
>
> This grace of Jesus, this example of Jesus, this virtue of Jesus, this spirit of Christ continues after the resurrection. It extends to history

and really goes on taking away the sins of the world; it attempts to take away the sins of the world; it attempts to convert hearts and convert society.[43]

In coming to understand the nature of Jesus' ministry and the significance of his death, Ellacuría models a reliance on the Scriptures and the tradition of the church as sources of revelation. However, Ellacuría does not relegate the crucifixion of Jesus and its significance to a past event that believers merely recall. Rather, he views the crucifixion of Jesus as possessing a sacramental character: in the reality of the poor today, we see a continuation of Jesus' crucifixion. They experience a crucifixion that demands the attention of believers and invites them on a path of historical discipleship seeking the Reign of God.

The Crucified People as Principle of Salvation

In his reading of the Gospels, Ellacuría notes what appears to be an obvious point: Jesus' ministry in the Gospels focuses on the poor and marginalized. A commentator would reasonably expect Ellacuría to develop a theology centered on the liberation of the poor. Yet while he envisions Christian discipleship as involving participation in historical struggles for liberation, Ellacuría does not treat the poor as passive receptors of liberation, nor even as active agents only of their own liberation. The role Ellacuría assigns to the poor moves beyond this notion in two ways. First, his various theological essays on contemporary poverty identify its significance in multiple layers: social, theologal, christological, soteriological, and ecclesiological.[44] This multilayered analysis indicates ways in which the poor serve as a theological "locus" of salvation.[45] Second, using the Old Testament figure of the Suffering Servant, Ellacuría articulates the salvific character of Jesus' crucifixion and finds a historical continuation of that crucifixion in the deaths of the poor today, in the ones he describes as the "crucified people." Though recognizing Christ's presence in the poor represents a motif present in the Bible and throughout the Christian tradition, the notion obtains soteriological weight in Ellacuría's thought. As suffering servants, the crucified people are a principle of salvation who illuminate salvation and call for discipleship.

The Poor as Theological Locus

Foremost among Ellacuría's theological claims about the poor stands his contention that they constitute a theological locus, a privileged place for theological reflection. "The poor in Latin America are a theological location inasmuch as they constitute the maximal scandalous presence, prophetic and apocalyptic, of the Christian God and, consequently, the privileged location of Christian praxis and reflection."[46] As this privileged locus, the poor and their reality disrupt complacency and force reevaluation of Christian theological themes. Ellacuría thus engages in a hermeneutics of the poor to understand their significance across a range of theological categories: socioeconomic, theologal, christological, soteriological, and ecclesiological.

Before ascribing any kind of theological meaning or nuance to the terms "poverty," or "the poor," Ellacuría understands poverty foremost as a socioeconomic reality.[47] The poor lack fundamental material needs, and this lack means death for the poor. Though Ellacuría acknowledges other meanings to the term "poverty," these cannot supplant this basic socioeconomic definition in his thought.[48] Since the death of the poor appears contradictory to the will of God, poverty involves sin and necessitates theological reflection. Indeed, since the majority of the globe's population suffers from poverty, it demands attention to poverty as a principal form of sin's domination in the world. The sinful character of poverty emerges as Ellacuría notes that "poverty" is descriptive not just of a privative state, but as indicative of a certain causation. The observation that the poor lack material needs leads to the question as to why that lack exists.

In moving to the causes of poverty, Ellacuría articulates the intrinsic link between poverty and wealth as a dialectic one: there are poor because there are rich.[49] This dialectic relationship plays such an important role that if the lack of material needs were universal, then poverty would not be an appropriate term for the condition. The term "poverty" should not be used even of simple inequality.

With allusion to his context in El Salvador (and that of Latin America and the so-called Third World in general), Ellacuría insists that poverty describes that situation in which people are dispossessed, denied what is rightfully theirs. "The material nature of poverty is the real, irreplaceable element. It consists not only in lacking what is indispensable but in being dispossessed dialectically of the fruit of one's work and the work itself, from social and political power by those who, with that plunder, have enriched themselves and taken power."[50]

Aware that a simplistic use of this dualism serves to demonize others, Ellacuría concedes that there are those among the "not poor" who do not so easily fall on the other side of the dialectic.[51] Yet this realization does not blunt the stinging critique for those who clearly fall on the other side of poverty's dialectic. If the poor are dispossessed, then these rich take possession. If the poor are oppressed and abused, then these rich are those who oppress and abuse. Of course, he does not acquit the former group entirely. These poor must still be on guard against the idolatry that devotion to wealth entails; furthermore, they must respond to the universal call to charity and transformation of society that the gospel announces.

Ellacuría invokes "theologal" language in order to speak about God's self-revelation in the world, God's will for the world.[52] It is a way to speak of God's transcendence "in" the world without collapsing divine transcendence. Therefore, he describes the theologal concept of the poor as "the personal and historical reality of human beings, and for this reality what the living and true God is, and what in reality God wishes to do among human beings and the poor."[53] To Ellacuría, biblical passages such as the Exodus and the Lucan beatitudes reveal this theologal concept because they proclaim a just God who promises to establish a just Reign, a God who hears the afflictions of the poor. As was the case in considering creation, Ellacuría's reflections on the theologal dimension of reality lead him to reflect on the Trinitarian God. Poverty is a negation of the Trinity. As a force of sin, it defies a Father who tenderly cares for the weakest children; it battles a Son who was sent to establish a Reign of justice and love; it pushes away the presence of the Spirit who animates the lives of all people.

The theologal dimension of poverty, while indicating the positive attributes of God for the poor, also presents a problem. For believers, the existence of the poor constitutes a challenge to faith; it implies a sort of apophatic moment in which the absence of God is most painfully felt. The cry of the poor for justice challenges belief in the Trinitarian God, and pushes the believer past the reality of present poverty to a hope in the promises of the God who saves.[54] So the poor simultaneously present the illuminating revelation of God and a call for conversion. As a presence both prophetic and apocalyptic, they illumine God's presence, but also indicate a hidden and scandalous dimension of this presence.

If Ellacuría's earliest christological reflections concentrated on Jesus' life and mission as the keys to understanding his death, then the poor, in turn, serve to clarify that life and mission and so serve as a location for christological reflection. Ellacuría notes that the Gospel of Luke has Jesus inaugurate his mission with a reading of the Isaiah scroll (Luke 4:16–21). If one understands that passage as signaling the "signs" of Jesus' mission (and his link to the prophetic tradition), then the poor reveal in what ways and to what degree that mission of announcing the good news to the poor, and liberty to captives, has been fulfilled. To the degree that Jesus' messianic mission remains unfulfilled, the church discovers its mission in the world: to announce the good news to the poor. For Ellacuría, the poor illuminate not just Jesus' messianic character, but his divine one as well. His reading of the parable of the Last Judgment (Matt. 25:31–46) places the poor at the heart of Christology because the heart of salvation/condemnation depends on the way one treats the poor. Jesus, as divine judge, identifies himself with the poor, revealing how they are an incarnation of God. Finally, Ellacuría notes that they reveal that Jesus' anointing, mission, and service to them is what put Jesus in conflict with those who would kill him.

As a theological locus, the poor provide a threefold interpretation of the central christological theme of *kenosis*. Here Ellacuría cites the classic canticle from Philippians 2 to underline the incarnation as a primary kenotic moment, but not as the only sense in which God's self-emptying is revealed. Ellacuría also identifies the ministry of Jesus as fundamentally a self-emptying praxis with and for the poor, a praxis that demonstrated God's love for all and one that put Jesus in conflict with authorities. Jesus' historical death, his crucifixion for the life and ministry that he carried out, constitutes the third moment of that kenotic dynamic. This *kenosis,* this self-emptying that reveals God's love for the poor, marks Jesus' divinity. "In Jesus' reality, in his praxis and his word, there is an essential connection between his Father (by means of himself), the poor (dialectically understood), and poverty itself. From this perspective of the poor comes the true confession that Jesus is God, and that God for us is the God of Jesus."[55]

Ellacuría indicates the salvific importance of the poor by examining the relationship of the poor to the gospel message. In some sense, the poor receive the gospel message; they are the evangelized because they hear good news. Yet as the privileged ones loved by God, the poor also evangelize the world. In working out how the poor are both evangelized and evangelizers, Ellacuría incorporates his christological and soteriological insights to call for a "civilization of poverty" that manifests the hope for the salvific Reign of God.

In developing this soteriological concept of the poor, Ellacuría builds on the insights of the Second Vatican Council's *Lumen gentium,* which states, "Just as Christ carried out the work of redemption in poverty and under oppression, so the church is called to follow the same path in communicating to human beings the fruits of salvation."[56] If Christ bore the sins of the world in poverty and oppression, then the poor today are the ones who bear that same sin. The work of implanting rights and justice then signals the dawning of a salvific order on earth.[57] This work evangelizes the poor and shows the way of conversion.

> Thus, the great salvific tasks consists in evangelizing the poor, so that from their material poverty they may reach the consciousness and spirit necessary to: first, escape indigence and oppression; second, end oppressive structures; and third, install a new heaven and earth where sharing takes precedence over accumulating, where there is time to listen and enjoy the voice of God in the heart of the material world and the heart of human history.[58]

Ellacuría's programmatic description requires the option for the poor as the basis for evangelization and so intimates the ecclesiological dimension of poverty. Like other Latin American liberation theologians, Ellacuría notes the importance of the phrase "the church of the poor." While this phrase comes from Vatican II, it finds its fuller elaboration in the ecclesial documents from Medellín as well as the work of liberation theologians themselves.[59] For Ellacuría, the "church of the poor" indicates not that a part of the church dedicates itself preferentially for the poor, still less a division of the church noted by some socioeconomic marker. For him the modifier "of the poor" designates "a constitutive and configuring feature of the entire church, such that it is either of the poor or it ceases to be the true and holy church wanted by God."[60] So the poor indicate the church's mission: its solidarity, its evangelization, and even its suffering from persecution, from which come its preferential option.

Ellacuría's exploration of poverty as a theological locus, as a socio-economic reality as well as its several theological dimensions, represents a crucial direction in his soteriology. Those victims of history, those insignificant ones, come to possess a theological power for Ellacuría. The paradoxical nature of the poor as evangelized and evangelizers leads Ellacuría to reflect on that greatest paradox of the Christian faith: that salvation comes through the cross of Jesus. This seeming defeat of Jesus' mission must actually be regarded as a triumph. The full *kenosis* of the Son takes form on the cross because the Reign of God confronts the reign of sin. Ultimately, Ellacuría's soteriological concept of the poor finds its climax in that historical link to the Reign, what he describes as the civilization of poverty. However, that link may be made only after exploring further how Ellacuría comes to understand the poor as the historical continuation of Jesus' crucifixion — to understand them as a crucified people.

Bearing the Weight of the Sin of the World

Ellacuría weaves together reflection on Jesus and on the poor in his image of the suffering poor as a "crucified people." In his essay of this title, Ellacuría recognizes that contemporary theology cannot escape the fact that the majority of the world's population languishes in suffering. This terrible reality of the poor leads him to examine how the poor relate to salvation history.[61] In order to answer this question, Ellacuría correlates the Christian tradition's central salvific figure, Jesus, understood in light of the Suffering Servant of Isaiah, with the poor as the "crucified people," who characterize the scandal of the present situation. Each figure illumines the other: the crucified people de-romanticize the passion of Jesus, while the passion of Jesus illumines the salvific importance of the crucified people today.

Ellacuría identifies this task of correlation as "historical soteriology," and he takes it as a methodological presupposition that any situation in history should be considered from the angle of its "corresponding" key in revelation.[62] This presupposition implies that both sides of this correlation illumine the other. While Christians have readily accepted the first part of the presupposition, that revelation sheds light on contemporary situations, Ellacuría emphasizes the complementary assertion that the contemporary situation enriches and makes present the fullness of revelation as well. With this methodological presupposition, Ellacuría hopes to bring out the historical nature of Jesus' passion and the salvific character of the people's crucifixion for theoretical and practical purposes.

Ellacuría explicitly chooses to focus on a soteriological, not ontological, consideration of what Jesus and the crucified people may mean for the salvation of humanity because of its implications for discipleship. He states that a historical soteriology must be one whose "essential reference point is the saving work of Jesus, but it must also be a soteriology that historicizes this saving work, and historicizes it as the continuation and following [*seguimiento*] of Jesus and his work."[63] The key to this historicization lies in the recovery of the scandalous character of Christian soteriology.

Ellacuría wants to reframe the scandal of Jesus' death, claiming that life comes from the death, by connecting it to the death of the poor. In an ahistorical soteriology, the scandal of Jesus' death comes from Jesus' nature as innocent victim. It is an abstract scandal that avoids the seeming failure of Jesus' proclamation of the Reign and leaves the consequences for Christian discipleship ambiguous at best. Consequently, the hope extended to the suffering poor of today involves participation in an ahistorical resurrection after death. In contrast, a historical soteriology acknowledges that Jesus maintained a hope for the Reign of God, but one that was tied to his life. The cross is the culmination of that life — the ultimate giving of self that confronts the reign of sin and illumines the path to salvation. Jesus' resurrection validates that life and death that proclaimed the Reign. In this model, Ellacuría wishes to demonstrate that the hope for the crucified people resides not solely in a transhistorical resurrection, but is a hope for that resurrection tied to a working for the Reign of God in the present.

The theological connection between Jesus and the crucified people indicates the importance of the mystery of the cross. Ellacuría remains wary of theories of creation or resurrection that obscure the meaning of the cross, that is, isolate the cross from Jesus' proclamation of the Reign of God. To those who associate with the cross a necessity derived from creation, he notes that creation and resurrection are not intrinsically connected; death and resurrection are. The resurrection of Jesus points back to his crucifixion. He does not rise as the terminus of an eternal cosmic plan; he rises because he was crucified. Since Jesus' life was taken away for proclaiming the Reign of God, he receives a new life as fulfillment of that Reign. The cross breaks the hold of the reign of sin. This emphasis on the cross corresponds to Ellacuría's view of Jesus' death and the crucifixion of the people as historical realities and the result of actions in history.

Following the same line of thought as his previous christological work, Ellacuría stresses that Jesus' death should be seen not as a natural necessity, but as a historical necessity. His death results from those oppressive powers who resist the proclamation of the Reign of God.[64] Viewing Jesus' death as a natural necessity eliminates the responsibility of those who killed him. In its tendency to either veil this aspect of sin or place everything under God's providence, this view advocates a fatalistic approach to human life and obscures the necessity for humans to act in history.

Ellacuría's overarching concern involves the danger resulting from a simplistic expiatory or sacrificial view of Christ's crucifixion, a view summarized in the schema "sin-offense-victim-expiation-forgiveness."[65] To counter this, Ellacuría's soteriology builds on the fundamental insight that Jesus is killed because of the historical life he led, not as an expiatory victim for sins that does not consider his historical life. Jesus lived this life because that was what truly proclaiming the Reign of God entailed, not because he was seeking a redemptive death. Therefore, what is salvific cannot be separated from what is historical. Ellacuría asserts, "Jesus' death is not the end of the meaning of his life, but rather the end of that pattern that must be reproduced and followed in new lives with the hope of resurrection and the seal of exaltation."[66] Ellacuría's logic indicates that the cross is the logical end-point for a life lived in confrontation with the reign of sin in history. Jesus' crucifixion does not mean the undoing of his proclamation and life — the cross completes them.

Ellacuría's historical soteriology ushers forth an imitative discipleship that seeks where and how the saving action of Jesus was carried out (in the past) in order to pursue it in history (in the present). Though Ellacuría acknowledges the importance of worship, particularly the sacramental presence of the Eucharist, he emphasizes that it cannot be considered the whole of the presence and continuity of Jesus. There must be a continuation in history of what Jesus carried out in his life and *as* he carried it out.

So who is it that continues the saving action of Jesus by bearing the weight of the world's sin? Ellacuría defines the "crucified people" simply as:

> that collective body, which being the majority of humankind owes its situation of crucifixion to a social order organized and maintained by a minority that exercises its domination through a conjunction of factors, which taken together and given their concrete, historical impact, must be regarded as sin.[67]

Ellacuría finds this designation of a collective body as the subject of salvation perfectly consonant with the Bible's use of the "people of Israel," delighting in how it counters a modern hyperindividualism that ignores the social dimension of human existence in reality. While he constantly adverts to the legitimacy of personal and psychological approaches to salvation, Ellacuría finds in his sociohistorical designation of the crucified people a way to make not just the relatively acceptable claim that they are collective receptors of salvation, but the more radical one that they function, in some sense, as a principle of salvation for the world.

> The subject of liberation is, ideally, the one who himself is the greatest victim of domination, the one who really carries the cross of history, because this cross is the mockery, not of the one who suffers, but of the one who imposes it. It carries in itself a process of death that can and should give way to a distinct way of life. The cross is the verification of the reign of nothing, of evil, that being defined negatively as "not-reality," is that which annihilates and makes all things evil. Yet because of the negated victim, it may give way to a new life that has the character of creation.[68]

In defining those who suffer poverty as a crucified people, Ellacuría does not hold illusory notions about their lack of complicity in sin. Indeed, many who are oppressed not only commit grave personal sins, but participate in the oppression and domination of others. Acknowledging this reality, Ellacuría points out how the structural nature of his analysis should not be interpreted as Manichean, in which one side is all good, the other all evil, but as complementary to a personal analysis that recognizes how the personal is affected by the structural and historical.

Ellacuría is not attempting to replace or relativize the salvific significance of Jesus Christ. The crucified people's suffering does not exonerate them, nor of itself save the world. Indeed, key to Ellacuría's analysis will be the extent to which he can demonstrate that while the fact of death does not possess a salvific character in itself nor bring about resurrection and life, Jesus' cross and resurrection are the culmination of his life and the definitive inauguration of the Reign of God. His death, as a victory over the reign of sin, means that God reveals Godself most fully in self-sacrificial love and in bearing the weight of the world's sin. Now, just as the mission of Jesus, the proclamation of Jesus, and the praxis of Jesus need to be continued in the liturgical and historical life of the church today, so, sadly, does the process of confronting sin. This latter principle continues in history in the suffering of the poor and oppressed today, the very ones with whom Jesus self-identifies in the Scriptures. Ellacuría turns to the figure of the Suffering Servant in the books of Isaiah to provide this soteriological insight to the death of the crucified.

Suffering Servants: Jesus and the Crucified People

Ellacuría carries out an analysis of the Suffering Servant songs in Isaiah (chapters 42–53) in order to discover characteristics of this servant that will deepen the soteriological reflection on Christ's death and the deaths of those he calls the crucified people. If he has been building a case for an alternative to an ahistorical theory of expiation that renders the historical life of Jesus, and therefore the historical lives of his followers, essentially irrelevant, then the Suffering Servant represents that biblical image that can assert expiation, but as the culmination of Jesus' historical life. Moreover, as a theological trope, the referential character of the Suffering Servant is not exhausted by Jesus, but fruitfully links the suffering of the poor to that of Jesus. Ellacuría performs this theological task both with appeal to the Bible, citing the Isaian theology in which YHWH's intimate and saving presence and the people's response is in history, and to tradition, as an imitation of primitive Christian use of these passages to interpret Jesus' death.[69]

To begin his task, Ellacuría discerns several "historico-theological" characteristics of the Suffering Servant that will serve to illuminate the expiatory nature of Jesus' crucifixion and to discern what or who serves as the historic continuation of that crucifixion. Ellacuría notes that the Servant suffers as a result of historical human actions, actions that are unjust. This treatment humiliates the Servant. Not only is the salvific potential of the Servant invisible, but the opposite seems true. The Servant appears to be a sinner.

Ellacuría contrasts this hostile, exterior view of the Servant with that of the cantor who recognizes the Servant's humiliation as undeserved, as the innocent taking on the sins of others. Though these sins mean the Servant's death, the Servant accepts this lot. Moreover, the songs portray God as accepting the Servant's sacrifice as expiatory of others' sins.[70] Because of the crucial nature of this characteristic, Ellacuría's reflection on expiation will be cited in full:

> The Lord himself accepts this situation: he places upon [the Servant] all of our crimes. Moreover, it says that the Lord chose to crush him with suffering and submit his life as expiation, although later on he would reward him and give him complete recompense. They are the strongest statements, but they do admit the interpretation that God accepts, as having been wished by Godself, as salutary, the sacrifice of one who has died in history because of human sin. Only in a difficult act of faith is the cantor of the Servant able to discover that which appears to be the opposite to the eyes of history. It is precisely because he sees one who, weighed by sin and the consequences of sin, did not commit them, that the singer dares, by the very injustice of the situation, to attribute what is happening to God. God must necessarily attribute a fully salvific value to this act of absolute, historical injustice. God may make this attribution because the Servant himself accepts his destiny to save, through his own suffering, those who cause it.[71]

It seems that to Ellacuría, the logic of the Gospel dictates that there must be continual bearing of the world's sins. The value of this bearing persists, no matter what the conscious state of the victims. Though occasionally Ellacuría differentiates between those who are mere victims and those who are victims because of their resistance, he does not do away with the former's salvific potential. Because they bear the weight of sin they did not commit, the crucified people serve as the historical location of that death that bears salvation.[72]

To be sure, Ellacuría considers Jesus the definitive Servant through whom God offers salvation. By emphasizing the Servant's role as leading to the removal of sin, Ellacuría echoes the liturgical acclamation of Jesus as the *Agnus Dei, qui tollis peccata mundi.* Now, this removal of sin extends not just from his death, but his entire life and ministry of proclaiming and manifesting the Reign of God that culminates in his death. The church's mission is to carry forward this mission, celebrating it in the Eucharist, but also historicizing it in action. Thus, just as there must be a historical continuation of that ministry, so must there be a bearing of sin. The crucified people continue the historicization of this salvation in their own unjust bearing of the world's sin, and in the efforts called forth from this fact, to transform the world to resemble the Reign more closely.

Their hope, a hope that must be historicized, resides in the promised and coming Reign of God, which represents the last crucial component of

Ellacuría's soteriology. In describing salvation in terms of the Reign of God, Ellacuría adopts the language of Scriptures to indicate a utopic vision of salvation and a prophetic discipleship that are historically transcendent.

The Reign of God

In his reflections on Jesus' ministry and death, on the contemporary poor as a "crucified people," and the correlation of these figures using the biblical image of the Suffering Servant, Ellacuría elaborates a historical soteriology that addresses a weakness latent in an abstract, ahistorical view of atonement or redemption. His soteriology, as historical, strives to overcome a view of salvation that ignores history, and consequently, either explicitly advocates or implicitly fosters a discipleship of passivity or evasion while the majority of the world's population languishes in poverty. Ellacuría's alternative grounds itself not just in a historical understanding of Jesus' death, but also in that central theme of Jesus' preaching: the Reign of God.

As a concept, the Reign of God incorporates the insights of Ellacuría's philosophical framework and culminates his christological reflections, revealing the need for a mode of discipleship engaged in history. Ellacuría prefers the biblical image of the Reign of God, rather than the language of heaven, eternal life, or individual salvation, precisely because it brings out the historical significance of theological concepts that might otherwise be interpreted in a purely "spiritual" or at least ahistorical manner. In articulating an understanding of the Reign of God, Ellacuría utilizes its polyvalent sense: the Reign brings together the historical and transcendent; it possesses a sense of both an "already" and a "not yet." Thus, Ellacuría never denies a transcendent or metahistorical character to the fullness of Christian hope; however, he assiduously maintains that that fullness cannot be conceived without a historical dimension.

The Reign represents both the goal and impetus for a genuine Christian historical discipleship. As such, Ellacuría associates the Reign with the language of utopia and prophecy as the historical continuation of Jesus' ministry. Jesus preached the Reign and manifested it in his ministry, and for the Reign, Jesus was killed. Jesus rose from the dead as a validation of his proclamation and as the definitive inauguration of the Reign. The poor today languish as victims of the anti-Reign, and by doing so, reveal the need and hope for the Reign. While believers are called to participate in the manifestation of the Reign, they can never equate it with any particular historical project. The Reign provides the impetus both for the prophetic unmasking of idolatries and false visions of hope, and the utopic activity that envisions and establishes a more just and loving world. In looking at the signs of his times, Ellacuría sees Latin America as a place for hope, a place where utopia and propheticism signal the advent of the Reign.

Characteristics of the Reign

Ellacuría's emphasis on the "historical Jesus" determines his interest in the concept "Reign of God."[73] As the central theme of Jesus' preaching, the Reign should rightfully be at the center of the church's proclamation of the good news, its carrying forward of Jesus' mission. Indeed, Ellacuría views the Reign as paramount to Christian faith and action. He describes the Reign as "the unifying object of all Christian theology...The greatest possible realization of the Reign of God in history should be what genuine followers of Jesus should pursue."[74] By directing attention to the Reign as a part of Christian discipleship, Ellacuría demonstrates the same "historical logos" he utilized in understanding the death of Jesus.[75]

Ellacuría claims about the Reign what he has about salvation itself — though the Reign represents much more than the historical, it cannot be described without some reference to the historical. "The Reign of God, although it does not remain reduced to being a purely historical project, demands [*pretende*] a historical realization, demands that the world of humans remain configured in a certain form."[76] The norms for this realization come from the life and proclamation of Jesus and the discerning of believers who carry forward Jesus' mission in the particularity of their own historical context.

In one essay, Ellacuría suggests five characteristics of the Reign that illustrate his understanding of this theological theme and how it relates to Christian discipleship.[77] First, Ellacuría notes that Jesus preached the Reign and not the church, nor himself, nor even what God is in Godself, apart from humanity. This indicates the parallel assertion that the church should not see its mission as proclaiming itself, nor even "the announcement of a Jesus or God apart from the real salvation of humanity and the world."[78] Ellacuría thus directs the church away from an obsession with ecclesial self-preservation and turns it to its real historical mission, a mission that may even call it to risk itself because it makes commitments in a divided society.

Because the Reign provides the church a mission involving present historical action, its eschatological character must lie, in part, within the purview of history. This historical sense comes through in Ellacuría's understanding of the Reign in a verbal sense. "The Reign is not a spatial concept, nor a static concept, but rather a dynamic reality: it is not a reign [*reino*], but rather the act of reigning [*reinado*], a permanent action affecting historical reality."[79] Here Ellacuría invokes that dynamic and interrelated notion of history inherited from Zubiri. Yet because history has a theologal dimension as well, this move allows Ellacuría to support and indeed deepen the claim that the source of the Reign is God. God transcends in history in the Reign, and humans are impelled to participation in the Reign's historical manifestation.

Ellacuría underscores the overcoming of seeming dualisms, for example, immanence-transcendence or horizontal-vertical, as a third characteristic of the Reign. In this, he simply continues a drive that runs throughout his entire theological corpus. Continually, Ellacuría strives to bring out the unity in seeming dualisms so that Christian discipleship will not be torn from faithful action in the world because of a supposed "spiritual" character. "The Reign of God is, at once, the active presence of God in history and the presence of history in God, the historicization of God, which does not have to sound any more scandalous than the incarnation of God and the divinization of history. It is truly God-with-us."[80] By linking it to the Incarnation and the salvation of humanity, Ellacuría parallels his claim that history must be viewed theologically not as the twin histories, sacred and profane, but one history of sin and grace.[81]

Ellacuría ties his reflections on the poor to the "scandalous" fourth characteristic of the Reign: namely, that the Reign must be a reign "of" the poor, the oppressed, those who have suffered persecution. Ellacuría draws upon his previous reflections both on the nature of Jesus' ministry and the soteriological significance of the crucified people to amplify the dynamic thrust of the Reign's manifestation. "When Jesus himself becomes the servant of Yahweh, destroyed by the world, broken in his battle against evil, victim of humanity's sin, he demonstrates God's way to establish the Reign in this world."[82] Not only do the poor represent those to whom the Reign was first preached, but in their suffering they indicate that divine dynamic of the Reign, the divine principle of salvation.

> As much as the concept of the poor and oppressed as the addressees of the Reign of God has been expanded, both the biblical tradition and even sociological reality demonstrate that the *analogatum princeps* is the one who really suffers upon herself or himself the effects of the world's sin, the negation of God's love in the negation of love to other humans; in sum, the poor person is Jesus himself, par excellence, dispossessed of everything on the cross.[83]

If the poor represent this crucial presence of the crucified in history, then the fifth characteristic of the Reign is its ability to overcome the duality between the personal and the structural through work on behalf of these poor. Ellacuría never denies the importance of the personal dimensions of faith and discipleship, but to the degree that he discerns his situation as one in which the asymmetrical emphasis on the personal dimension serves to overshadow any sense of wider commitments, he emphasizes these wider implications through theological concepts such as the Reign. By situating the gift of God to humanity in the Reign, and by viewing humanity's "return" to God through the Reign, Ellacuría sees that "the 'relations' are personal, but the mediation that puts them in contact is not purely individual. Here one can see that the Reign is not purely a question of faith and obedience, but also a question of works, of works that with faith establish the objective presence of God among human beings, which should not only be believed in, but should also be done."[84]

In order to speak of those works that should be done, Ellacuría turns to historicize his reflections on the Reign of God within the context of Latin America. This context will demonstrate how these five characteristics of the Reign find their historical shape and fuel the hope of the poor, the oppressed, and those in solidarity with them for the ever-increasing manifestation of that Reign.

Utopia and Prophetic Activity

In the last essay published before his assassination, Ellacuría produced an expansive treatment of both "theological" notions like the Reign of God and "political" ideas like the weaknesses of capitalism in Latin America. The piece serves to conclude a life and career dedicated to what is summed up well by its subtitle: "A Concrete Essay of Historical Soteriology."[85] This essay of historical soteriology concentrates on that ultimate hope of Christian soteriology: the Reign of God. Rooted in the example of Jesus' own proclamation of the Reign, Ellacuría understands the necessity for both a negative condemnation of idolatry and the positive vision of hope for the fullness of salvation. He identifies these two tasks with the terms "propheticism" and "utopia."[86]

While each of these two concepts presents possibilities when reflecting on renewal and liberation, Ellacuría notes that if they are separated, they risk idealistic escapism in either subjective reductionism or transcendental idealism.[87] So Ellacuría situates them in a historical context that allows for the thrust of reality to make itself present in each; namely, that utopia and prophecy as dialectical terms refer to the method (prophecy) and horizon (utopia) of liberation-salvation in Latin America. In doing so, Ellacuría historicizes his reflections on the Reign of God in terms of the signs of the times he discerns in Latin America.

Ellacuría brings out the soteriological dimension of the term "utopia," and specifically a Christian utopia, by understanding it in relationship to the reality called the "Reign of God."[88] At times, Ellacuría appears to use the term "utopia" as synonymous with the Reign of God.[89] However, Ellacuría also states that the Christian utopia is "operative for historicizing the Reign of God."[90] Despite this ambiguity, it seems that Ellacuría names as utopia that Christian imagination, rooted in revelation and the tradition, which attempts to name and identify the contours of the Reign without equating that imagination with the actual Reign of God.[91] In considering Christian discipleship, he claims, the concretizing (*concreción*) of utopia is the historicizing of the Reign of God, an activity that occurs in both hearts and structures. If, in a general way, the Christian utopia has been proclaimed in the Scriptures and other sources in the tradition, then the question becomes how the utopia achieves its concretion. Prophetic activity makes this possible.

Ellacuría views the critical function of propheticism to be that of contrasting the Reign of God with the present historical reality. "Propheticism is the critical contrast between the announcement of the fullness of the Reign of God and a determinate historical situation."[92] In its proclamation, Christian propheticism illumines the limitations and evils of the present historical situation and encourages movement toward (*hacia*) the Reign.[93] While Ellacuría never identifies the Reign of God with any specific historical project, he sees propheticism as that link which demonstrates the necessary relationship between history and transcendence in the Reign. The Reign of God possesses a historical transcendence that parallels the life of Jesus, and indeed, God's self-revelation. History involves transcendence because God's transcendence, as a "transcendence-in," has become history ever since the beginning of creation.[94]

In relating prophecy, utopia, and historical commitment, Ellacuría differentiates his vision of Christian discipleship from a secular Marxist utopia. Ellacuría's understanding of faith that produces prophetic action stands in direct contrast to an assessment of religion as the pacifying "pie-in-the-sky." Moreover, the Christian prophetic action that Ellacuría espouses always retains a humility about its possible accomplishments. Here the Christian utopia differentiates itself from a Marxist utopia by retaining humility about its ultimate efficacy in history.[95] Utopia may represent an ideal vision that enlivens praxis, a vision whose embodiment signals the incipient presence of the Reign, but it does so without being equal to the Reign.

Ultimately, Ellacuría understands the relationship between utopia and the Reign through the Zubirian principle of "actualization."[96] Playing on a Spanish definition of *actualizar* as "to bring up to date," Ellacuría argues that what is given in revelation must be actualized, not by bringing it up to date, but by giving present reality to what is formally a historically possibility (as option).[97] Actualization arises in the signs of the times, but what these "signs" signify transcends the historical. Ellacuría expresses utopia as "asymptotically realizable," while prophecy "gathers and expresses the historical-transcendent intercession of the Spirit," demonstrating the way that Ellacuría employs his philosophical framework to treat the historical and transcendent as related without conflating them.[98]

In Ellacuría's philosophical framework, all concepts must be historicized. So he turns to Latin America as providing important signs of the times, and performs a prophetic analysis of the situation that demonstrates the function of utopia and prophecy for contemporary theology. In his context, Ellacuría contrasts the historical reality of the poor with the hope found in Christian revelation. This utopic vision and its concomitant prophetic activity indicate the content of salvation for Ellacuría, if only in an incipient way.

Ellacuría utilizes analysis of the crucified people of Latin America, such as that they possesses characteristics like the Servant of YHWH, to demonstrate how the poor and those who work in solidarity with them embody propheticism.[99] Though (and because) it has endured great suffering, Latin America has nourished resistance, manifested in the figures of prophets and martyrs. As Latin America struggles to realize a new order, the prophets and martyrs indicate that the reality of the actual historical order cannot be duplicated or widened. They reveal that the developed world is not the utopia; it is quite distant from the Reign. On the other hand, these prophets and martyrs positively reveal that through the option for the poor, the church may participate in the actualization of the Christian utopia in history, an actualization that requires discernment to reject the many pseudo-utopias that exist.

Though he sees hopeful signs in Latin America, Ellacuría views its reality with no illusions about its innocence. The sin of the world shapes Latin America, which is not just passive victim but an active subject-participant of structural sin. Capitalist and socialist pseudo-utopias indicate the sin present in Latin America. Ellacuría widens the prophetic indictment to the world order, and he denounces current international relations, the capitalist system, and even the manner in which the institutional church is structured.[100] Though Ellacuría notes nominal improvements in the hierarchical acceptance of the notion of the preferential option for the poor, he notes that even many church leaders passively accept or actively promote social structures that mean suffering and death for the majority of Latin Americans. In this situation, a new vision needs to irrupt: denouncing the present order and announcing a vision for a new world. Latin America, indeed the world, needs prophecy.

While Ellacuría, like many of his other Latin American colleagues, incorporates dependency theorists' critiques of the Western capitalist system into his prophetic denunciations, he notes how the same insights exist in magisterial documents of the Roman Catholic Church, including Vatican II's *Gaudium et spes,* Paul VI's *Populorum progressio,* and John Paul II's *Sollicitudo rei socialis.* Invoking this tradition of Catholic social teaching, Ellacuría emphasizes the problem of debt for the Third World with echoes of the "civilization of capital/wealth" vs. the "civilization of work/poverty" that appear elsewhere in his work. Clearly, for Ellacuría, the civilization of capital represents the negation of the Reign of God. If prophecy consists in a proclamation of the present situation, then Ellacuría feels compelled to denounce capitalism because it has caused the most harm in Latin America.[101] Noting that John Paul II criticizes both socialist and capitalist systems in *Sollicitudo rei socialis,* Ellacuría argues for a local determination as to which system has done more harm. Here he goes on to make the stronger case against capitalism, ending with a powerful contrast between its values and Christian ones.

Not stopping at economics, Ellacuría's prophetic denunciation of the current world order includes a protest against the way the (Roman Catholic) Church is structured and behaves. Too often, in Ellacuría's view, the church tolerates structural injustice and institutional violence. Even though the episcopal conferences of Medellín and Puebla mark progress, they have had little real effect on church structures and behavior. Ellacuría finds that even the strong critique of capitalism in John Paul II's *Sollicitudo* has no developed pastoral dimension. If the church speaks of mercy to the exclusion of justice, then it ignores a principal theme of prophecy. Even in issues of inculturation, Ellacuría would add stark economic differences to the list of cultural factors that need attention when considering the evangelization of a region or people.

The reality of the church that Ellacuría identifies stands in marked contrast to the ideal of his prophetic and utopic vision that the church, through the preferential option for the poor, should declare for the salvation of all humanity:

> The "no" of prophecy, prophecy's negation which overcomes [*la negación superadora*], goes generating the "yes" of utopia, in virtue of the promise, which is the Reign of God, already present among human beings, above all in the life, death, and resurrection of Jesus, who has sent his Spirit for the renovation, through death, of all humanity and of all things.[102]

Ellacuría identifies universalism as a characteristic of a Christian utopia. By universal, Ellacuría does not mean the expansive thirst to dominate the globe evident in capitalist nations, whose consumption and inequality demonstrate that the system cannot be made universal.[103] For him, the preferential option for the poor becomes the principle for a true universalization. As the poor become active subjects, they manifest their salvific-historical value. In his reflections on the poor, Ellacuría views them as a theological locus, as the real presence of Jesus; their participation in the concretion of a universal utopia signals their capacity for salvation.

The move from oppression is received as grace but grows in praxis sustained by hope. Rather than understanding Christian hope as a calculated plan or idealistic dream, Ellacuría defines it as "the accepting of the liberative promise of God, a foundational [*fundamentante*] promise that propels [*lanza*] to an exodus in which historical objectives and goals conjoin with trans-historical certainties."[104] Here Ellacuría differentiates a subset of the general term "the poor" and refers to the "poor-with-spirit" who possess faith and derive hope from the promise of the Christian utopia. While these poor historicize this promise in the transformation of society, they also manifest it in the celebration of life.[105]

Even though the universality of the hope Ellacuría describes has affinities to Kantian thought, Ellacuría contrasts the hope of Latin American prophecy with that of the liberal Enlightenment ideal. While both visions may espouse a hope for freedom and justice, they differ in their conception of the historical process to that end. Ellacuría denies that the future-directed hope of the poor implies a complete rejection of the past; however, he also recognizes that it rejects a necessarily linear development he sees in some forms of liberal positivism. Furthermore, prophecy indicates not only freedom as a "freedom from" restraint or oppression, but a "freedom for" others, a freedom for solidarity not readily apparent in many forms of modern utopic thought. Christian liberative prophecy goes against any historical order in which sin prevails over grace, and instead proposes a new human and new world. It emphasizes life, in persons and structures, beginning in material life and reaching to the fullness of life. Liberation involves:

> a march toward the utopia of freedom through a real process of pro-phetic liberation, which would involve the liberation from sin, the law, and death (Rom. 6–8), and whose goal consists in the revealing of what it means to be a child of God, something possible only through a permanent process of conversion and liberation (Rom. 8:18–26) in the following of Jesus through the personal reproduction of the features of his Son, so that he would be the eldest of a multitude of siblings (Rom. 8:29).[106]

Ellacuría contrasts the anthropological dimension of Christian utopia with that of the modern, Western ideal. He asserts that the Western and so-called Christian ideal for the human being is in fact anti-Christian. In citing Hobbes, Ellacuría indicts the Enlightenment image, and in particular, how Christianity has succumbed to it. "When official Christianity converts into optional or intentional virtues what should be the real negation of anti-Christian attitudes and acts, it is also making an interested [biased] reading of the faith that annuls its real truth and effectiveness."[107]

Nowhere does the contrast between modern Western ideals and Christian utopia appear more obvious to Ellacuría than in the conception of wealth. A "historical realism" recognizes the dialectical relationship between wealth and poverty that makes it impossible to rationalize wealth away. Ellacuría invokes the language of a "culture of wealth" whose allure [*señuelo*] threat-ens the marks [*señas*] of identity. Its dangers include: machismo, violence, deviations in sexual and family life, etc., and the mechanisms by which these are ideologized. Yet this enumerating of the negative aspects of this culture of wealth points to what will be the positive features of utopia. "The central point concerns the preferential option for the poor as a fundamental mode of battling the priority of wealth in the configuration of the human being." This shows the poor as a "privileged place of humanization and Christian divinization."[108]

Ellacuría's articulation of the utopic "new earth" challenges those visions that would attempt to improve the structural whole solely by the improve-ment of each individual. Here the language of a "civilization of poverty" returns with force as he contrasts it with a civilization of wealth.[109] In con-trast to that civilization of wealth, which views the accumulation of capital as the primary dynamism and goal of history, Ellacuría proposes a civi-lization of poverty that prefers the universal satisfaction of basic material needs. This latter civilization, also called a civilization of work, values shared solidarity as the process of becoming fully human, not the possession and enjoyment of wealth. Self-realization that takes place through labor in the context of community supplants the hyper-individualism of wealth's pursuit.

While Ellacuría's analysis of Latin America leads him to a greater sympathy for socialist systems, he notes that one must be critical of all systems, even scolding liberation theologians for being too meek in their criticisms of socialism.

In his vision of a new social order, Ellacuría hopes to evade the evils of individualism and statism, not in a middle position, but by dreaming of a communal social order in which social groups are considered and active. Likewise, a new political order does not represent another attempt at a "third way," a path espoused by many Christian political parties in Latin America's history, but a vision for liberation in which freedom derives from justice and justice leads to freedom. Ellacuría does not see liberal democracy as the solution, preferring to implement the principle that the reality experienced by the mass of the people is to be imposed as selection criterion leading to genuine self-determination. He expresses a cynicism toward Christian attempts to correct capitalism as usually making the church more worldly and capitalist than vice versa.

The new human, social, and political orders correspond to a new cultural order in which fulfillment consists in the joy brought about by work rather than the incessant need for entertainment characteristic of the civilization of wealth. This cultural order advocates communication and contemplation as desired activities rather than the active product consumption or pure passivity and receptivity of the civilization of capital.

The Christian utopic vision announces a new heaven as well as a new earth. Ellacuría proposes an understanding of heaven not as abstract, but as present in history. He defines it as "the historical and increasingly operative and visible presence of God among human beings and public human structures."[110] This vision requires a committed, historical discipleship on the part of Christians. Ellacuría envisions the church as a sacramental presence that historicizes the new heaven as "the historical body of Jesus crucified and risen." While including the celebration of cultic ritual, this view of sacramentality goes beyond it to a sacramentality in which the church carries forward the mission of the historical Jesus, a spirituality that views historical corporeity as a demand of the Spirit.

To summarize his investigation, Ellacuría concludes:

> The prophetic negation of a Church as the old heaven of a civilization of wealth and empire, and the utopic affirmation of a Church as the new heaven of a civilization of poverty is an irrecusable reclaiming of the signs of the times and of the soteriological dynamism of the Christian faith historicized in new human beings, who continue announcing firmly, although always in the dark, an always-greater future. Because beyond successive historical futures one may observe the saving God, the liberating God.[111]

The soteriological hope for the Reign of God, historicized in a civilization of poverty, ultimately rests in the saving, liberating God, but it also calls for a faithful discipleship on the part of believers. Indeed, it is with an eye to the nature of discipleship that Ellacuría nurtures his soteriological vision. The shift to a so-called "historical logos" guides several interpretive features of Ellacuría's soteriology.

Conclusion

Ellacuría focuses on a "historicized" view of the Jesus portrayed in the Gospels. This involves understanding Jesus not simply in terms of the divine and human natures, but in terms of the way that Ellacuría views every human being's existence: as a multidimensional network of relationships in historical reality. Ellacuría turns to the sociopolitical dimensions of Jesus' messianic ministry to unearth elements of the Jesus portrait easily overlooked by earlier "natural" analyses. Ellacuría does not deny Jesus' divinity, but he articulates the incarnational mystery with a view of God's transcendence in, not away from, history. He discovers a Jesus whose ministry possessed a singular focus: the proclamation, in words and deeds, of the Reign of God.

While this ministry evidenced signs and wonders, particularly as a preferential option for the marginalized of society, it also engendered fierce opposition from social, political, economic, and religious powers who perceived Jesus as a threat. As a consequence and culmination of his prophetic ministry, Jesus was killed by these authorities. However, despite the seeming failure of his ministry, Jesus was raised from the dead as a divine validation of his ministry and the definitive moment of the Reign's inauguration. Generations of believers thus confess him as the Son of God, as the Redeemer who took upon himself the sins of the world. The cross reveals the fullest moment of God's transcendence in the world, and the paradox that the reign of sin is defeated in a victory of self-sacrifice.

In Ellacuría's treatment of these christological mysteries, he indicates a connection between Jesus' ministry and crucifixion that possesses significant implications for discipleship. Believers not only take up the invitation to follow (*seguir*) Christ, but they carry forward (*proseguir*) his mission of proclaiming the Reign of God, a proclamation in word and deeds. This dictates a faith that, like Jesus' own ministry, possesses sociopolitical dimensions.

Contemporary Christian discipleship finds its wellspring in the life of the poor for whom, as the Scriptures reveal, God has a preferential love. The poor, considered in all their complexity, thus become the crucial theological locus for our times. Proclaiming the gospel of life to those who are in the shadow of death defines the mission of the church in the world. Moreover, as the poor take up their struggle in faith, as a spiritual task of participating in God's will for the world, they evangelize the church by calling it to conversion. They call it to the *kenosis* that characterized Jesus' own historical existence and the manner by which God reveals Godself.

By the way that they bear the brunt of the world's sin, the poor are a crucified people who become a principle of salvation for the whole world.

In this view, the crucifixion of the poor, as a historical continuation of that definitive crucifixion of Jesus, calls forth a redemptive process that nourishes active discipleship, not passivity. Indeed, as all are called to participate in the greater presence of God's justice, some are even called to share in that inevitable consequence of confronting sinful powers: martyrdom.

The sacrifice of martyrdom finds its meaning in light of the Reign of God. In particular, utopia and propheticism signal that the Reign is neither an abstract heaven, nor a strictly historical or realizable project, but a historical-transcendent reality in whose coming we are called to participate in an anticipatory fashion. Ellacuría recognizes that this calls for prayer and the scrupulous resistance to the temptation that leads to personal sin. He also seeks a wider aperture, however, one that recognizes sin in its social dimensions. So utopia and propheticism also call Christians to discern whether and how political and economic structures at the local, national, and international level contribute to the Reign of God or represent the reign of sin.

So far, this book has described both the framework and central theological motifs of Ellacuría's soteriology as directed toward a historical discipleship. While the previous chapter established Ellacuría's understanding of historical reality, God's transcendence, and salvation history as a salvation in history, the present chapter turned to that definitive moment of salvation history for Christians: the life, crucifixion, and resurrection of Jesus Christ. At the foot of that cross, each generation of Christians is asked to follow the one who was slain for proclaiming the Reign. For Ellacuría, only through historicizing that crucifixion do we know its meaning. Thus, the presence of the crucified people today signal that place of conversion and discipleship. In the next chapter, the characteristics of that historical discipleship will emerge as the way that the church is called to an ecclesial praxis that carries forward the mission of Jesus.

Chapter Four

Ecclesial Praxis as Real Discipleship

PERHAPS NO CONCEPT summarizes the confusion and controversy surrounding Latin American liberation theology more than "praxis." In contemporary theology and philosophy, the turn to praxis emerges as a critique of exclusively theoretical criteria for norms of action and reflection.[1] Posited negatively, the turn to praxis rejects conceiving of human action in mechanical terms, as the mere application of theoretical exercise.[2] Theologically, attention to praxis engages centuries-long debates about the nature and relationship between divine and human agency in the economy of salvation. In addition, however, it serves as a polarizing element in liberation theologies because of its significance in the work of Karl Marx and subsequent Marxist thought.[3] For those critics who accuse Latin American liberation theologians of reductionist tendencies, the turn to praxis entails a range of perils from an almost Pelagian emphasis on human activity to the reduction of Christian discipleship to violent revolutionary action.[4]

This chapter takes up the meaning and function of praxis in the theology of Ignacio Ellacuría. If the previous chapters have established soteriology as the proper frame with which to analyze Ellacuría's thought, then this analysis will reveal how Ellacuría's account of Christian discipleship, which he describes in the language of praxis, cannot be understood apart from his wider account of salvation. Viewed within the logic of his theological method, Ellacuría's understanding of praxis indicates the moment he calls "taking charge of the weight" (*encargarse de*) of reality, a moment mutually dependent on the previous moments, "realizing the weight" (*hacerse cargo*) of reality, and "shouldering the weight" (*cargar con*) of reality.[5]

In order to explicate Ellacuría's view of Christian praxis or discipleship, the chapter will begin by analyzing Ellacuría's working definition of the term "praxis" within his philosophical system. While Ellacuría's thought demonstrates an informed dialogue with Marxist philosophy, his understanding of praxis represents a mediating position that inherits Marxist critiques of idealism while possessing its own criticisms of a materialism that would minimize personal action in favor of larger historical collectives. Ellacuría situates praxis within the dynamisms of historical reality to move beyond hyper-individualism without sublating human activity into a determined or teleological historical movement. Moreover, since he posits praxis as a unity of diverse moments, Ellacuría understands theory as an important moment of praxis, one that both grounds and finds its validation in other forms of praxis. The exercise of theology, then, represents a crucial ideological moment of ecclesial praxis.

The chapter then investigates Ellacuría's understanding of ecclesial praxis. Because Ellacuría envisions Christian activity primarily in the communal context of the church, rather than in an individualistic notion dominant in many modern theologies, he most frequently speaks of discipleship in terms of an ecclesial praxis. For him, the church, dynamically interrelated in history with others, lives as a sacrament of salvation in its following of Jesus and carrying forward of his mission to proclaim and manifest the Reign of God. It mediates the presence of the Trinitarian life of God in history. Therefore, the church and its ecclesial praxis represents another moment where transcendence involves movement "in" history, rather than "away" from it.

Finally, the chapter concludes with a look at Ellacuría's writings on personal spirituality. Though Ellacuría prefers to speak in collective terms about Christian discipleship, he does not overlook the important personal dimensions of ecclesial praxis. In particular, Ellacuría fashions a view of personal discipleship profoundly affected by the spirituality of Ignatius of Loyola. Drawing from the language of the *Spiritual Exercises,* Ellacuría posits the Christian mission in terms of a contemplation in action for justice. Like theologians of past eras, Ellacuría draws inspiration and finds a model for his view of discipleship incarnated in a historical person. For him, Archbishop Oscar Romero demonstrates the crucial dimensions of Christian praxis and embodies the ultimate destiny of those who would follow Jesus and carry forward his mission: death at the hands of oppressive powers, but with hope in resurrection.

Praxis in Ellacuría's Philosophy

Commentators on Ellacuría generally agree that praxis occupies a central place in his philosophy.[6] The way that Ellacuría treats praxis reveals not just how he assimilates his intellectual influences, but also how he moves beyond them creatively to fashion his own philosophical and theological vision. While Ellacuría's philosophy always reflects the primary influence of Xavier Zubiri, his understanding of praxis signals an engagement with other important figures as well. In particular, Ellacuría frames his understanding of praxis as an attempt to overcome two extremes: Hegelian idealism, and the materialism of the so-called "left-wing" Hegelians, Feuerbach and Marx.[7] Understood this way, Ellacuría's philosophical articulation of praxis grounds a view of ecclesial praxis and discipleship that, in turn, attempt to overcome the extremes of a disengaged "spiritual" Christianity and a reductive, exclusively political understanding of Christian life.

Some commentators claim that Ellacuría's use of the term "praxis" marks a continuation of what had been a project of Spanish philosophy for at least two generations.[8] José Castellón identifies a trajectory of philosophers, from Ortega y Gasset, through Zubiri, to Ellacuría, trying to overcome the nature-subject dualism of previous Western philosophy.[9] His narrative follows in this manner: if Greek and medieval philosophy saw being (*ser*) as nature, or *physis*, a category that described all reality, then modern philosophy (Kant et al.) counters that humans know this reality only within the bounds of subjectivity. To the moderns, philosophy must claim the structures of knowledge and human subjectivity as its proper starting point. In response to these "classical" and "modern" models, and their inherent opposition, the Spaniards endeavor to find a starting point for philosophy that synthesizes the insights of the two positions.[10]

Diego Gracia, a fellow student of Zubiri who worked with Ellacuría in the 1970s, describes their turn to praxis as the result of elucidating a practical drive latent in Zubiri's work. Gracia identifies his efforts with Ellacuría in that time as the pursuit of "practical philosophy," a philosophy that rejected idealism's philosophical project.[11] He suggests that Zubiri had an enormous appreciation for philosophical pragmatism, an appreciation that while undeveloped in his early work, *Naturaleza, Historia, Dios*, would come to fruition in his more mature work. Indeed, as part of that "second generation" of Zubiri's students influenced by his *Sobre la esencia*, Gracia describes his efforts with Ellacuría as trying to "frame and interpret" the important points of Zubiri's pragmatism to produce a practical philosophy.[12]

Gracia describes the weekly gatherings with Zubiri as being focused primarily on his theory of knowledge, although he acknowledges that Zubiri preferred the terminology of "theory of intelligence" or what he later called *noology*. In particular, Zubiri's students sought to understand what he meant by the phrase "impression of reality." While some students focused on the term "reality," Ellacuría concentrated on the other term, "impression." Rather than trying to understand this term in a classical/medieval (Aquinas) or idealist (Hegel) sense, Ellacuría preferred to view Zubiri's "apprehension of reality" as closer to the thought of Feuerbach, and Marx's critique of Feuerbach.

If Hegel had interpreted knowledge from the senses as that which is most immediate and certain (*sinnliche Gewißheit*), yet that which when absolutized produces the worst error (materialism), then Feuerbach inverts this insight to affirm, "Truth should be actual, real, sensible, visible, human. ... Only the real, the sensible and the human is true."[13] While Feuerbach appeared closer to Zubiri's emphasis on the apprehension of reality than Hegel, Ellacuría and Gracia did not remain satisfied with it, but wanted to accept Marx's critique as well. For Marx, Feuerbach's *Sinnlichkeit* should rather be understood as *sinnlich menschliche Tätigkeit* — that is, not simply as sensorial, but related to sensorial human activity.[14] So if for Feuerbach criteria for truth resided in the sensorial, then Marx located these criteria in praxis.

While some have accused Ellacuría and Gracia of "Marx-izing" the work of Zubiri, they themselves preferred to see it as "Zubiri-izing" Marx:

> Our objective was to see if one could, from Zubiri's perspective, reinterpret some of the principal theses of the young Marx, the philosopher Marx, which were the ones that interested us at the time. Was it so crazy to think that *praxis* as the origin of knowledge [*conocimiento*] did not necessarily lead to dialectical and historical "materialism," but could be reinterpreted usefully in the sense of Zubirian "realism"?[15]

For Ellacuría, Zubirian realism informs a view of praxis that addresses the profound need for transformation in Latin America, but accounts for that transformation within the complex dynamism of historical reality. While he wishes to overcome an individualism that ignores the larger social and historical factors that condition human action, Ellacuría does not want to do so in a way that would have history, or some sort of historical collective, eviscerate the contribution and significance of personal biographies and cultural and religious practices. In order to accomplish this task, Ellacuría draws from his philosophy of historical reality to situate praxis within the dynamic interrelated structure of historical reality. In doing so, Ellacuría underscores the importance of all human activity, even its theoretical exercise, in determining the shape of historical reality without compromising the view of reality as "religated" to the creating, saving God.

Praxis within the Dynamisms of Historical Reality

When Ellacuría takes up the notion of praxis, he incorporates Zubiri's insights regarding the dynamism of reality into the ongoing idealist-materialist debates concerning history.[16] Ellacuría poses historical reality as that intra-mundane reality in which all other reality is rooted, but he recognizes that real beings have a relative autonomy.[17] Thus, Ellacuría speaks of praxis as "historical praxis" — a notion that, while placing great emphasis on human activity, places praxis within a wider view of history as the concrete form of reality's dynamic process.

If one adopts Zubiri's dynamic and "respective" characterization of reality, then the forces of history constitute a unitary structure within which human freedom operates. Thus, this should not be confused with any modern notion of history as teleological, as a linear and progressive project oriented to culmination in a final reconciliation that nullifies individual activity. Rather, this view understands the unitary nature of history as constituted by a multiplicity of dynamisms. Ellacuría's priority in articulating praxis will be to account for the unitary nature of history without neglecting the importance of individual/personal activity or practice. A brief survey of Ellacuría's account of history's complex dynamisms will indicate how he balances these two priorities.

In his *Filosofía de la realidad histórica,* Ellacuría concludes with an analysis of the dynamisms inherent in the historical process and how they culminate in historical praxis.[18] Ellacuría distinguishes distinct levels at which these dynamisms occur, which correspond to different features of real beings.[19] At the most basic level, Ellacuría identifies change or variation (*variación*), which indicates how the features of any real thing change respectively to other things.[20] When speaking of the dynamism that affects not just the inherent features but the very structure of a thing, Ellacuría refers to alteration (*alteración*), which has the subcategories of transformation, repetition, and creative evolution, that may be evidenced in a wide spectrum from the physical and biological level to the personal and psychological.

Even though things may be described by dynamisms such as variation and alteration, many also maintain their proper identity in some form of stable structure. Sameness or stabilization (*mismidad* or *estabilización*) indicates this dynamism, whose application may range from inanimate objects merely maintaining a proper material identity, to living things that maintain a dynamic equilibrium. In the latter case, the *mismidad* does not suggest a static entity. Though indicating an integral continuity, *mismidad* includes a formal dynamic equilibrium. As Ellacuría suggests, "Life is a dynamism that enables one to continue being the same thing without staying the same."[21] The description of *mismidad* underscores a principal characteristic of history to Ellacuría, namely, that history constantly changes, but in this incessant change it possesses a mode of continuity. This implies a great value to all human activity, which is never lost in history, but becomes an intrinsic part of that which is handed on.

Ellacuría notes that in human beings sameness has a distinct transcendental character such that *mismidad* becomes the dynamism of "ownness" (*suidad*). This dynamism describes the difference between being a "formalized animal," whose actions are assured by its proper structures, and one that transcends this state to become a "hyper-formalized animal" or "personal animal" in whom the structures do not dictate a prescribed response. It speaks of that crucial phenomenon called personalization. As Ellacuría avers,

> In personalization, the very being (*ser*) of the human is in play: that "suchness" (*talitativamente*) which supposes being in one mode or the other, the living a life of these or other contents, transcendentally supposes putting into play (*poner en juego*) the very being of my proper reality. This is where the dynamism of freedom takes on its weight, which progressively determines that being opted from the proper reality, the shape of reality proper. The dynamism of personalization goes forging the personality of the human with each possibility that it appropriates and to which in that appropriation derives power over itself; it is a dynamism of "possibilitation" (*posibilitación*), before one of execution.[22]

Ellacuría roots the possible contribution of each person to the system of historical possibilities in personalization. This personal dynamism, as a self-possession or self-realization, affects and is affected by others as others, or what Zubiri has termed "respectivity." This respectivity signals not just an interaction of separate entities, but a real living together (*con-vivencia*), a dynamism that constitutes the social body. The actualization of this system of social possibilities constitutes the social world, but does not reduce history merely to this actualization, a danger often associated with crude readings of Marx. In respectivity, Ellacuría attempts to speak coherently of the personal and social without conflating them. "It is possible to absorb the social world without being absorbed by it; that is why, more radically, it is possible to constitute a personal communion without leaving the social world, which leads to the existence of a truly personal community."[23]

Ellacuría places history at the pinnacle of these dynamisms. He describes the dynamism of history as that of offering possibilities and capacities (*posibilitación y capacitación*), a dynamism in which all of the prior dynamisms remain integrated, and in which all the other dynamisms make themselves present.[24] As Ellacuría states,

> Nothing is still. All is in perpetual transformation [*devenir*]. Everything is becoming itself, including that which is already constituted. Just as reality itself is transcendental, so is the dynamicity of reality, such that any static and tranquilizing [*quieta y quietadora*] conception of reality is not just an escape of reality, but a reaction against it, a veritable counter-realization.[25]

These lines indicate Ellacuría's deep suspicion of static or passive philosophies or theologies. They also emphasize the importance that Ellacuría places on the realization or historicization of concepts. There can be no conceiving of history or reality without dynamism, and that dynamism extends even to those forces that would deny its very existence.

With his profoundly dynamic view of historical praxis, Ellacuría finds a reading of the Aristotelian mutually exclusive counterposition of praxis and *poiesis* to be ultimately untenable. If Aristotle differentiates *poiesis,* as activity performed to a certain product or end, from praxis, as that activity performed as its own end, then for Ellacuría the latter category is an empty set. Because of reality's integral dynamism, Ellacuría views all activity, even that done for its own sake, as possessing some dimension of transformation and self-realization.[26] As he suggests, "Only the human being formally 'realizes' that which she or he does and realizes while self-realizing, and it is within the scope of formal realization that one should situate praxis."[27] Ellacuría would not deny that different forms of praxis exist, some more interior to the human person than others, but he will not place any form of praxis outside the dynamism of historical reality. All human activity generates a ripple that affects the wide ocean of historical reality.

Ellacuría differentiates "biographical" and "social" forms within praxis. With the former, Ellacuría affirms a close cognate to Aristotelian praxis or Kantian practical reason, the dimensions of personal transformation and realization. However, he faults any view of the personal that is purely "spiritual" or "contemplative."

> All biography is the biography of an individual directed toward others, constituting a social body and situated in a determined historical context from which it not only receives conditioning and possibilities, but is its real field [*campo*] of insertion. This field is not merely contemplative and spiritual in the sense of a praxis that leaves historical reality untouched because there is no biography without the material. . . . All contemplation is sensible activity and a principle of action or reaction before reality's dynamism and the dynamism of other biographical praxes or social praxis.[28]

Ellacuría emphasizes biographical praxis as the dynamically interrelated activity of human persons, and he describes social praxis as that which conditions praxis in terms of providing (or denying) a system of possibilities for biographical praxis. The option for the poor, considered at a structural or institutional level, provides a system of possibilities within which persons and communities then shape a praxis. In describing social praxis in this way, he does not wish to eliminate or sublate human activity under a notion of history or Spirit as actor; however, he realizes the larger structures that affect biographical praxis.

> By praxis we mean here the totality of the social process, such that it is transformative of reality, both natural and historical. In it, subject-object relations are not always unidirectional. For that reason, it is preferable to speak of a "co-determinant respectivity," in which the social whole adopts more the characteristics of an object, which obviously not only reacts, but positively acts and determines. Yet the social subject (that does not exclude personal subjects, but presupposes them) has a certain primacy in the direction of the process.[29]

Ellacuría's identification of praxis with the productive and transformative dimensions of the historical process does not reduce praxis to a determined set of actions or social structures. On the contrary, Ellacuría acknowledges a plurality of praxes. "That some forms of praxis, for example the political or economic, can have a major and immediate efficacy in some forms of social transformation, is not proof that they always do so, nor that they exhaust the necessity for other real transformations."[30] So while maintaining the importance of political and economic transformation, Ellacuría opens the door for a number of forms of praxis as crucial to human, and indeed Christian, existence.[31]

By situating praxis within the dynamisms of historical reality, Ellacuría moves away from conceptions of human action that are either atomistic or overly determined by a historical collective. Ellacuría's understanding of praxis protects the integrity of personal action, but places the human person in a wider net of mutual interrelatedness. This provides a better account of the wider structural forces that affect history, forces that have a particularly negative force in Ellacuría's El Salvador. Without dissolving individuals into a collective whole, Ellacuría's understanding of praxis as social process allows him to suggest its application to the notions of social sin and liberation.

> Without going into the problem of praxis in its depth, it appears that one can say without exaggeration that phenomena of oppression have a structural-social character, and in turn, the processes of liberation should have a structural-social character as well.[32]

Yet in accounting for praxis and particularly in envisioning a praxis of resistance to forces of oppression, Ellacuría does not descend into a material instrumentalism. As an intellectual, particularly as president of a university that saw its mission in terms of bringing the national reality to light, Ellacuría does not advocate strict activism as the ideal praxis. Rather, he places a great deal of importance on the exercise of theory as an important moment of praxis. An analysis of Ellacuría's understanding of the theory-praxis relationship will serve to illuminate this important notion and provide a transition to how Ellacuría understands theology's relationship to the wider notion of ecclesial praxis.

The Theoretical Moment of Praxis

As a philosopher and theologian, Ellacuría recognizes the value in the theoretical enterprise, but ultimately views it within the wider circle of praxis.[33] Seeing praxis as the unity of all that the social whole (*el conjunto social*) does in its transformation, Ellacuría argues that this praxis has theoretical moments of different grades. These may range from the simple consciousness that accompanies all activity, to moments of conscious reflection in distinct forms. For him, all theory transforms in some manner. Yet this is a long way from claiming that pure theory is the strongest force for transformation.

> It is more convenient to speak of the theoretical moment of praxis, which can have different grades of autonomy and should seek them out, to be sure, by seeking the correct relation to praxis as a whole, which it [the theoretical moment] can orient in part, though perhaps not direct it [praxis], and from which in turn the theoretical moment receives direction and orientation.[34]

In positing a theoretical moment of praxis, Ellacuría demands attention to the unity of praxis. Yet this unity must be understood in the same way that Ellacuría posits the unity of historical reality: namely, as a unity that is not an identity, but a structural unity of diverse moments.[35] As a moment of praxis, the exercise of theory — say, in philosophy or theology — must then pay attention to this unity.

> What is crucial in these praxes is that they are moments of one praxis and therefore, they do not allow for Robinsonian isolations. . . . So, for example, when philosophy or theology do not speak about [the violation of] human rights, they diminish the importance of this question and make it easier for them to be violated.[36]

As a moment of historical praxis, theory exercises a certain power and influence. Rather than seeing theory as the opposite of praxis, Ellacuría views it as an initial moment that deals with the conscious character of praxis.[37] For Ellacuría, the theoretical moment of praxis has the form of ideology, but not in the pejorative sense. It is accompanied by a series of representations, valuations, and justifications that give it sense and impulse and produce some sort of system. Yet even in this account of theory's importance, Ellacuría acknowledges that theory looks to historical praxis as a principle of reality.

> Historical praxis is itself a principle of reality and of truth in its supreme grade. It is a principle of reality in that within it, integrally understood, the *summum* of reality is given; it is the principle of truth, as much as the principle of reality, because the historicization of theoretical formulation is what definitively demonstrates its degree of truth and of reality.[38]

The assertion that theory must be historicized reflects Ellacuría's conviction that while theory is valuable, that value can often be overestimated.[39] Praxis, then, serves as a check, a principle of verification of theoretical assertions. This underscores the necessity for the intellectual to possess a critical distance.[40] In a logic similar to his explication of transcendence (as "in" and not "away from" history), Ellacuría understands this critical distance not as separation nor as lack of commitment, but "only [as] the confirmation that not even the best of actions reach their proper *telos* in one blow, and probably stagnate or stray long before having approximated it."[41] So whether one's primary task is theory or activity, Ellacuría advocates a humility in regard to each of their ends.

Ellacuría's ideas on the reflexive interrelation between theory and praxis, and how he locates the norms for truth and genuine human living in praxis, become more clear in his advocacy of a "Christian" philosophy — a philosophy that contributes to a genuine *metanoia* of both consciousness and social structures.[42] Crucial to his Christian philosophy is the place from which it does its reflection. Here Ellacuría's emphasis on the optative moment echoes his theological method. For the philosopher who wishes to find that place-that-reveals-truth, Ellacuría identifies not only a theoretical discernment but an optative moment. "The moment of option, which seeks the place-that-reveals-truth [*lugar-que-da-verdad*] and does the truth, should not be blind but illuminated — illuminated, in the first place, by an ethical valorization of justice and freedom, or more correctly, of the denial of justice and freedom that are the primary facts in our situation."[43]

Ellacuría's invocation of themes such as conversion and option signals the important ecclesial dimension that praxis possesses for him. The elaboration of praxis within the complexity of historical reality requires that the church's existence be taken seriously in all its depth. The church does not float above the world, but finds itself immersed within it. To the degree then that Ellacuría has presented a view of praxis within historical reality that includes a transcendent dimension, he provides a way to account for the church's worldly existence and mission that can overcome dangerous separations. Without reducing the church to an exclusively sociological entity, Ellacuría attempts to account for ecclesial identity and mission that takes seriously historical reality and avoids the dangers of passive escapism and elitist sectarianism.

Ecclesial Praxis

When Ellacuría turns to theological usage of the term "praxis," he applies the insights of his philosophical work, particularly focusing on attacking a similar set of dualisms present in much contemporary theology. Just as Ellacuría articulates a view of praxis that avoids both a hyper-individualistic subjectivity and a collectivity that annuls the human person, he demands a similar balance when discussing Christian praxis. While he does speak in the language of personal spirituality, Ellacuría avoids speaking in individualistic terminology and prefers to speak of Christian discipleship in ecclesiological terms, most frequently using the language of "ecclesial praxis."[44] While attempting to overcome the individual-collective dualism, Ellacuría also uses "ecclesial praxis" to overcome that dualism against which his entire soteriology is aimed — a dualism of the transcendent and the historical — now with an eye to ecclesiology and discipleship.

Ellacuría situates ecclesial praxis, and indeed the church itself, within the dynamism of history. All that he has said regarding the human embeddedness in historical reality and the depth of historical praxis must apply to the church in its members and as institution. So, positively, Ellacuría defines ecclesial praxis as "every historical action of the church, understood as a community of human beings that in some way realizes the Reign of God...that is, the transforming action that the church necessarily undertakes on its historical pilgrimage."[45] Ecclesial praxis, then, includes the dynamically interrelated sense that Ellacuría attributes to praxis at large, but places it within a vision of the church's salvific historical mission: historicizing the Reign of God. All the church's activity, including the theoretical moment of theology, shapes an ecclesial praxis that occurs in history, but is not merely equated with it.

While the previous usage of "ecclesial praxis" dominates Ellacuría's writings, some passages reflect a reticence on his part to offer an exclusively positive connotation to the term. Aware of the danger of ecclesial triumphalism, Ellacuría makes it clear that the church's praxis, in its individual members or as an institution, sometimes falls short of realizing the Reign. Indeed, he identifies the possibility that "ecclesial praxis could be moving against the current not just of historical salvation, but against salvation history itself."[46] So while occasionally Ellacuría uses "ecclesial praxis" with a critical edge in order to avoid both a naiveté regarding sin and a triumphalism regarding the church, this chapter will concentrate on his more frequent prescriptive usage that asserts the church's important historical role.[47]

While he acknowledges a structural unity between historical and ecclesial praxis, Ellacuría also recognizes a certain autonomy in the church's constitution and self-understanding. Ellacuría's "historical" understanding of the church does not settle for mere sociological definitions of the church, but recognizes its transcendent dimension as well. He posits the church's autonomy against those who would claim that all of the church's activity is but a reflection of economic, social, and political conditions, a point that emerges as part of Ellacuría's critical dialogue with Marxist thought. "The theological foundation of this autonomy rests on the postulated presence of something 'more' in history that is made effective in it."[48] We have seen Ellacuría indicate this "more" in history already with the language of *religación* — the acknowledgment of God as creator, sustainer, and savior of all — and the central thesis of his soteriology: salvation history is a salvation in history. In his view of ecclesial praxis, Ellacuría concentrates on the relation of personal and ecclesial action and the Reign of God.

Because Ellacuría's view of *religación* grounds a theo-logical view of reality that provides the church its priority and mission, he need not impose an ecclesiology that violates the basic dynamisms of history. Rather than expressing the theological priority of the church in ontological terms, the temptation latent in past forms of Christendom, Ellacuría prefers the language of sacramentality. This move also underscores Ellacuría's continuity with Catholic thought of the 1960s and 1970s and the influence of his studies with Karl Rahner, the documents of the Second Vatican Council, and those of the CELAM meetings in Medellín and Puebla. The church is a visible sign and efficacious sacrament of salvation as it fulfills its twofold calling: to follow (*seguir*) Jesus Christ and carry forward (*proseguir*) his mission to proclaim and manifest the Reign of God. Ellacuría understands the actualization of the Reign as both a negative and positive process: both the removal of sin and the divinization of humanity. Therefore, ecclesial praxis demands the prophetic confrontation of the sin that means death for the majority of the world's population. It also requires a continual conversion to incarnate the presence of God in the weakest members of the human community. It carries out this sacramental mission as a leaven in the world.

Church as Sign or Sacrament of Salvation

Above all, Ellacuría wishes to convey an understanding of church that takes seriously its historical character and mission without denying its transcendent element as well. To clarify this desire, he relies on a rhetorical device to which he regularly turns: Ellacuría situates his understanding of the church in opposition to problematic ones. In an early article, he critiques the claim that the church "has been, is, and always should be, the same in all times, identical in all places."[49] Elsewhere, his diagnosis involves twin extremes that he wishes to avoid: a "spiritual" view of the church that does not occupy itself at all with temporal things, and a "worldly" view that reduces the church's activity only to the political sphere.[50]

Ellacuría finds these formulations flawed because they identify the church within a framework that downplays or negates history. To conceive of the church as a static social reality denies the dynamisms that are present in all historical reality, and in which the church finds itself. Yet to divorce the church from its past misconceives not only the nature of religious traditions, but of the traditional nature of history itself as a *trasmición tradente*. Similarly, to separate the "spiritual" and "political," prioritizing either one of them, involves denying the "religated" character of historical reality. It separates the historical and transcendent. As a remedy to these flawed positions, Ellacuría articulates a historical understanding of the church's character and salvific mission.

In his ecclesiological essays, Ellacuría turns first to the Christian notion of salvation as the proper framework to understand the church's historical and transcendent character. Lest he be understood as advocating a reductionistic view of salvation, Ellacuría speaks of salvation that "is humanity's, but not of humanity," describing it as a "free and historical irruption rather than something deducible *a priori* from the nature of the world or humanity."[51] Christians declare that Jesus, the Word of God, is a historical Word outside of which there can be no salvation, but which, as divine initiative, transcends humanity. Yet, in addition, the saving word of God is also a personal and changing word because it is addressed to hearers who live in different historical circumstances.[52] Therefore, salvation itself is historical. Again, avoiding the polar dangers of a salvation either divorced from history or identical with history, Ellacuría asserts that salvation-as-historical has two implications: "Salvation would be different according to the time and place it is realized, and it should be realized in history and in historical human beings."[53]

Ellacuría draws on the understanding of salvation as historical not just as a reference for his ecclesiology, but in order to give that ecclesiology content. It is not simply that the church is historical and transcendent in the same manner as salvation, but that the church derives its mission and self-understanding in the task of "realizing" salvation. Ecclesial praxis, then, involves the church's "historicization" of Christian salvation. In one instance, Ellacuría defines this historicization as "communicating in a real way to each human being the presence and demand of the historical word of God. Historicization requires incarnation in time and in location."[54] Yet how is this ecclesial form an authentically Christian understanding of praxis? What differentiates this formulation from the Marxist praxis of social transformation? Once again, Ellacuría situates himself between extremes that would either spiritualize ecclesial praxis or see it exclusively in political terms.

To situate himself rhetorically, Ellacuría sets up a spectrum of positions with reference both to biblical exegesis and to the differences between Feuerbach and Marx on praxis. In looking to the Scriptures, Ellacuría posits a view of the Hebrew Bible's early writings that show a clear, if not exclusive, political connotation to YHWH's deliverance/protection of Israel.[55] Though Ellacuría contrasts this "early" view of "politicization" with a prophetic heritage that more properly balanced the political and religious, he understands this reading of the early Hebrew Bible as operative in the debate on praxis between Feuerbach and Marx. Marx criticizes Feuerbach for prioritizing the interior and contemplative act of theory over praxis because he holds "too Jewish" a notion of praxis.[56] While he admits that Feuerbach does well to abandon that form of religious praxis, Marx faults him for abandoning transformative praxis altogether. In light of this argument, Ellacuría stakes out his own position as distinct from ancient politicization, interiorization, and Marxist praxis.[57]

Ellacuría paves the way for this "fourth option" by establishing the connection between the Reign of God, the divinely initiated process of humanity's liberation from sin and divinization for life, and the church's call to participate in this salvation as its herald and sacramental mediator. As Ellacuría insists,

> The active subject of salvation, par excellence, is God and his mediator Jesus Christ. God is the beginning and end of humanity's salvation, and God has chosen to offer it to humanity definitively in the incarnation, life, death, and resurrection of God's Son.... The subject subordinate to the principal subject (which is God and God's mediator Jesus Christ with the Holy Spirit) is the Church in the totality of its salvific actions.[58]

As salvific-historical action, ecclesial praxis avoids the error of idle interiorization, while advocating a transformation that is more than a merely intramundane human project. "If the church, then, is capable of constituting itself historically as a historical sign, in its historical conduct [*proceder*], of the Reign of God's presence among human beings, its apparent duality would be overcome: its theologal aspect and historical aspect, without being identified, would be unified."[59] As a hallmark of his entire theological method, Ellacuría once again argues here for a unity-in-difference in "theologal" concepts that views transcendence "in," not "away from," history.

In this framework, ecclesial praxis represents the principal component of the sacramental character of the church.

In a move that echoes the ecclesiology of the Second Vatican Council, Ellacuría articulates the role of the church in relation to the Reign as that of sacrament or sign.[60] Though he does not articulate a fully developed sacramental theology, Ellacuría stresses the sacrament's making present, in a *real* way, that which it mediates. Just as the Eucharist is the real presence of Christ, so the church must be the real sacrament of salvation. He claims, "The church, as the gatekeeper of salvation, should be that sign that makes salvation historically present and effective."[61] The church fulfills its "signifying" or sacramental function, then, precisely by historicizing the salvation that Ellacuría has previously described as the Trinitarian life of God. While there are moments in Ellacuría's theology where he indicates how even non-believers might contribute to this process of historicizing salvation, he assigns a distinctive and essential role to the church. "One should see that action transformative of the world and society from its proper Christian inspiration is the constitutive sign outside of which salvation, the divinization of humanity, is not made present."[62]

Following Jesus and Carrying Forward His Mission

As a sign, the church represents the visible continuation of the mystery of Jesus Christ in history. Because Ellacuría locates Jesus Christ within the larger salvation history that began at creation and ends at the eschaton, he describes the passion, death, and resurrection of Jesus as the culminating, but not final, moment of salvation. This preserves not only a profoundly eschatological edge to his understanding of Christ, but a sacramental one as well. "Jesus is the sign of the saving God, par excellence, but he is also the efficacious sign, the sign that truly realizes what it announces: God's salvation in history."[63] Christians follow Jesus because he is the definitive sacrament of salvation, but this following requires more than devotion. It demands that the church assume the same task of realizing what it announces.

This sacramental understanding of Jesus sets up a parallel crucial to Ellacuría's understanding of ecclesial praxis: just as Jesus made the Father present, so the church makes Jesus present — it must continue or carry forward (*proseguir*) his mission. This move does not relativize the role of Jesus, but rather, it provides the church the twofold path to faithfully historicize the salvation he brought: Salvation comes in the following (*seguimiento*) of Jesus as the Way to salvation and the carrying forward (*proseguimiento*) of his mission.[64]

If in the previous chapter we have seen the importance that Ellacuría places on the "historical Jesus," here we see how Ellacuría draws on the historical Jesus to describe the contours of faithful Christian discipleship.[65] By first asking the question "Why was Jesus killed?" instead of "Why did Jesus die?" Ellacuría clarified how the soteriological importance of Jesus' death cannot be separated from its historical character.[66] By linking ecclesial praxis to the carrying forward (*proseguimiento*) of Jesus' mission, Ellacuría demonstrates that historical embodiment of that mission constitutes the church's principal sacramental mediation of Christian salvation.[67] In order to describe the nature of salvation, Jesus' ministry, or the mission of the church, he most frequently turns to the twofold formulation: liberation from sin and divinization of humanity.[68] These actions, as understood within the specific historical circumstances of the church in a given place and time, constitute the heart of ecclesial praxis.

Ellacuría repeatedly asserts that one may not speak about salvation without including a corresponding deliverance from sin. "There is no salvation without the disappearance of sin, and sin, in order to be pardoned, must be removed."[69] If the Catholic liturgy proclaims that Jesus Christ is the *Agnus Dei, qui tollis peccata mundi* (the Lamb of God who takes away the sin of the world), then Ellacuría takes seriously the mission of removing sin as a fundamental element of ecclesial praxis. In Ellacuría's eyes, ecclesial praxis must discern the presence of sin in historical reality, confront that sin prophetically, and participate in its removal.

While Ellacuría holds a graced vision of creation, using terminology of the presence of the Trinitarian life, he cannot deny the pervasive reality of sin in the world. The manner in which he accounts for that sin reflects the way that he has positioned salvation as transcendent and historical. Ellacuría's "theologal" view of sin, then, analyzing sin in relation to the presence of God in history, reads the reality of Latin America as "the negation of the loving essence of God, that which is the ultimate and grounding (*fundante*) reality of all reality."[70] This negation of God's presence, that from which humanity needs salvation, represents the sin of the world. Yet this theologal concept of sin cannot stand alone, lest it be read abstractly apart from the world's reality.

By equating the world's massive poverty and suffering with sin, Ellacuría does not "horizontalize" sin, but rather historicizes it. While the former would mean a reductionism that does not recognize the depths of sin, the latter recognizes that sin as a concept does not reach its depth unless it is recognized historically.[71] Though Ellacuría acknowledges a personal dimension when speaking about sin, the exigencies of historical reality move him to emphasize the structural dimensions of sin.[72] Indeed, if some speak of a modern forgetting of sin, Ellacuría represents the recovering of the sense of sin not by intensifying the hyper-individualism latent in this modern amnesia, but by retrieving the notion of social sin, a sin that means death for the majority of the world's population.[73] Likewise, since the diagnosis of sin varies, the discernment in each time and place as to what negates the Trinitarian life of God in history, Ellacuría naturally emphasizes that sin he sees overwhelmingly in El Salvador and the Third World: massive poverty due to structural injustice.

Clearly, Ellacuría believes that greed and the pursuit of wealth constitute the sin that most shapes the reality of the world.[74] Moreover, he views this sin, particularly as a form of idolatry, as the most frequently condemned in the Scriptures. Because of this understanding, Ellacuría's "political" writings can be seen in a theological light. They represent the attempt to identify and denounce prophetically the grave inequalities that mean death for so many Salvadorans.[75]

For example, the sin of greed for wealth often entails the distorting of truth. Ellacuría knew all too well how his country's media covered over and distorted the reality of the country to deny this sin. So ecclesial praxis, and the ecclesial praxis that he and the other staff members of the UCA personally chose, involved the "de-ideologization" of those who would distort reality. This indicates a prophetic dimension to ecclesial praxis that has internal consequences as well. Not only does the church critique the wider society, but prophetic praxis leads to the church's own conversion to the place in reality that most clearly reveals the presence of God: the world of the poor.

In its commitment to the preferential option for the poor, the church not only fulfills the negative call to remove sin but positively historicizes the divinization of itself and humanity. Though Ellacuría does not expand the nature of this divinization at length, he often invokes the language of conversion and incarnation to characterize the positive transformation of the church. When the church imitates the *kenosis* of Christ by responding to the reality of the poor, it is purified.[76]

Incarnating itself in the world of the poor, the church discovers the nature of Christian love.

> Although love cannot be reduced to doing good for one's neighbor, this doing of good, when it is generous, when it has no borders, when it is humble and kind, is a historical form of active love. Not every struggle for justice is the incarnation of Christian love, but when the historical situation is defined in terms of injustice and oppression, Christian love does not exist without the struggle for justice. It is here that the Church, as sacrament of salvation, has the twofold task to awaken and encourage the struggle for justice. It does so among those who have not committed to the struggle, and among those who have, it urges them to do so from Christian love.[77]

Ironically, this reveals a rather "high" ecclesiology in Ellacuría's work. The church can never cease being the sign of Jesus Christ's divinity. Yet this mediation does not lead to triumphalism or naïveté regarding the capability of the church to be complicit with grave sin. He and other Latin Americans know all too clearly the church's long history on the continent of siding with those who oppress the weak. Moreover, the fundamentally Catholic drive latent in his ecclesiology prevents him from conceiving of the church in sectarian terms. To avoid sectarian logic while preserving a prophetic drive, Ellacuría prefers to speak of the church as a leaven within the mass of the larger society.[78] The image of the leaven in the dough provides Ellacuría a way to preserve the historically dense understanding of ecclesial praxis articulated thus far.

> Ecclesial praxis, by virtue of its own real nature, lacks the material conditions to be the dominant instance of the course of history, although it has tried to be such.... That ecclesial praxis should influence history and not only the souls of individuals or through conversation between persons, does not mean that it should or could be the determining moment in the historical process.[79]

Ellacuría invokes an ecclesiology that fulfills the vivid command given by Jesus in the Gospel of John: Be in the world but not of the world. Because Ellacuría emphasizes a transcendence in history, he offers a notion of ecclesial praxis that emphasizes the struggle for justice without being reduced to it. As leaven in the dough of the world, the church transforms the world through its faithful praxis — its imitation of Jesus and carrying forward his mission. Sadly, the carrying forward of this mission often dictates the same fate that Jesus suffered. Ellacuría would come to know, as would many Salvadorans who participated in the church's struggle for justice, the painful consequences for the faithful disciple.

> The fight against sin that does injustice to the most needy is the locus of God's revelation and communication. It is the place of witness and of efficacy, the place of martyrdom, because persecution by the powerful of this world, by those who possess that sinful structure of this world, that persecution makes true the mission of the Church.[80]

Where does this concept leave those Christians who find themselves in wealthy parts of the world? If liberation theology affirms that the church of the poor is the privileged place for theological reflection and for the realization of the Reign of God, does this nullify the reality/praxis of the church in wealthy countries? Ellacuría's insistence on the importance of the poor does not indicate his nullification of the reality or praxis of the church in wealthy countries. On the contrary, Ellacuría notes that Christians in these areas have their own problems that need to be recognized and responded to by their own theologians. This does, however, indicate how European theology is not theology par excellence, but represents a "local" theology as much as liberation theology does.[81]

Ellacuría feels comfortable asserting the concept of the "church of the poor" because he recognizes the poor and oppressed as the privileged addressees of the New Testament. Moreover, poverty/oppression represents the current situation of the great majority of humanity. In order for the church to fulfill its "catholicity," it must address that universal problem. In wealthy countries, this implies a recognition of participation in sin. "The churches of the rich countries should seriously consider the parable of the Good Samaritan, so that they not be so focused on 'more elevated and religious' concerns that they pass by Jesus himself crucified in history."[82]

Thus, Ellacuría identifies a universal ecclesial praxis directed toward the manifestation of God's presence in history. As a sacrament, the church continually experiences a call to conversion, a call to make the same kenotic journey as Jesus Christ to proclaim and efficaciously manifest the Reign of God. In this mission to follow Jesus and carry forward his mission, the church embodies the transcendent-in-history that lies at the heart of the Christian mystery. In identifying the mission of the church within the complex dynamisms of historical reality, Ellacuría overcomes a temptation to view Christian discipleship in individualistic terms. What remains of the analysis will be to identify the ways that Ellacuría describes the personal dimensions of this ecclesial praxis.

Personal Spirituality

Though Ellacuría emphasizes the collective dimension of Christian discipleship, preferring the language of ecclesial praxis, he does write on issues of personal spirituality. As a priest, and having spent four years directing formation of the Central American Jesuits, Ellacuría understood the importance of prayer and spirituality in the Christian life.[83] Though articulated in personal terms, Ellacuría's understanding of spirituality continues his response to the danger he sees latent in all contemporary theology: to "spiritualize" in a way that disengages the Christian from the world and reality. Thus, Ellacuría draws on the long Christian tradition of linking contemplation and action.[84] His formulation of contemplation in action for justice represents his "historicized" vision of Christian discipleship. Furthermore, it draws from the great historical example that Ellacuría experienced personally: the brief but significant episcopacy of Archbishop Oscar Arnulfo Romero. In Romero's legacy, Ellacuría possesses an incarnation of the great calling to discipleship.

Spirituality as Making the Spirit Present in History

Ellacuría recognizes a twofold challenge to contemporary spirituality.[85] It must overcome a dualism that completely separates the spiritual from the material, and it must resist a "monism" that conflates one into the other. To carry out this task, Ellacuría recasts the spiritual and material as two mutually dependent dimensions of a unity. This involves comprehending the biblical notion of the Spirit's presence as a historical presence. This presence of the Spirit takes away the world's sins and so represents the gift of God to the poor. Since Christians receive this Spirit as the Spirit of Christ, they comprehend spirituality as conforming to christological criteria. These include Jesus' announcement of the Reign; his teachings, among which the

Beatitudes of the Sermon on the Mount receive emphasis; and the cardinal virtues of faith, hope, and love.

Ellacuría's analysis of the term "Spirit" in the Bible leads him to conclude that Christian spirituality rests not on so-called "spiritual practices," but on the affirmation that God is becoming present in history, the affirmation of the Reign of God. So "spiritual ones" are those who perform actions that conform to the Spirit of Christ who came to proclaim and manifest that Reign.

> Those who are spiritual are not the ones who perform many "spiritual" practices, but those who, filled with the Spirit, reach its creative and renovating impetus, its overcoming of sin and death, its power of resurrection and greater life; those who reach for the fullness and freedom of God's children; those who inspire and illumine others and help them live more simply and freely.[86]

Ellacuría does not shy away from admitting the diversity of the above task. If true Christian spirituality involves mediating the living presence of God in history, then the task necessarily dictates a multiplicity of forms depending on the particular calling and circumstances in which Christians find themselves.[87] Yet if spirituality directs itself to the living presence of the Spirit in history, a presence that means the removal of sin, then spirituality, like ecclesial praxis, must be committed to the removal of sin everywhere in the world. Furthermore, the Christian discovers the fundamental criteria for this praxis in the ministry of Jesus as portrayed in the Gospels. Christian spirituality discovers its Christian sense by conforming to the example of Christ.

> The grace of God is received in the world of the poor in a *praxis* that responds efficaciously to the great task of removing the sin of the world, the death of the world, so that the world and humanity might have more life.... Any spirituality that does not come from and lead to a *praxis* that liberates from sin and its consequences does not respond to the life of Jesus.[88]

So Ellacuría's sense of spirituality follows an ancient and traditional method: look to the Scriptures, particularly the Gospels, to discover a norm for Christian behavior. Because the Gospels portray Jesus as understanding his mission in terms of the Reign of God, so then spirituality should focus on mission. Once again, Ellacuría understands Christian mission as an ecclesial praxis of announcing and realizing the Reign of God in history. This mission involves the entire church body and each Christian personally.[89] Practically, the turn to the Scriptures reveals the special place that the Beatitudes occupy for Ellacuría. He stands in an ancient tradition of seeing in Matthew's Sermon on the Mount a summary of the entire Gospel message.[90]

For Ellacuría, the norm of Jesus' ministry, and of the theological notion of incarnation as well, may be summed up in the preferential option for the poor. The gracious self-giving that characterizes the *kenosis* of Jesus also roots many of the great Christian lives throughout history. Ellacuría, noting how periods of reformation in the church's history have come through a renewed commitment to the imitation of Jesus' poverty, offers a new appropriation of this theme relevant to the reality of his situation. Ellacuría's interpretation of the Beatitudes boils down to one simple theme: "Make yourselves poor while there are poor in the world; place yourselves in the field of the poor."[91] This directs the evangelical virtue to the place where poverty exists, to that place of weakness that God has chosen to reveal Godself.

Ellacuría interprets evangelical poverty as that option, the location indicated by the "shouldering of the weight of reality," for the poor that often means the struggle for justice. In order to obviate the distortion of Matthew's first beatitude, Ellacuría suggests that the phrase "poor in spirit" be understood as "poor with spirit." This signifies that poverty should come to be understood by Christians as the place of commitment, the principle of liberation. While not imposing a mechanical or determined reading of the Beatitudes, Ellacuría's reading of the contemporary global situation leads him to define this poverty with spirit in opposition to the perceived "civilization of wealth" he discerns as the operative *zeitgeist* of the capitalist order.[92] Part of Christian spirituality then involves the struggle for justice. How it does so leads Ellacuría into the discussion of the relationship between faith and justice, contemplation and action.

Contemplation in Action for Justice

Taking up the important theme of the Society of Jesus' General Congregation XXXII (1975), Ellacuría devotes attention to the relationship between faith and justice within Christian life. For him, this question represents a variation of the fundamental problem that he has diagnosed: the temptation to separate the spiritual from the material. By understanding faith and justice as forms of praxis, Ellacuría attempts to overcome deficient understandings of these categories and to contribute to a superior orientation of Christian discipleship.

Once again, Ellacuría reveals his own priority by identifying a deficient notion which he hopes to overcome. In this case, he warns against a dualistic understanding of faith and justice without advocating a unitary understanding that conflates them. Ellacuría provisionally defines faith in this perspective as "what is an explicit cult of Christian inspiration, as the relations between God and humanity, by way of Jesus Christ," and conversely, he suggests justice should be understood as "the effort to do away with [*desterrar*] injustice that exists in the relations among human beings, social classes, and nations."[93] Already latent in this proposal lies the temptation to define faith exclusively with the divine, and justice with the human — a suggestion Ellacuría rejects outright. Yet rather than simply trying to clarify the terms positively, Ellacuría directs his readers to look at the "false consequences" that result from this deficient dualistic view.

By asking whether faith or justice should take priority, Ellacuría gets at the basic problem of posing them dualistically. At one level, Ellacuría reasons that conscience, and above all, love dictate that justice appears to be the priority. It would seem that the person who, even without explicit faith in Jesus Christ, acts according to conscience and commits no injustice is more likely to be saved than the believer who commits injustice. In making this claim, Ellacuría appears to confirm the suspicions of those who would warn against liberation theology's propensity to reduce salvation. However, Ellacuría argues that it is the inherent dualism in the proposition that makes for the problematic conclusion.

Ellacuría attacks the aporia posed by the dualistic view of faith and justice by expanding the imagination of the terms. With reference to the Pauline priority of love over faith (1 Cor. 13:13), he defines justice as the historical form of love. "Justice is that form that love adopts in a world of oppression and sin. . . . In justice, one is dealing with the historical form of objectivized love, of love realized in a historical situation."[94] To those who would object that it is the love of God that is highest, Ellacuría counters with a classic Christian trope: the love of God and love of human should not be separated.

This Christian definition of love indicates the manner in which Ellacuría correspondingly expands the meaning of the term "justice" far beyond the modern, Enlightenment virtue.[95] Ellacuría avers, "If one treats justice as a virtue that simply means giving each person what is her or his due, pre-scinding from the totality in which this call has its concretion, then it does not make sense to discuss priorities, much less relation. . . . Can one have justice if it is not the work of God? Is not justice the presence of God's grace?"[96] In Ellacuría's view, justice and faith receive their fullest meaning within an overarching perspective that does not separate and valorize them, but rather aligns them within an understanding of salvation history as a salvation in history, of the transcendence of God as a transcendence "in" history. Thus, Ellacuría invokes what are by now familiar themes of his soteriology to illumine the path of discipleship.

Ellacuría's soteriology leads him to conclude that "the promotion of justice is the relevant and constitutive sign of the realization of the Reign of God in our history."[97] The logic that supports this statement comes from his previous assertions regarding the significatory or sacramental role of the church. If justice reveals the presence of God, and it is something constitutive of that presence, then justice is not only something related to faith, but it reveals faith. Ellacuría believes that justice marks a basic element of the realization of Christianity. Though he claims a necessity for justice, he does allow that the historical form that justice takes may be considered relative. This calls for discernment as to how best to realize the Reign within a particular historical situation.

In reflecting on how Christians best realize the Reign, Ellacuría draws on one of the great themes of Ignatian spirituality: the "contemplation to attain love" toward the end of the *Spiritual Exercises*.[98] Ellacuría appropriates this reflection in order to formulate properly the relationship between faith and justice. He claims, "contemplation . . . in action for justice would be the Christian mode of access to God and of bringing God to humanity."[99] In making this claim, Ellacuría selects the Dominican slogan *contemplata aliis tradere* as a counterposition against which he can define his own approach to this topic in Christian spirituality.[100]

For Ellacuría, the motto "transmitting to others that which is contemplated" implies the separation and prioritization of theory over praxis that he discerns as the primary danger in contemporary spirituality. This phrase assumes that contemplation possesses a fullness that need merely be communicated to others, rather than a more circular conception of knowledge that Ellacuría proposes. Furthermore, beyond merely an assumption of knowledge, the phrase strikes at the heart of Ellacuría's conception of revelation. His emphasis on the revelation of God in others, particularly the poor, views others as active agents rather than simply passive objects of contemplation.

> Others, above all the oppressed, are already in themselves the sacrament of Christ, the historical body of Christ, the history of his crucified divinity. They are the place where one should focus one's contemplation, but not treating them simply as an object of contemplation, but as a reality that captivates and obligates one to partake of their historical journey and their personal problems. They require an immersion in what they are and what they do.[101]

Faith, in this conception, does not appear as something possessed beforehand that is then transmitted so that believers will convert it into works. Rather, faith itself is a historical enterprise that calls for discerning the presence of God in history.

Ellacuría suggests that the pair faith-justice possesses the same unity-in-distinction that he sees operative in salvation history in the pair transcendent-historical. In order to bring out the fullest implications of this realization for Christian discipleship, he turns to revise the provisional understanding of contemplation and action offered above. Instead, he suggests:

> Contemplation and action are not understood here as two separate activities — whatever the mechanisms through which they are realized — but as a unity, in which the element "action" would be that action or conjunction of actions that attempt to eradicate injustice from this world, as much in its structures as in the human heart. Meanwhile, the element "contemplation" would be that action or conjunction of actions that illuminate, from the faith, the real struggle for justice; that discover how and under what conditions God the Savior and God's salvation are made present in the struggle for justice.[102]

Ellacuría has reconfigured the moment of faith, beyond a merely conceptual act of assent to a fully participative and historical praxis. Yet this reconfiguration does not mean reducing faith to the doing of justice. Repeatedly, Ellacuría emphasizes that faith provides a fullness to the seeking of justice without which it remains not only incomplete, but not properly Christian. He uses the metaphor of faith as light that illumines the struggle for justice. "Faith is like the light, thanks to which whatever is the real sign of God, the revealing presence of God, is made plainly transparent; however, even though this presence is illuminating in itself, it does not actualize its luminosity without faith."[103] This reference to light hints at why he appears to equate faith and contemplation.

By invoking the language of contemplation-action as a correlate to the pair faith-justice, Ellacuría draws on an important moment in the *Exercises* to bring out the fullness of Christian discipleship. In doing so, he revises the traditional understanding of contemplation. He describes contemplation as "the moment of faith" and "the explicit exercise and proclamation of faith."[104] The truth of contemplation is in action, but contemplation permits that action to demonstrate the salvation announced by Jesus. Contemplation serves, then, as a light that properly illumines and orients action as Christian. If the hope of contemplation is often described traditionally as the vision of God, then Ellacuría reorients that vision to the historical presence of God, the caring for the "least ones" who are the presence of God.

> Consequently, the role of faith is not reduced: faith is the Christian vision and strength that give rise and impetus to proper historical action, where that historical action already includes the message of revelation within it. There would be an advance in faith in proportion to an advance in contemplated action; and there would be an advance in action in proportion to the growth of contemplation on it.[105]

Ellacuría concludes by suggesting four characteristics of contemplation in action for justice. The first is a basic understanding of contemplation as the desire and attempt to discover the saving presence of God.[106] This desire manifests itself in the second characteristic, a constant call to conversion that means a movement away from sin. The great historical sins of poverty and oppression indicate that Christian contemplation cannot reach its fullness without a conversion to the poor. They demonstrate the historical presence of God in a way that faith/contemplation cannot ignore.

A third characteristic of contemplation is that it presumes "effective intervention" in the course of history. This follows naturally from Ellacuría's reflections on praxis. Contemplation is part of a human life, and that life/praxis provides the adequate place for contemplation. Yet this notion brings out an ambiguity in Ellacuría's thought regarding the possibility of "pure" contemplation. On the one hand, he makes strong claims regarding the need for activity. "Only in active, *praxical,* insertion in a situation are there possibilities for an adequate contemplation."[107] On the other hand,

Ellacuría allows leeway for a wide range of actions such that "this proposal does not deny even the possibility of pure contemplatives.... The history of the great contemplatives demonstrates how their real intervention in the course of other people's lives is plainly seen."[108] Unfortunately, Ellacuría does not explain the form of this intervention.

The fourth and final characteristic Ellacuría assigns to contemplation is that it assumes "authentic contemplation." In explaining this authenticity, he returns to the *Spiritual Exercises* to better substantiate the internal moment normally connoted by the term "contemplation." He notes, "Everything that Ignatius put in the *Spiritual Exercises* before proposing his 'contemplation to attain love' is necessary. There is no Christian contemplation without the first three weeks, without the leaving of sin, the world, one's passions and interests, etc."[109] Action on behalf of justice, in itself, does not cause faith, but like the reception of the sacraments, reaches a depth when the participation comes from faith.

In light of the original problem of understanding faith and justice, Ellacuría concludes, "Contemplation in action for justice can be the praxis and the adequate spirituality of the one who unifies and does not separate what is unified in itself: faith and justice."[110] If all that Ellacuría meant by justice or action were the attempt to destroy unjust structures, then his suggestions would be reductionistic. Since Ellacuría has defined justice as the historical form of Christian love, however, then faith takes on a new historical depth.

Even though Ellacuría often concedes the importance of interiority, it would be easy to dismiss these moments in light of the enormous emphasis he places on questions of structural sin and ecclesial praxis as a response to it. Yet this emphasis seems the only logical outcome of a spirituality that is predicated upon response to the specific historical situation. Be that the case, it remains unfair to caricature Ellacuría as an activist interested only in social change at the expense of the vitality of the Christian faith. His account of Christian spirituality serves to ground Christian faith in a life dedicated to seeking the presence of God. This requires faith; this requires prayer.

Although Ellacuría's treatment of contemplation differs from many traditional approaches, beneath the surface there are lines of thought that, without passing over the difficulties in Ellacuría's presentation, offer possibilities for contemporary appropriation of the contemplative tradition. Traditionally, contemplation has been described in terms of the threefold way of purgation, illumination, and union. While Ellacuría avoids this interior language, he shows a sensitivity to that underlying movement in stressing the need for conversion that is often a *kenosis,* an active option for the poor that provides illumination, and finally the same desire for union with God. Yet these moments are historicized in his thought. Perhaps the best way to access this dimension of Ellacuría's theology would be to turn to that historical incarnation of Christian discipleship, whom it seems Ellacuría would call a contemplative in action for justice par excellence: Archbishop Oscar Romero of El Salvador.

Romero as Exemplar of Christian Discipleship

Even though Ellacuría spends many pages describing ecclesial and personal Christian praxis, he found it best exemplified in the remarkable episcopacy of Oscar Romero.[111] Although it lasted only three years, Romero's term as archbishop showed one man's extraordinary conversion from being what Ellacuría describes as a relatively ineffective priest to a universally acclaimed pastor of his people. Substantiating the reason for this change and the elements that characterized Romero's witness provides Ellacuría an incarnated portrait of proper Christian discipleship.[112]

For Ellacuría, Romero's life and ministry embody the very threefold confrontation with reality that underlies his theological method. The key to understanding Romero's legacy lies in recognizing how he changed the location/situation from which (and for which) he performed his ministry because of that confrontation. The crucifixion of the poor, starkly incarnated in the assassination of Rutilio Grande, an elderly man, and a young boy, confronted Romero with a reality to which he had to respond. The realization of the weight of this reality meant transformation — both Romero's personal transformation and that of his episcopacy. Listening to the plight of the poor meant opting for them such that the preaching and ministry of the church was nourished by this commitment, by its carrying of the weight of reality. This option led to an ecclesial praxis that itself would deepen the realization of reality's weight.[113] Once the poor became Romero's focus, his work became fruitful because it genuinely historicized the salvation of God.

The ministry of Archbishop Oscar Romero demonstrates the notion of conversion operative in Ellacuría's understanding of Christian discipleship. This conversion meant not just an initial acceptance of faith, but the ongoing process in Romero's life that led him to historicize the force of the Gospel. Ellacuría notes that while Romero may have had sympathy for the poor earlier in his career, he did not signify anything to the poor themselves because he did not know how to historicize the truth of the Gospel.[114]

Ellacuría, along with most commentators, cites the assassination of the Jesuit Rutilio Grande, which occurred in the same month that Romero was installed as archbishop, as the crucial turning point in Romero's ministry.[115] Grande's death caused Romero to see something objectively new, and this is what transformed him. So for Ellacuría it is not that Romero was transformed and was then able to see, but that the martyr's witness opened Romero's eyes to a reality that would transform him and his ministry. The death of a priest who had tried to evangelize the poor, to historicize salvation, and to give historical flesh to the word of God interrupted and called Romero to conversion.

Ellacuría speaks of Romero's conversion as merely the beginning of a new phase that provided Romero a mission: Whereas he once was concerned with the poor "as well," they now become the orienting center of his work.[116] He begins to see in them the historicized Jesus; and as the poor become significant in this way to Romero, he likewise becomes significant to them. Romero saw "in the people without a voice, the very voice of God; in the crucified people, God the savior; in the struggles for liberation, the way for the arrival of the new heaven and new earth."[117] If one accepts Ellacuría's perspective, then the common appellation given to Romero, that he was "voice of the voiceless," takes on a new meaning.

For Ellacuría, Oscar Romero is the "voice of the voiceless," but not in a heroic sense in which Romero functions merely as some sort of spokesperson or representative. If that were the case, then one could argue that the voiceless do not need someone to be their voice, but should gain their own voice(s). However, understood within the framework of Ellacuría's concepts of conversion and *kenosis,* Romero becomes a voice of the voiceless by surrendering his own voice for theirs. By learning humility and an overwhelming concern for the poor, Romero engages the power and voice of the archbishop's *cathedra,* not in a way that represents *mundanización,* a surrender to assimilation to the world, but a surrender to the voice of those who suffer the pain of crucifixion today. The voiceless do gain their own voice because of Romero's kenotic understanding of his ministry. Moreover, their suffering serves as a principle of salvation to those who would hear it and take on the path of Christian discipleship of announcing and manifesting the Reign of God.

Romero's ministry represents the transcendence-in-history that lies at the heart of Ellacuría's understanding of salvation. Ellacuría notes that Romero never refrained from invoking the transcendent: in his homilies it is the word and action of God that breaks through all human limits.[118] Romero's idea of transcendence does not abandon the human but perfects it. Romero tried to break the grip of sin and open up possibilities. He countered the absolutization of power and wealth, but also that of ideas (dogmatism) and of one's organization (sectarianism). Of course, this confrontation, which indicates the carrying forward of Jesus' mission that also confronted these powers, led to Romero's martyrdom.[119]

> One can and should say that with [Romero] the salvation of the historical process that is being fulfilled in El Salvador began to be realized in a surprisingly efficacious mode. He gave impulse to that process in its concrete historical reality because in him was seen more light than darkness, more life than violence. He took a position through that process, inasmuch as he favored the oppressed people. Yet the process cannot be identified with him exclusively, because the Gospel requires incarnation "in," but not identification "with" any determined historical process.[120]

In Romero's person, Ellacuría sees a Christian moved by compassion. Encountering the reality of the poor, Romero enters into a process of continual conversion, a conversion that calls him to an incarnational immersion into that reality. This incarnation takes the shape of a defense of the poor, a condemnation of those powers and structures that oppress the poor, and a working to remove those elements that further their suffering and early death. Romero's encounter with the living God comes through his encounter with the weakest ones, and a redemptive process is engaged through his contemplation-in-action tied to this encounter. It meant Romero's own salvation and an important moment in the salvific process of the Salvadoran church. In Romero, the different dimensions of Christian spirituality, including prayer, liturgy, immersion in reality, work for justice, and the call to peace, come together. Romero proclaimed a Christian hope built on "two pillars": one historical and the other transcendent.[121]

Like Romero's, Ellacuría's life of discipleship, committed to proclaiming a Christian transcendent-historical hope, ended in martyrdom. Those two lives, and their deaths, cannot be understood outside of the complex web of dynamisms in which they emerged. These men, their personal biographies, their ecclesiastical standing, their respective political roles, the social, political, economic situation of El Salvador at the time, and even the geopolitical conflict between the United States and the Soviet Union are among the many pieces that make up the intricate story of their discipleship and the power of their legacy. Accounting for this power and complexity drives Ellacuría's own understanding of Christian discipleship as an ecclesial praxis.

Conclusion

Ellacuría situates praxis in historical reality to stress the importance of human activity without treating that action in a mechanistic or utilitarian manner. To be sure, Ellacuría's transformative vision shows the influence of Marx, and though Ellacuría posits history as the highest form of praxis, the image that it conjures is one of a web of interconnected praxes rather than a dominant force or collective overrunning the human person. The thrust of Ellacuría's reflection on praxis resides in overcoming forces, and their ideological justifications, that continue to mean the oppression of the majority of the world's population. This transformation, one that is personal, social, and structural, represents not just a humanistic goal, but to the degree that this transformation conforms to the teachings of Jesus, the prophets, and the church's understanding of salvation, it indicates the importance of an ecclesial praxis engaged in transforming history.

Ellacuría's notion of ecclesial praxis cannot be separated from his notion of salvation history as a salvation in history. If salvation has a historical dimension, then the church that proclaims and hopes for this salvation must discern the manner in which it acts in history. A church embedded in history must configure its preaching and action to the historicization of the Reign of God. In doing so, it becomes an efficacious sacrament of salvation. In Ellacuría's understanding, this sacramental mission means both participating in the process of removing sin and the divinization of human persons. While the manner in which this mission is configured will differ with respect to different historical conditions, the norms for ecclesial praxis reside in the life and ministry of Jesus of Nazareth.

For Ellacuría, a twin set of verbs convey the nature of ecclesial praxis in light of Jesus' example. The church must follow (*seguir*) him, and must carry forward (*proseguir*) his mission of proclaiming and manifesting the Reign of God. In Ellacuría's reading, this must involve the transformation of societies where injustice rules. Ecclesial praxis involves more than the struggle for justice, but one cannot speak of ecclesial praxis in a world of injustice without that struggle. Ellacuría envisions a church that adopts an active, historical form of love that realizes in part the salvific hope proclaimed in the Gospels.

Ellacuría's rhetoric against passivity and his relative emphasis on active love could lead many readers to think he denigrates prayer and other practices as part of the Christian life. In Ellacuría's writing, ecclesial praxis does not mean the subordination of prayer and other practices to the pursuance of social justice; rather, the dynamic interpretation of history serves to demonstrate how prayer, practices, and the seeking of a more just society are interdependent — each possessing an importance and serving to condition the others. Ellacuría strongly criticizes those who would reduce the church's mission to a mere political task, but he cannot advocate a spirituality that ignores that task. Indeed, given his interrelated understanding of praxis, Ellacuría recognizes how those so-called "non-political" practices are in fact political, and can be used to obfuscate the workings of an unjust society.

Ultimately, Ellacuría argues for a Christian discipleship that transforms historical reality. Christians, and the Christian body that is the church, cannot speak of the Christian life in otherworldy terms because they are embedded in the historical reality of this world. Yet this does not mean reducing the activity of the church to exclusively sociological or political categories. By identifying a theologal dimension to historical reality, which springs from the fundamental belief in a Creator-Savior God, Ellacuría characterizes Christian ecclesial praxis as a participation in the Trinitarian life. While the ultimate fulfillment of salvation may be metahistorical, in Ellacuría's view, salvation possesses a historical character in which the church is called to participate.

That Ellacuría's understanding of praxis, and the way he and the others at the UCA carried it out, possessed a certain power finds verification in his assassination. Committed to a vision of Christian salvation in history, the *kenosis* of these intellectuals who deployed the intellectual gifts and institutional strength of a Christian university in service to the weakest members of Salvadoran society, enacted a carrying forward of Jesus' mission that was rewarded with his same fate—martyrdom. Yet the hope they engendered is a resurrection hope. Transformed by the reality of El Salvador, they sought to transform that reality so that it might conform more closely to that Reign of justice and love proclaimed by the prophets, by Jesus, and by followers throughout the centuries.

Assessing Ellacuría's legacy decades after his assassination requires a historicization of its own. The ground that this book has covered thus far, recognizing the interaction of the significant concepts in Ellacuría's constellation of theological ideas and placing them in the historical context of the liberation theology debates of the last century, could serve simply as a historical piece. Yet the ongoing relevance of Ellacuría's thought resides in the ability to historicize his reflection in new and ever-changing moments.

The subsequent, and concluding, chapter offers a first step in this historicization by posing the questions of a new generation to Ellacuría's theology. The circle of thinkers of the so-called "radical orthodoxy" challenge contemporary theology to reflect on the very themes with which Ellacuría concerned himself: how to articulate properly the understanding of Christian salvation and its implications for Christian life. Their engagement in a new historical situation, and drawing from a different set of intellectual sources, offers a critical engagement that could draw out those parts of Ellacuría's thought fruitful to ongoing theological reflection.

Chapter Five

Transforming Realities
and Contesting Orthodoxies

T O SOME DEGREE, the preceding chapters could stand on their own
as a historical, descriptive analysis of Ellacuría's soteriology. Considering his work within the debates about Latin American liberation
theology that raged during the 1970s and 1980s, this book began with the
claim that soteriology represents a fertile way for understanding different
positions within those debates and, considering Ellacuría's own concentra-
tion of writing on this theme, a most helpful manner to examine his own
theological output within the larger debate about liberation theology's legiti-
macy. Thus, after identifying some of liberation theologians' key themes and
Vatican counterclaims of this period as precisely soteriological, in the heart
of the text, chapters 2–4, I elucidated Ellacuría's soteriology by accounting
for its philosophical, christological, and ecclesiological dimensions.

While this analysis performs the important task of retrieving the thought
of a remarkable theologian-martyr, it has strayed little from what could
have been attempted already in the years immediately following Ellacuría's
assassination. By 1990, not only had assassins taken Ellacuría's life, but the
Vatican's International Theological Commission and the Congregation for
the Doctrine of the Faith had already published their responses to liberation
theology. So one could consider the preceding chapters the recitation of
a theology whose content, while not necessarily irrelevant, resides in an
ever-receding past as other movements such as the Tübingen school or the
Nouvelle Théologie.

Yet a question lingers. In a period in which the "death" of liberation
theology has been declared, does retrieval of Ellacuría's theology possess
any prescriptive value for current and future theological conversation? Any
answer to this question requires identifying which issues are relevant to contemporary theological debate. The debates of the 1970s and 1980s cannot
simply be rehashed. If liberation theologies in general, and Ellacuría's theology specifically, have something vital to say in the new millennium, with
whom must they converse?

The Challenge of Radical Orthodoxy

If Ellacuría's assassination in 1989 marked the closing of a first phase of liberation theology's development (and its concomitant critiques), then the following decade began with the emergence of a theological school that would present an entirely new set of questions to liberation theology. With the publication of his *Theology and Social Theory*, John Milbank boldly announced the arrival of "radical orthodoxy."[1] In many ways, the critique of liberation theology found in radical orthodoxy sounded familiar: liberation theology conceives of salvation in a reductionist manner, particularly in its dependence on Marxist theory. Milbank and others, including Daniel Bell Jr. and William Cavanaugh, arrived at their critiques drawing from a much different set of intellectual sources, however — sources that coalesce around a deep suspicion of the entire modern liberal "project." Their assertions regarding Christian salvation and the nature of Christian behavior in the world present a significant challenge to and opportunity for liberation theology to deepen its reflections. This chapter organizes these challenges to mirror the philosophical-christological-ecclesiological matrix utilized in the presentation of Ellacuría's thought in the previous chapters.

Thus, this final chapter begins with Milbank's philosophical diagnosis of liberation theology as excessively dependent on modern secular reason. His insights on Continental philosophy are then supplemented by two thinkers influenced by the U.S. ethicist Stanley Hauerwas. So consideration will be given to Bell's claim that liberation theologians' emphasis on justice misconstrues the proper way to combat capitalism and its evils. Instead, the christological notion of forgiveness provides the proper "therapy of desire" to counteract capitalism's pernicious technologies. Finally, Cavanaugh's ecclesiological invocation of Eucharistic performance as the church's true calling completes the complex challenge that radical orthodoxy thinkers pose to Latin American liberation theologians.

The point of this treatment is neither to offer an exhaustive examination of radical orthodoxy nor to construct a complete response from the perspective of one liberation theologian (Ellacuría). Such an undertaking would, of course, require its own monograph. Rather, by offering some preliminary responses to the radical orthodoxy thinkers from the perspective of Ellacuría's work, this book concludes with a twofold claim: first, that Latin American liberation theology remains a vibrant source of reflection, and second, that Ellacuría's work in particular possesses rich possibilities for present and future theological conversation.

Trapped in Secular Reason

In *Theology and Social Theory*, Milbank positions Latin American liberation theology within a larger trajectory of criticism.[2] In this text, Milbank pursues a deconstruction of a modern ontology of conflict and violence that is, he argues, "a reading of the world which assumes the priority of force and tells how this force is best managed and confined by counter-force."[3] In part, this modern metanarrative stems from a sociology of religion, originating in figures such as Comte, Malebranche, and Durkheim and following through to Kant and Weber, that bestows a metaphysical status to "social facts."[4] In the guise of science, this sociology asserts a latent, but no less significant, set of theological claims that have disastrous results for those forms of modern theology, including liberation theology, that embrace its assumptions.

The more proximate figures relevant to Milbank's scrutiny of liberation theology include Hegel and Marx. Milbank focuses on their use of dialectics, which, although possessing an important critical value, inevitably remain trapped within modern secular reason. Having argued that modern political theory rests on three great denials — of "Baroque *poeisis*" (in which human making is not merely instrumental but a route to the transcendent), of the Christian doctrine of creation, and finally of Aristotelian ethics and politics — Milbank assesses Hegel as both questioning and reinforcing these denials.[5] Hegel's "myth of negation" drives a reading of society and history that requires denial to lead to a new positive result. Hegel misconstrues infinity by sublating the opposition of infinite to finite as identity.[6] So Hegel's attempt to support the transcendence of the creator God unwittingly confuses the distinction between creator and created.

In the area of human behavior, Hegel's mistaken attempt to overcome modernity's denials continues to lead to their inadvertent reinforcement. Milbank argues that because of Hegel's inability to posit a proper *telos* for human activity beyond the Cartesian subject and its freedom, he cannot posit a *Sittlichkeit* that embodies true Aristotelian *praxis*.[7] At the wider social level, Hegel's version of Christian history reinforces the "new science of politics" in which the possibilities for Christians in society get reduced to a metanarrative of evolution and privatized action. Even justice becomes "something to do with upholding laws that can be ultimately connected with the freedom of person and property."[8]

In his comments on Marx, Milbank maintains a dialectical sympathy-critique that mirrors his reflections on Hegel. Just as Hegel falters by not escaping a wider metanarrative, so Marx remains captive to a positivist, reductionist story. Though he acknowledges the importance of Marx's trenchant critique of capitalism, Milbank concludes that Marx ultimately misconstrues the proper solution by viewing capitalism as "a necessary phase within the process of human becoming."[9] Marx's vision of a single realm of human production remains inevitably locked within a positivist vision of modern natural law and the modern secular order. This vision dictates at best a critique of capitalism, but not a declaration of it as irrational. Moreover, it directs the critique of religion to an unstated but accepted theological understanding. Milbank notes the irony that Marx's critique of Christianity itself functions by " 'situating' it within a metanarrative which has itself a quasi-religious and 'heretical' character."[10]

If, according to Milbank, Marx possesses an important insight into the logic of capitalism as a secular logic, then his undoing resides in an unacceptable account of history and anthropology. Rather than Marx's dialectical argument that resides within a wider modern metanarrative, Milbank's vision consists in a critique that is *traditional* in character, in the fullest sense of the word. It would be a critique that David Burrell rightly characterizes in these words: "There is nothing necessary about it, but one is confronted with an alternative view of the *humanum* which identifies an excellence which capitalism is dedicated to eliminate."[11] That both Hegel and Marx cannot substantiate a truly alternative vision sets up Milbank's analysis of the twentieth-century theologies that inherit their legacy — in particular, Latin American liberation theology.

Milbank correctly situates the beginnings of Latin American liberation theology in relation to the monumental changes to the Roman Catholic Church during the Second Vatican Council.[12] Specifically, he claims that this theology emerges in the wake of the "integralist revolution" embraced by the council: that every person has always already been worked upon by grace, so that one cannot separate "pure nature" from the integral unity of natural and supernatural. Milbank agrees with this distinction from "integrist" clerical dominance over all affairs. Thus, he accounts for the reasoning behind the "distinction of planes" theology that created space for lay involvement, but also lauds the liberationists for insights into how this distinction ultimately breaks down in Latin Americans' experience. However, having supported the overarching motivations behind liberation theologians' inheritance of the "integralist revolution," Milbank faults them for embracing the wrong form of integralism.

For Milbank's narrative the integralist revolution has two sources: a French source (de Lubac, Blondel), that by "supernaturalizing the natural" recovers a premodern sense of the Christianized person as a fully real person; and the German (Rahner), which "naturalizes the supernatural" through a mediating theology, a rapprochement with Enlightenment that makes of the supernatural a permanent area of human life.[13] In Milbank's diagnosis, the "main proponents" of liberation theology follow the German tradition and so remain trapped in secular reason and its foundationalist propositions.[14] In short, he views liberation theologians as relying on the view that "the social is an autonomous sphere which does not need to turn to theology for its self-understanding, and yet it is already a grace-imbued sphere, and therefore it is *upon* pre-theological sociology or Marxist social theory, that theology must be founded."[15]

This allegiance to a modern, sociological metanarrative empties liberation theologians' attempts to formulate Christian praxis. Milbank characterizes their attempts as a "foundational praxis which appeals either to an impossible practice 'without theory,' or else to a specifically 'political' practice, which is a practice outside Christian tradition." In contrast to this stands Blondel's " 'supernatural pragmatism,' which makes practice fundamental in the sense that thought and action are inseparably fused in the development of a tradition."[16] So rather than espousing a praxis that is "genuinely historical and open," liberation theologians unwittingly inhabit a space "theoretically marked out as secular political practice."[17]

The specifics of Milbank's argument appear in a section tellingly entitled "Salvation or Liberation."[18] Rather than arguing whether liberation theology considers salvation as individual or collective, Milbank focuses on the manner that he believes liberation theology gives salvation content in social terms, but treats the experience in an entirely individualistic fashion. He regards this split as due to liberation theologians' reliance on an abstract sociological opposition between the social and the individual. Two consequences stem from this reliance: (1) Salvation remains a separate "religious" category that concerns a particular dimension of individual *a priori* experience (which really indicates an a-social notion of salvation itself); and (2) the juxtaposition of society to the individual permits a realm of religious experience which remains unaffected by social processes.

Milbank claims that liberation theologians reduce salvation to a "private transcendence" because of their reliance on a Rahnerian account of grace that universalizes natural human ontology.[19] While correctly dismissing a notion of divine self-revelation as extrinsic to human existence, liberation theologians neglect a truly gratuitous account of grace by adherence to a Rahnerian vision of the supernatural existential. Milbank rejects the anonymous dimensions of this theological anthropology as conceding an autonomous sociological sphere, or worse, baptizing an essentially modern, secular view of the person as individual.

In dissecting Clodovis Boff's proposal for a "first theology," Milbank concludes, "all Boff is doing is renaming the categorical imperative as 'faith.' "[20] Milbank views in liberationists' efforts nothing more than a baptizing of an individualist ethic that replaces any serious social or political theory. Indeed, Milbank believes that if pushed to define how something like the love of neighbor might be socially instantiated (or indeed, what love itself *is*), liberation theology must fall back to a position requiring either a utilitarian, sociological, or Marxist diagnosis of proper conduct.

If Milbank maintains that theoretical flaws haunt liberation theologians at the level of philosophy and social theory, then he believes that they make a direct impact on the theological articulation of Christology and proper Christian discipleship. For example, Milbank rejects the reading that many liberation theologians offer for the parable of the last judgment in the Gospel of Matthew (Matt. 25:31–46).[21] Not only does Milbank view in their understanding of this parable an appeal to an anonymous form of love, in contrast to Milbank's notion of Christian love as a "highly complex, learned practice," but he believes it provides a basis for an approach to Christ far too general and susceptible to ideologization. Milbank alleges that "the liberation theologians only acknowledge in Christ a perfection of subjective *motivation."*[22] This reduces evaluation and repetition of Christ's example to the level of strategy or motivation.

In contrast, Milbank advocates an adherence to certain "persistent features of Jesus' practice" that define Christian discipleship. The difference between this position and what Milbank identifies in liberation theology strikes at the very core of his criticism. He declares,

> It is not that we are to exercise the same motivation of love within different historical circumstances which we interpret theoretically, but that we are to "repeat" precisely what Jesus did in practice, but in different historical circumstances, which we interpret practically through subsuming them into our "performance" of the original Christic text.[23]

In particular, Milbank stresses Jesus' "peaceableness" as a key distinguishing feature of Christian discipleship, and in the end, as the notion that reveals the fatal mistake of liberation theology. "Liberation theologians attempt to reduce Jesus' peaceableness to the strategic level: arguing that violent struggle was not the path which love could conveniently take in Jesus' day before industrialization and proletarianization made revolution a serious possibility."[24] Therefore, Milbank views in liberation theology the culmination to his overall theory concerning the modern secular metanarrative as advocating an ontology of violence.

The compromised views of salvation and Christian praxis found in liberation theology move Milbank to conclude that liberation theology also possesses a flawed ecclesiological view. Because they are caught in the modern sociological metanarrative, liberation theologians remain unable to mount a serious critique of the current capitalist system. "What they really say is what they claim not to say: namely that Christians should say their prayers, be decent citizens, and otherwise just accept society as it is."[25] For Milbank, only by recovering a sense of theology as an autonomous account of human existence, free from the dependence on the social sciences, can contemporary theology escape the modern sociological trap.

Ironically, Milbank suggests that an outstanding ecclesiological example lies right under the noses of liberation theologians. In the attempt to recover the view of the church as a "society of friends" that represents an anticipation of a possible socialist community, Milbank notes, "this may be to say that liberation theology has not properly theorized the significance of the 'base communities' in Latin America."[26] While Milbank elects not to elaborate on this point, he signals a route that subsequent analyses will take in relation to exploring liberation theology.

Milbank's criticism of Latin American liberation theology, though wide-ranging, coheres around his wider indictment of modern theology as trapped within secular reason. For Milbank, it is in the sources, in the manner that liberation theologians frame their thought and conception of reality, that they make a fatal error. Thus, he spends little time developing a sustained analysis of theological concepts or of any particular liberation theologian's thought. He has lifted the veil of philosophical assumption within modern, liberal theology. Whether they be considered valid or not, Milbank's critiques represent important philosophical questions with which not just liberation theologians, but all contemporary theologies should wrestle.

The Refusal to Cease Suffering

While John Milbank's critique of liberation theology in *Theology and Social Theory* represents a preliminary salvo that concentrates primarily at the level of sources, subsequent efforts by a group of younger scholars influenced by his work turn attention to more specific questions of theological and ethical content. These scholars, specifically Daniel M. Bell Jr. and William T. Cavanaugh, have produced full-length monographs that represent the most substantial critical engagement of Latin American liberation theology in recent literature.[27] They also represent an important way that Milbank's European thought has been received in the United States. Both Bell and Cavanaugh, students under Stanley Hauerwas, bring to liberation theology not only the profound suspicion of modern, liberal presumptions, but a communitarian ecclesiology that emphasizes the importance of distinctive Christian witness.[28]

Bell agrees with Milbank's central conviction that Latin American liberation theology suffers the pernicious effects of engagement with and assumption of modern thought. Rather than focusing on philosophical sources such as Hegel and Marx, however, Bell utilizes postmodern thinkers, such as Foucault and Deleuze, to suggest an alternative diagnosis of capitalism's evil, and to offer the correct prescription for Christian action in the world. In particular, Bell claims that liberation theologians offer a mistaken account of justice that eclipses the more proper Christian emphasis on forgiveness. He also asserts that liberation theology cannot seriously challenge capitalism's hegemony because the practice it advocates relegates the Christian community to a status subordinate to the modern liberal state.

Sadly, liberation theology is "embedded in the modern narrative that divorces religion from social-political-economic dimensions of life."[29] The so-called "church of the poor" about which liberationists speak remains only indirectly political because it exists within a metanarrative that relegates politics to statecraft. For Bell, Christianity represents the true politics, the church a true polity. He advocates a vision of the Christian community as a public *sui generis* (a social-political-economic formation in its own right) whose primary goal consists in forgiveness rather than seeking justice.[30]

Situating his analysis in the period after Francis Fukuyama's famous declaration of the "end of history," Bell identifies the present moment as one of crisis for liberation theology.[31] He notes the apparent triumph of "savage capitalism" as the gravest challenge to all contemporary Christian discipleship.[32] Though sympathetic to liberationist efforts, Bell concludes that liberation theology fails because its critique of capitalism is not radical enough.[33] Drawing heavily on the work of Foucault and Deleuze, Bell identifies capitalism not simply as an economic system but as an order of desire.[34] Liberation theologians, who have not arrived at this conclusion and so hand revolutionary expectations to the state, remain trapped within the capitalist order, never able to overcome its power.

If history shows that Latin American liberation theologians emerged both from and as a reaction to the "New Christendom" of the early twentieth century, then Bell suggests, in a rhetorical move reminiscent of Milbank, that liberation theologians have mistakenly adopted the very position they criticized. Even though liberation theologians claim to disapprove of the "separation of planes" that characterized Maritain's New Christendom model, they end up with an ecclesiology that separates the theological and social, religion and politics. Attacking precisely the connection between salvation and politics, Bell suggests that liberation theology casts the denunciation of injustice and the annunciation of the Gospel's values as only indirectly political. Thus, liberation theology construes the church as an "apolitical custodian of disembodied moral values."[35]

Bell insists that the practice of the faith should be seen as intrinsically social, political, and economic. So the church is the exemplary form of human community. Christianity is a fully material reality whose practices transform circumstances. "The church is a public in its own right; it is a public *sui generis*."[36] Making this formulation, Bell explicitly cites and opposes Ellacuría's description of the church as "just another power in history, which follows the dynamics of other historical powers."[37] No — for Bell, the church represents an exemplary form of human community. Ironically, though, Bell does not (or cannot) identify communities in the United States that instantiate his descriptions. He, like Milbank, claims that the liberation theologians have the perfect example of proper Christian behavior in the Latin American *comunidades de base*.

The qualities Bell praises in the base communities reflect those he sees in his historical example of the ideal community — the monastic community of Bernard of Clairvaux and the Cistercians. The medieval monastic community demonstrates Christianity as that fully material reality, an ensemble of technologies that provides "the moral space for the release of desire from the bonds of violence, pride, and sensuality."[38] This idealization of medieval monasticism functions within a narrative of mourning indicting modern Christianity. In speaking of "the distance separating medieval feudal and modern liberal polities," Bell makes the extraordinary claim:

> Perhaps the difference that matters is not that which is created by the absence of monastic institutions but that which is rooted in the limitation of Christians' willingness to have their everyday lives shaped by the grace of God. In other words, the real obstacle to living Christianity

as an ensemble of technologies of desire is not the dearth of monastic orders but the lack of persons who are willing to place themselves
in the types of relations with others and with God that characterized
Cistercian life.[39]

Sadly, according to this narrative, liberation theology draws its notion of
justice not from the monastic trajectory, which reaches its zenith in the vision
of justice articulated by Aquinas, but from a defective form found in modern
Catholic social teaching.[40] This latter vision of justice falls into the trap of
casting proper Christian behavior in terms of "individual rights," a move
that eclipses the importance of that therapy able to overcome capitalism's
control of desire: forgiveness.[41]

The heart of Bell's criticism lies in his identifying the liberationist concept
of justice with that which "has been broadly conceived in terms of the ancient phrase *suum cuique:* to each what is due."[42] Understanding liberation
theology this way, Bell prosecutes it, and the modern Catholic social teaching tradition, for equating the common good with a cache of rights. Justice
understood this way leads to Christian practice that forgets the principles
of mercy and forgiveness. At its worst, especially to this group of pacifist
thinkers, it leads to Christians adopting violence to secure and enforce the
claims of justice. Bell must evaluate the concept of justice as "each getting
her or his due" as theologically incomplete.

In identifying the theological flaw behind liberation theology's view of justice, Bell turns to the importance of soteriological claims. "The importance
bestowed upon justice in liberationist accounts of contemporary Christianity is such that justice becomes synonymous with salvation."[43] In part, Bell
bases this claim on Gustavo Gutiérrez's assertion that "without justice there
is no salvation."[44] Bell assumes a connection between the way theologians
conceive of justice and the way they understand salvation by the way that
he turns his attention to Christian soteriological tropes. Though Bell ap-
provingly cites and utilizes Ellacuría's notion of the crucified people, he
cannot agree with Jon Sobrino's characterization of the resurrection as the
triumph of God's justice. The overcoming of sin, of injustice in the resurrection "must be understood as an overcoming that is something other than
justice conceived as *suum cuique.*"[45] To find that more proper understanding
of resurrection, and indeed of Christian salvation, Bell turns his attention to
the key moment where justice and salvation meet in the Christian mystery:
the notion of Christ's crucifixion as an atonement.

For Bell, the atonement, properly understood, indicates the displacement
of justice in favor of grace. To develop this idea, Bell turns to the classic
treatment of atonement in Anselm's *Cur Deus homo?* With a reading of
Anselm heavily dependent on David Hart, Bell suggests that Christ's atoning work means not a substitutionary sacrifice (according to the notion of
justice as *suum cuique*), but a recapitulatory vision in which God's rejected
offer of love is made again in the person of Christ.[46] For Bell, what "God

accomplished in Christ" must be summed up in terms of forgiveness, not justice. "Justice in the classic sense of *suum cuique* would refuse to have suffered the injustice of sin and the cross.... Accordingly, the atoning grace of God in Christ displaces such justice as the modality of God's overcoming of sin and sets in its place forgiveness."[47] Through the forgiveness forged by Christ's sacrifice, humanity participates "in the divine life of the Trinity through participation in Christ, in Christ's body, the church."[48] The logic of this forgiveness not only displaces the logic of justice, it does so in the communally instantiated capacity to forgive. Bell emphasizes the ecclesiological nature of this atonement theory and its relation to the Reign of God.

> To paraphrase the Gospel of Mark, because the Reign of God has drawn near, forgiveness is possible (Mark 1:15). The advent of the Kingdom interrupts the progress of sin and creates spaces (called "Church") where desire can escape from its captivity to sin through the enactment of God's forgiveness.[49]

If capitalism's technologies of desire serve to entrap and enslave humanity, then Christianity must be seen as that ensemble of technologies that serve as a therapy of desire. The Christian church *is that space* where desire escapes captivity. Through confession, repentance, and penance, the Christian church possesses those powers that can truly overcome capitalism's hegemony, a power not found in liberation theology if it adheres to justice as providing each his or her own due. For example, Bell understands the claim that "forgiveness of social injustice is incomplete without reparations" merely to continue the destructive logic of justice.[50] Only through the logic of forgiveness may Christianity shed its (modern) identity as apolitical custodian of abstract values and preferential options and assume its proper place in the temporal realm as the true politics, the exemplary form of human community.[51]

Although much of Bell's rhetoric decries the centrality of justice in Christian discourse, Bell realizes that he cannot ignore so rich a biblical theme. So he concludes his work with a "repositioning of justice within the an-economic order of the divine gift of forgiveness."[52] Ironically, the theologians from which he draws to make his case are the Latin American liberation theologians.[53] He then notes sadly, "These insights, unfortunately, are not sustained; eventually the liberationists corral them into line with their conception of justice as the guarantor of rights."[54] This conclusion sums up nicely the rhetoric at work throughout Bell's text: too often, liberationist insights show promise but are ultimately undone by their fundamental theoretical deficiencies.

Though Bell seems quite sympathetic to many of the liberation theologians, in the end, he builds his case on an accusation of fundamental ignorance. They do not understand capitalism properly, they do not understand justice properly, and finally, they do not understand the salvific importance of forgiveness as the key to Christian life in the world. The ecclesiological ramifications of this ignorance come to the fore in the work of another radical orthodoxy writer, William Cavanaugh.

Eucharistic Performance

Among the radical orthodoxy writers, William Cavanaugh has marked out a space that appears most proximate to that occupied by Latin American liberation theologians. His book-length consideration of the Eucharist analyzes the Chilean Catholic Church during the Pinochet regime.[55] His various articles draw upon Medellín, base communities, and Salvadoran martyrs Rutilio Grande and Oscar Romero as touchstones for reflection and often as bases for prescriptive declarations for the wider church body he addresses.[56] Indeed, one surface reading might identify Cavanaugh as part of a new generation of liberation theologians who wish to deepen the insights of a previous generation's work. Such, however, is not the case.

A closer analysis of Cavanaugh's work reveals that despite a general sympathy with the efforts of liberation theologians, he retains a deep suspicion of both their theoretical underpinnings and ecclesiological conclusions. In many ways, this suspicion echoes, and indeed emerges from, a reliance on Milbank's philosophical critiques and a Hauerwas-influenced ecclesiology similar to that of Bell.[57] Cavanaugh excoriates any theology indebted to the modern *mythos,* particularly to the degree that the church cedes political activity either to the state or as the task of individual lay people with only a general ecclesiological blessing from a church more occupied with "spiritual" salvation.[58]

Cavanaugh's principal contribution resides in a provocative reading of the Eucharist as the discipline of a church body, a body that serves as a contrast society. Drawing from the work of Foucault in a way shared by Bell, Cavanaugh scrutinizes the state as a disciplinary regime whose power derives, in part, from its ability to strip persons from communities and so leave them as "atomic individuals."[59] Despite a strong affinity with the liberation theologians, Cavanaugh maintains that only Eucharistic performance, and not appeals to abstract principles such as love and justice, possesses resources powerful enough to resist the hegemony of the state and its co-opting practices and ideology.[60] By relying too strongly on a modern theoretical and ecclesiological framework that dissolves the church into the world, liberation theologians merely play into the state's disciplinary power.

Cavanaugh's central claims, particularly those that function to differentiate his positions explicitly from those of liberation theologians, center on his alternative ecclesiology. Cavanaugh, like Milbank and Bell, discerns in Latin American liberation theology too close a dependence on modern thought. For Cavanaugh, the tragic outcome of this reliance is an ecclesiology that too easily dissolves the distinctive character of the church into the world.[61] Sadly, the modern state will quickly accept authority and activity under its pernicious hegemony. While *Torture and Eucharist* details the weakness of this ecclesiology vis-à-vis the Pinochet regime in Chile, that serves only as a demonstration of a more thorough account of the nature of the modern state and its insidious mythos of salvation.

Rather than continuing the liberationist vision as he sees it, that is, dissolving the church into the world in a social scientific reading of reality, Cavanaugh articulates a retrieval of a "church practice of the political" within a specifically Christian discourse. Ultimately, Cavanaugh offers an alternative ecclesiology to that of liberation theology in his insistence that the church be seen as a contrast society that, through the performance of the Eucharist, enacts a counter-performance to that of the modern state.

To make his argument, Cavanaugh contrasts the modern state and the Christian church by their alternative soteriologies.[62] What he finds in common in these soteriologies is that both the modern state and Christianity possess stories that have a similar goal: namely, "salvation of humankind from the divisions which plague us."[63] While both the state and "the church" pursue peace and an end to division by enactment of a social body, Cavanaugh consider the state's body a "false copy" of the body of Christ. Therefore, he asserts the Eucharist as a key practice for a "Christian anarchism" that can overcome the state's soteriological story.

Before delving into the state's soteriology, Cavanaugh summarizes the Christian story. For him it begins with the natural unity of the human race founded in the creation story in Genesis. Following de Lubac, Cavanaugh claims that "the effect of sin is the very creation of individuals as such, that is, the creation of an ontological distinction between individual and group."[64] Thus, redemption occurs by restoration of unity through participation in Christ's Body. This permits Cavanaugh to introduce the reading of Augustine's *civitatis Dei* as the "true politics" as opposed to the *civitas terrena*.

In Augustine's vision of the two cities, the reunification of the human race depends on Christians locating true citizenship beyond the confines of the earthly empire. We journey through the *civitas terrena* always aware that our true home is in heaven. This communion with our fellow-citizens in heaven is not, however, an escape from this-worldly politics, but rather a radical interruption by the Church of the false politics of the earthly city.[65]

In contrast to this Christian story, Cavanaugh, relying on Milbank, asserts that "modern politics is founded on the voluntarist replacement of a theology of participation with a theology of will."[66] Human government is established not on a primal unity, but on the irreducible individuality of the members of the human race. Despite variations in the stories of Locke, Hobbes, and Rousseau, they concur that salvation involves making peace among competing individuals. Moreover, part of the myth of the modern state includes the claim that it exists to save humanity precisely from the conflicts brought about by religion.

Cavanaugh argues that the false modern myth that the state delivered Europe from the "Wars of Religion" resulted from fifteenth- and sixteenth-century constructions of religion as a system of beliefs rather than what it was earlier, "a virtue located within a set of theological claims and practices which assume a social form called church."[67] If this is so, then the wars were not a fight between members of different religions, but a battle of the state over a transnational ecclesial order. Since individuals in the modern state share no ends in common, the state's *religio* (its habitual discipline for binding one to another) becomes violence. Thus, Hobbes has Leviathan swallow the church, leaving to the latter only the task of producing obedience to the laws of the state.

In light of this reading of modernity, Cavanaugh identifies the grave challenge for the contemporary church not simply as secularization, the stripping of the sacred with a profane remainder, but a capitulation to the powerful state soteriology, "the substitution of one *mythos* of salvation for another."[68] In his analysis of the situation in Chile, Cavanaugh assigns blame primarily to that "New Christendom" ecclesiology that saw as its major source the writings of Jacques Maritain. With this model's "separation of planes," the Chilean hierarchy too comfortably asserted its responsibility for the souls of citizens while leaving their bodies at the mercy of the state, tragically rendering the laity isolated individuals unable to counter the power of Pinochet's regime.

He implicates liberation theologians as primary inheritors of the "New Christendom" model, noting how figures like Gustavo Gutiérrez and Juan Luis Segundo "began their social activism in Catholic Action."[69] Cavanaugh connects the "See-Judge-Act" methodology of Catholic Action with the way that "liberation theologians emphasize a first moment of social scientific reading of the situation before a theological analysis is applied."[70] While Cavanaugh appreciates how liberation theologians have criticized Maritain, he believes that too often they only compound the problem by positing the unity of history, sacred and profane, as an alternative to the separation of planes. It is a view of history's unity that Gutiérrez and others see as moving the church away from an "ecclesiastical narcissism" in which the church, as the only true vehicle of salvation, existed in history in an almost accidental way. It is one, however, that Cavanaugh rejects. "The world has absorbed the church into itself. This signals both the final destruction of a church practice of the political, and the abandonment of specifically Christian discourse in favor of a social scientific reading of reality."[71]

As an alternative to the legacy of Maritain, in which protecting the "spiritual" character of the church yields an "autonomy of the temporal" to the state, Cavanaugh prefers to envision the church as a "culture" possessing an alternative set of specific social practices.[72] In short, Christianity should not try to influence the state, the apparent fatal flaw behind liberationist thinking, but should participate in the heart of its true *religio*: the Eucharist.

When Cavanaugh considers the Eucharist, he does not countenance an opposition between symbolic, ritual performance and what occurs "in reality." Rather, he claims, "for Catholic Christianity there is nothing more real than the real presence of Jesus Christ in the Eucharist."[73] The reality of this presence alone, which transforms the assembled body into the body of Christ, possesses the power to resist the discipline of the modern state. Therefore, Cavanaugh sees in the Eucharist an anti-logic to that of the modern state's use of torture. Where torture isolates individuals, Eucharist calls them to one body. "Torture creates victims; Eucharist creates witnesses, martyrs."[74]

A central way that Eucharist counters the narrative of the state involves its creation of unity. For Cavanaugh, Eucharist creates a catholicity that, rather than playing on the usual understanding of "catholic" as a universal spreading out, implies instead a gathering together.[75] Though the Eucharist may be celebrated in scattered communities, it gathers them together in a collapsing of spatial barriers that counters modern mapping. Furthermore, in the Eucharist, "A story is not simply told but performed; space is organized by a body in movement.... As such, the spatial story is not simply descriptive, but prescriptive."[76] The practices that originate in this alternative spatial story bring unity and guide the church's behavior.

While Cavanaugh advocates understanding the Eucharist as an alternative spatial and temporal order, he affirms that this still implies an engagement in this world. As an alternative to modern mapping, represented most clearly in different globalization frameworks, Eucharistic mapping does not abandon, but transforms spaces. "The City of God makes use of this world as it moves through it on pilgrimage to its heavenly home."[77] Eucharist, however, transforms time in its eschatological expectation of the Kingdom. This anticipation of the Kingdom overcomes the individuality of worldly historical imagination incorporating persons into a communion that is simultaneously past and future.[78]

This vision of the Eucharist relies on a notion of God's transcendence. If signs and locations become interchangeable in the modern state, then the Eucharist tells and performs a counternarrative that restores humanity's proper longing for God.

> Augustine saw that one's true identity is only found in desire for God, who is beyond the fleeting things of this world. We might add that it is precisely God's transcendence of the world that allows liturgical difference, for where God cannot be fully grasped, a diversity of locations and practices is necessary to imply the transcendent. Nevertheless, liturgical difference is possible not because all the particular signs are interchangeable. On the contrary, in the Eucharist the particular is of the utmost importance, for this particular piece of bread at this particular place and time is the body of Christ, and is not merely a pointer to some abstract transcendent standing behind the sign.[79]

The manner in which the particularity of the Eucharist manifests as a witness signals the fundamental differences between Cavanaugh's account and that of liberation theology.

While Cavanaugh agrees with those liberation theologians, for example, Leonardo Boff and Jon Sobrino, who underscore the Christoformic nature of contemporary martyrdom, he believes that other norms condition the way they articulate the Christian character of martyrdom. Cavanaugh views their account of martyrdom as an *imitatio Christi* circumscribed by abstract (modern) notions of love and justice. Cavanaugh's irritation with Sobrino's suggestion that martyrdom may be defined simply as an "unjustly inflicted death for love's sake" reveals his basic disagreement with liberation theology: namely, that this "leaves [Sobrino] no choice but to recognize even those who resort to armed violence as potential 'martyrs by analogy.'"[80] Cavanaugh cannot reconcile this possibility with his view of the ancient martyrs as being defined by their nonviolence. Thus, he formulates a counter-vision of martyrdom itself.

Rather than a view of martyrdom that appeals to abstract principles, Cavanaugh defines the imitation of Christ in martyrdom as "a highly skilled performance learned in a disciplined community of virtue by careful attention to the concrete contours of the Christian life and death as borne out by Jesus and the saints."[81] Cavanaugh sees this enacted in the early church precisely because early Christians saw themselves as an alternative community. Martyrdom makes this alternative community/body visible, disciplining the community and helping it claim its identity. To Cavanaugh, this function of martyrdom dictates a de-emphasis of the individual intentions of the martyr. "It is not the heroism of the individual which is most significant, but rather the naming of the martyr by those who recognize Christ in the martyr's life and death."[82]

Ultimately, what the community recognizes in the martyr involves a foretaste of eschatological expectations. Cavanaugh views the martyr as a "bridge between heaven and earth" because she or he incarnates Christ's victory over death. "A martyr is one who lives imaginatively as if death does not exist."[83] This victory over death delineates the Christian body from a worldly body under the reign of death. Thus, in the Eucharistic performance and incarnation of Christ's victory over death, Cavanaugh concludes that alternative vision of the Christian body that he believes liberation theology cannot generate if wed to a modern state's narrative.

Though Milbank does not continue any engagement with liberation theology after *Theology and Social Theory,* the work of Bell and Cavanaugh demonstrate that radical orthodoxy has a continuing interest in the claims of liberation theologians, and this interest entails the possibility that what up to this point has been a monologue can be converted into a dialogue of theological exchange. The next portion of this chapter will focus on what that dialogue might look like if one of the interlocutors were Ignacio Ellacuría.

Seeds for a Radical Response

Given the extent and gravity of the accusations levied against liberation theology by radical orthodoxy thinkers, a full response from the perspective of liberation theology would require a number of responses from its respective authors.[84] Although those liberation theologians who are still alive could engage radical orthodoxy thinkers in debate, in the case of Ellacuría, it must be an imagined one. Obviously Ellacuría never saw the publication of Milbank's text nor any of the subsequent material. Yet by suggesting themes in Ellacuría's written corpus as seeds for a response, this section attempts to demonstrate both the distinctive nature of Ellacuría's vision and its ongoing relevance for fruitful dialogue with contemporary theological movements.

Many factors indicate possible lines of convergence between Ellacuría's theology and that of radical orthodoxy. Ellacuría repeatedly positions his philosophy and theology as a critique of dangers he sees present in modern Enlightenment thought. His criticisms of separations and dualisms in certain strains of modern thought seem to occupy a space proximate to his radical orthodoxy counterparts. Ellacuría's stinging critique of capitalism and his call for a Christian ecclesial body that enacts an imitative and creative Christian discipleship also appear to find a correspondence in these critics. Indeed, his legacy, raising the UCA's prophetic voice in criticism of both an oppressive military regime and a violent guerrilla opposition, looks as if it would be advocated as radically orthodox.

Despite these areas of seeming proximity, a basic impetus separates Ellacuría from radical orthodoxy. Even though Ellacuría often engages in an argumentative rhetoric, his fundamental worldview tends to be inclusive. The profound interrelatedness of historical reality and unity of praxis in his thought stand in marked contrast to the claims of radical orthodoxy thinkers who tend to speak in oppositions. Milbank, Bell, and Cavanaugh emphasize the distinctiveness, the otherness of the Christian narrative and Christian body in a world that has uncertain meaning outside of this narrative and body.

Therefore, putting Ellacuría's theology in dialogue with radical orthodoxy engages the areas of affinity and disparity while examining worthy critiques of Ellacuría, areas in which Ellacuría's thought acquits itself of accusations, and finally ways in which Ellacuría's theology poses questions to radical orthodoxy.

Escaping the Non-Secular Trap

The central accusation against liberation theologians from the radical orthodoxy concerns attention to the philosophical sources of its reflection and the underlying suppositions attached to differing visions of the world. Certainly, one of Milbank's great contributions consists in reminding contemporary theologians of the ideological narratives latent in other theoretical and especially social scientific disciplines.[85] Theologians risk troubling compromises, and outright capitulation, if they accept social-scientific data naïvely without devoting corresponding attention to these underlying narratives.

Turning to Ellacuría's thought, one might suggest that his use of Marxist thought, and not coincidentally his theological tutelage under Karl Rahner, makes him a clear example of that erroneous form of Catholic integralism that attempts to "naturalize the supernatural." Bracketing the validity of Milbank's claims in regards to Rahner, one can still argue that Ellacuría acquits himself of relying on a non-Christian metanarrative in his articulation of Christian salvation. His reliance on Zubiri provides a way to offer a thick description of historical reality without succumbing to a metanarrative in conflict with the Christian story.[86]

While Ellacuría's (and Zubiri's) analysis of historical reality is open to and even demands knowledge from the social sciences, his proposition of reality's theologal dimension appears to be that overarching Christian logos that provides meaning for this encounter. Because of the theologal underpinnings of Ellacuría's thought, it is always already tied to a fundamentally Christian vision, thus avoiding any capitulation to pure secularism. Ellacuría's own methodological debate with Clodovis Boff illustrates one way in which he eschews the simple acceptance, or even the dichotomization, of the social sciences and theology.[87] Ellacuría frames his entire consideration of human existence by naming God, a God beyond being, as that which religates all reality. Furthermore, by describing salvation as participation in the *plasmación ad extra* of the Trinitarian life, Ellacuría avoids the individualism that is Milbank's irritant and offers interesting points of contact to Milbank's own Trinitarian turn.

Milbank's focus on competing metanarratives calls attention to the ways that Ellacurían theology could better develop the notion of tradition. In particular, the important roles of culture and language could be explicated more clearly. While Ellacuría offers a strong account of how ecclesial praxis consists in a faithful lived interpretation of the Scriptures and ties that to a basic thrust of reality itself, he does not spend time attending to the formative role of language and culture.[88] Because Ellacuría's elaboration of these concepts would spring from a unitary notion of history, however, it seems that it would appear in quite a different form than the combative view that Milbank puts forward.

Because Ellacuría locates historical reality's relative autonomy within the theologal, his account of the Christian logos of creation, while open to enrichment by other narratives, is not fundamentally threatened by them. This openness challenges that tendency in Milbank's thought that Aidan Nichols describes as "hermeticism."[89] Ellacuría's constant attempt to overcome dualisms stems precisely from a realization of the ultimate unity of all historical reality. That unity implies an interconnectedness that the "either/or" narrative of the radical orthodoxy thinkers has trouble addressing. Though he retains a conflictive sense in his use of the "Reign vs. anti-Reign" language,

Ellacuría does not essentialize this distinction so as to automatically disqualify any particular strain of thought outright.[90] Ellacuría's critical use of Marx does not necessarily entangle him in a non-Christian metanarrative, any more than Bell's or Cavanaugh's utilization of Foucault and Deleuze betrays their reading of the contemporary situation.

Ellacuría's view of historical reality permits him to accept the contributions of non-Christians in understanding all of intramundane reality without consigning that reality to a strictly intramundane view. Here the force of his language concerning transcendence "in" history turns on his would-be critics. Ellacuría would not only reject Milbank's accusation that salvation is a private transcendence in liberation theology, but he would question the implied understanding of transcendence that connotes a separation or distanciation. Indeed, Ellacuría's thought suggests ways that radical orthodoxy's oppositional rhetoric might be misconstrued to posit a corresponding oppositional view of transcendence. These concerns become clearer still when considering ecclesiology and the Christian body's transcendence; before broaching this subject, however, attention turns to the disagreements on the articulation of soteriology.

Forgiveness and Justice

While Bell proposes a creative reading of capitalism as an order of desire, his central contribution lies in focusing attention on the question of justice and its relation to Christian salvation. He rightly points out how easily talk of justice can be proposed from an individualistic view that demands redress and forgets the Christian principle of forgiveness. Any reading of liberation theology that contents itself with justice as a mere cache of rights misunderstands the significance of Christian forgiveness. In trying to overcome this viewpoint, Bell correctly focuses on the mystery of the cross. Yet turning to Ellacuría's theology reveals that many of Bell's critiques lose their potency when put under the lens of historical reality.

The primary accusation that Bell levies against liberation theology is that it relegates the role of social transformation to the state, leaving the church a mere custodian of values. In examining the role of the Catholic Church in El Salvador during the ministries of Archbishops Oscar Romero and Arturo Rivera y Damas, and the role played by the UCA during the civil war, one cannot support Bell's claim that religion was divorced from the social, political, and economic dimensions of life.[91] If that is so, the question then becomes not *whether* the church was engaged in these dimensions, but *how* it was engaged. Here the profound differences between liberation theology and radical orthodoxy's visions for the church's engagement emerge.

Certainly, when Ellacuría calls for the transformation of social structures he advocates a participation in statecraft. Yet because his understanding of historical reality accepts the notion of human persons with multiple and intertwining commitments, the participation in statecraft does not necessarily doom the value or even distinctiveness of the Christian vocation. Ellacuría's notion of the prophetic church, one embedded in historical reality, allows him to avoid Bell's claim regarding the church as a public *sui generis* without compromising its sacramental and transcendent character.[92] Ellacuría understands the church as leaven in the world that demands that all its ecclesial praxis be understood as social, political, and economic.[93] In fact, it was precisely to those in El Salvador who wanted to limit the church's mission to the "spiritual" that Ellacuría often found himself opposed. Ellacuría takes up *precisely* this issue when he claims that making the option for the poor consistently and without compromise is the way the church can be appropriately "secular" (e.g., engaged in this-worldly projects) without becoming worldly, what he calls *mundanización*.[94]

Bell casts a doubtful eye on this proposition of a prophetic community, in part, because he believes that the rhetoric of justice used by liberation theologians represents a compromise of Christian resources. To Bell, Christianity cannot be that source of alternative technologies of desire in opposition to capitalism if its goal remains at the level of justice understood as each individual receiving his or her due. If this were an accurate characterization of Ellacuría's understanding of justice, then, in Bell's eyes, even Ellacuría's appeals to propheticism cannot surmount this fundamental flaw.

However, Ellacuría's vision extends much further than simply justice as each getting her or his due or as a cache of rights; rather, he describes the goal of justice within the larger vision of the Reign of God.[95] Ellacuría's understanding of justice springs not from an Enlightenment view of the individual, but from a reading of the Bible, particularly the prophets and the teachings of Jesus.[96] Justice is desired as a sign of the twofold process of removing sin, rejecting the oppression that means an untimely death for the majority of the world's population, and divinizing humanity, participating more fully in the Trinitarian life.[97] This eschatological hope goes far beyond a mere calculus of equality; that calculus, however, may retain value in discerning the historicization of that hope. To use a common Ellacurían trope, justice may not equal salvation, but one should not speak about salvation without justice.

Bell's ultimate worry concerning justice regards how it serves as a "prerequisite" for forgiveness in liberation theology. Because of this, according to Bell, liberation theologians misunderstand the mystery of the cross. On the surface, Bell's charge appears to be a simple misreading of liberation theologians. In truth, Ellacuría never developed the theme of forgiveness, perhaps because of his historical context. One might argue that had Ellacuría survived to see the end of the civil war, he would have reflected more on forgiveness in the context of the peace accords and the general amnesty in El Salvador. To claim justice as a prerequisite for forgiveness, though, is different from the sort of claim that Ellacuría might make, that forgiveness is not complete unless it possesses the restoration of justice. On a deeper level, the way Bell points to the mystery of the cross poses more serious questions to Ellacuría's soteriology.

Unexpectedly, Bell's reading of Christ's atonement reveals a similarity to Ellacuría's thought. One could argue that it is precisely that economy of justice, as giving each his due, that leads both Ellacuría and Bell to reinterpret atonement theory. Yet Bell's invocation of Anselm in chapter 3 of *Liberation Theology after the End of History* offers an explanation of how and why the manner of Jesus' death was salvific in a way that Ellacuría has trouble explaining. For Bell, Jesus' "refusal to cease suffering" recapitulates God's offer of forgiveness such that the whole economy of justice is transformed. The cross, in itself, thus enacts salvation in a distinctive way.

Ellacuría would be wary of Bell's proposal because it makes no explicit connection between the cross and Jesus' life and ministry. Since Ellacuría views salvation as the prophetic denunciation and removal of sin and the participation in divine life that is characterized by self-sacrificial love, then the cross enacts that process in a definitive way, but one that cannot be separated from that life and the vindication of resurrection. Bell's proposal suggests that the cross is a choice, where Ellacuría understands the cross as the culmination of a lifetime of choices.

Bell's invocation of the cross pushes Ellacuría's theology to make more explicit the definitive nature of Jesus' cross, especially when trying to articulate the significance of the "crucified people." In particular, with its reading of the contemporary poor as a "Suffering Servant," Ellacuría's theology must account more clearly for the suffering of victims who do not demonstrate the volitional character of the servant's suffering. At most, it seems, the victims of history serve as a principle of salvation in their power to call for conversion. Their bearing of sin beckons those who would listen to take up the path of following Jesus and carrying forward his mission.

The Church's Practice

If Ellacuría's theology demonstrates an often overlooked connection between soteriology and discipleship, then it is natural that the differences between his liberation theology and that of radical orthodoxy figures center on different conceptions of the church's behavior in the world. Cavanaugh, himself a Roman Catholic, demonstrates the closest affinity to the thought of Ellacuría, and indeed, of the Catholic liberation theologians in general. His main contribution lies in the creative engagement of liturgical and aesthetic imagination by contrasting Eucharistic performance with the torture of the oppressive military state. In doing so, Cavanaugh points out an area that receives relatively less attention in Ellacuría's writings. For Ellacuría, sacramentality resides in the church's being a credible and efficacious sign of the Reign. Cavanaugh's thought serves to spark creative ways in which the liturgical celebration of sacraments, and particularly the Eucharist, enacts a counter-imagination useful in resisting states not unlike the El Salvador of Ellacuría's time.

Cavanaugh worries that the legacy of New Christendom's separation of planes renders the church impotent in the political sphere. By clinging to a role governing the spiritual realm, the church cannot resist the coercive power of the modern capitalist state that atomizes its population in order to subdue it. In contrast, Ellacuría's proposal that salvation history is a salvation in history does not accept the "separation of planes" and so does not render the Christian body unable to act in the political sphere. Few if any contemporary theologians can claim a knowledge of and prominence in the political workings of their respective countries that rivals that of Ellacuría. At the same time, Ellacuría never allowed for the church's mission to be interpreted in an exclusively political or "horizontal" way. Hence, the debate focuses once again not on whether the church is engaged, but how.

Cavanaugh, skeptical of the church's ability to engage in politics without compromise, employs the now familiar rhetoric of opposition: Eucharist becomes an alternative set of practices that disciplines a community now able to resist the modern state. In his articulation of this opposition, a rich vision of Eucharistic participation and performance emerges. Indeed, in light of Ellacuría's emphasis on the church as a sacrament of salvation, Cavanaugh's development of the Eucharist provides a provocative historicization of Eucharistic belief and reveals an area that could receive more attention in Ellacuría's writings. Though he often adverts to the practices of prayer and liturgy, Ellacuría seldom reflects on how participation in these practices disciplines the discipleship of members of the community.

While Cavanaugh might lead Ellacuría's theology to reflect more on liturgical practice, Ellacuría's appeals to the ministry of Jesus and its historicization provide a verification principle lacking in the lofty Eucharistic rhetoric of Cavanaugh's theology. Because Eucharistic performance lacks a tie to historical reality, Cavanaugh's concept of liturgical participation remains radically ambiguous. Cavanaugh cannot account for how participation in the Eucharist fosters the disciplined behavior he desires.[98] For the most part, Cavanaugh's claims concerning the Eucharist do not, in principle, exclude the devout Catholics who also participated in death squad activity. Neither can it account for members of the Christian body who would also produce flyers reading, "Be a patriot, kill a priest!" Though Cavanaugh occasionally appeals to producing visible actions in conjunction with Eucharistic participation, he cannot provide the criteria for what constitutes these actions. Ellacuría's call for adherence to the Reign and its presence in history serves just as reliably as Cavanaugh's appeal for a disciplined Eucharistic community. At the same time, Ellacuría is able to account for elements in the church who are not "disciplined," and who in fact, under the guise of imitating Christ, serve the anti-Reign.

Though only a preliminary suggestion, an "Ellacurían" response to the criticisms of Latin American liberation theology levied by the radical orthodoxy reveals both interesting lines of continuity and significant points of contention. Both theologies recognize the countless victims left in the wake of capitalism's savage advance. Both seek to provide a coherent account of Christian behavior that can properly enact that alternative vision found in the Christian announcement of good news. In trying to provide this account, both theologies recognize that at its basis, a vision for Christian life rests on a corresponding vision of salvation. Along with these similarities, these theologies make distinct claims that challenge and ultimately help enrich what, as fellow Christians, should be the shared hope of salvation.

Dialogue with the theologians of radical orthodoxy challenges Ellacuría's theology to maintain the distinctive character of Christianity when thinking through the mystery of salvation and the nature of the Christian life that flows from that mystery. In light of Ellacuría's openness to other philosophical and social scientific accounts of reality, radical orthodoxy serves to warn of possible compromises to the Christian story. This distinctiveness extends even to the practices within Christianity, especially the Eucharist, which provide for the ongoing formation of a community able to carry forward Jesus' teaching and example faithfully.

For his part, Ellacuría's robust understanding of historical reality and its theologal dimension serves to counter a triumphalism latent in radical orthodoxy's emphasis on distinctiveness. By not defining the church exclusively as over against the world, while still recognizing the temptation to worldliness, Ellacuría offers sufficient ground for a prophetic Christian witness while retaining a humility founded in the recognition of human interrelatedness. The awareness of sin demands a parallel and humble awareness of Christian complicity with it. Rather than a response of withdrawal or rejection of the world, however, the possibilities of which are doubtful given the interrelatedness of historical reality, Ellacuría prefers a transformative view that takes being leaven in the bread as its primary metaphor. This serves to balance the sectarian tendencies in some strains of radical orthodoxy and belies an important rhetorical strategy in its approach.

All three radical orthodoxy writers treated here have evaluated the Latin American *comunidades eclesiales de base* in a favorable light. They have done so, however, while positing them as something apart from or in distinction to the phenomenon of liberation theology. In this view, a proper Christian discipleship lies under the noses of liberation theologians who have either ignored them or interpreted them incorrectly. This strategy not only misconstrues the relationship between liberation theology and the *comunidades,* but dismisses an interesting place for rapprochement between liberation theologians and those of the radical orthodoxy.

For if they conceive of the *comunidades* as intrinsic to liberation theology, one that nourished its reflection and in turn was nurtured by that reflection, then radical orthodoxy's theologians would have reason to revisit some of their critiques. If they see value in the witness of Salvadoran *comunidades,* then seeing, for example, Ellacuría's soteriology, Sobrino's Christology, Romero's pastoral letters, and Grande's homilies within that context might generate an appreciation of that theology. Proper discipleship would direct them to proper theology.

Furthermore, that liberation theology found life in the transforming reality of the *comunidades* challenges theologians of radical orthodoxy to ground their theological reflection in the lived experience of their own communities. They could then bolster their arguments and deepen their insights within that community's dynamic engagement with historical reality. Involvement and commitment in communities would ground radical orthodoxy's theology, making it more orthodox and truly radical.

Conclusion:
A Martyr's Theological Legacy

In reflecting on Justin Martyr, one of the earliest theologian-martyrs, Jaroslav Pelikan cites Moritz von Engelhardt's comment: "It is equally certain that Justin's own faith was nourished more by that which the congregation confessed and taught concerning Christ its Lord than by that which he himself interpreted in a theoretical way." Pelikan adds, "He was, after all, ready to lay down his life for Christ; and his martyrdom speaks louder, even doctrinally, than does his apologetics."[99] This book assumes that Ellacuría's experience in El Salvador and his theological work possess a symbiotic, mutually enriching character. Whether Ellacuría's martyrdom or his "apologetics" speaks louder, only time and tradition will tell, but certainly one cannot be considered without the other.

This book takes that meeting of Ellacuría's martyrdom and apologetics as its starting point. The details of Ellacuría's remarkable life and brutal assassination give a certain weight to his theological reflections on Christian discipleship. Ellacuría stands along with other twentieth-century figures such as Martin Luther King Jr., Dietrich Bonhoeffer, and Mohandas Gandhi, whose intellectual contributions were complemented and even fulfilled in a personal commitment that ultimately meant their own deaths. To date, literature on Ellacuría in the English-speaking world has concentrated on his martyrdom more than his theology; therefore, this book serves as a complement to this literature by exploring Ellacuría's theological understanding of Christian discipleship as tied to the basic proclamation of the good news of salvation. It indicates how Ellacuría's life and theology were not incidental to each other, but were mutually constitutive.

A close examination of someone like Ellacuría runs the danger of devolving into facile connections or hagiography that flattens out a complex figure.[100] Ellacuría had personal liabilities, and his intellectual work possesses certain limitations as well. Kevin Burke points to some general problems in investigating Ellacuría's theology.[101] One issue concerns the problematic nature of his reliance on Xavier Zubiri's thought. Zubiri's scholarly isolation, which results in an idiosyncratic philosophical lexicon, threatens to leave Ellacuría either misunderstood or isolated himself. A second problem involves the fragmentary nature of Ellacuría's corpus of writings. Ellacuría leaves behind no full-length theological monograph; his writings consist almost entirely of essays that never achieve the synthesis of a classic work or definitive statement.[102] While these might be described as problems of accessibility to Ellacuría's writings, attention to his context also reveals problems inherent to the writings themselves.

Even though the late 1970s through the 1980s represents the peak period of Ellacuría's scholarly output, his theological writings constitute a mere fraction of the many tasks he took on during this period. As rector of the UCA, particularly during the civil war, Ellacuría had to juggle research and writing with a myriad of administrative duties and a host of responsibilities tied to his public role in attempting to find a peaceful settlement to the war. Ellacuría wrote his theology under great pressure, prompted by exigent circumstances that required immediate response. This imparts a fragmentary character to much of his writing. Although he was able to complete some major articles, the remainder of his writings often do not reflect the polish or thoroughness of the more outstanding examples.[103]

The context of the war, moreover, often lends a polemical edge to his essays that requires us to read them with caution. As noted in previous chapters, Ellacuría frequently employs a rhetorical strategy in which he lays out an argument by first identifying a position he wishes to correct. Whether due to time or space constraints, Ellacuría's descriptions of these counter-points at times lack proper substantiation.[104] While Ellacuría describes well what he seeks to oppose, the question of whether and which opponents actually make these claims needs further investigation.

Despite these shortcomings, Ellacuría's theology deserves further analysis and elaboration. The years since his assassination have seen select works initiate this task.[105] Because a general introduction to Ellacuría's thought has already appeared, this book marks a next step, focusing on a specific aspect of that thought. Given his extraordinary biography, it seems logical to explore how someone who personified Christian discipleship reflected on that theme in a scholarly way. Reading his thoughts on discipleship/praxis reveals that Ellacuría constantly speaks of this in relation to a set of assumptions concerning Christian salvation. Soteriology, then, broadly conceived as the salvific relationship between God and human beings, frames what Ellacuría has to say about the Christian life.

Traditionally, soteriology has focused specifically on the redemptive act wrought by Jesus Christ. However, this work suggests that soteriology refers to a broader "logos" about Christian salvation that deploys a whole constellation of ideas surrounding the divine-human relationship. In a certain sense, Christian theology at its core is soteriological, and the manner in which a Christian theologian understands salvation often reflects underlying assumptions behind such theological themes as God's transcendence, the mission of Christ, and the nature of the church. Perhaps most importantly, this broad sense of soteriology animates Christian behavior, forming a kind of soteriological circle in which the Christian account of salvation spurs a discipleship which in turn deepens the notion of Christian salvation. This book's thesis is that Ellacuría's notion of Christian discipleship cannot be understood outside of the philosophical, christological, and ecclesiological dimensions of his soteriology.

The distinguishing characteristic of Ellacuría's soteriology is the way that he describes salvation as both historical and transcendent without conflating these characteristics. Drawing on Zubiri's philosophy, Ellacuría portrays the multiplicity of dynamisms at work in historical reality. In particular he draws out the implications, indeed the demands, resulting from the human confrontation with reality. But his description of reality does not end there. Ellacuría describes historical reality as possessing a *theologal* dimension, a vision of the world as *religated,* or tied to God. This involves portraying God neither as subsumed in reality, as just another being or part, nor as apart from reality. Rather, Ellacuría speaks of a God who transcends *in* history at its very depths.

Ellacuría's view of transcendence dictates a reexamination of theological concepts that might otherwise be interpreted in a way that removes them from history. Without reducing the theologal content, Ellacuría insists that theological concepts must find historicization. Thus, for him, salvation history is a salvation in history. Jesus' death is a death in history; Christian discipleship is a discipleship that carries Jesus' mission forward in history. In all these instances, Ellacuría would not deny a metahistorical character, the "more" of salvation, Christology, or ecclesiology, but he cannot countenance their fullness being expressed while excluding the historical dimension.

Ellacuría follows the biblical tradition by describing salvation in terms of the Reign of God. Certainly, the Reign is God's work and ultimately eschatological. Ellacuría finds a strong impulse for Christian behavior, however, by emphasizing the anticipatory nature of the Reign. The Reign is irrupting in history. Inaugurated in a definitive way in the life, death, and resurrection of Jesus Christ, the Reign exhibits two primary characteristics: the removal of sin in the world, and the divinization of human beings such that they enjoy a fullness of life. In envisioning the dynamics of this salvific process, of the way humans are brought into this twofold movement of the Reign, Ellacuría directs attention to the crucial role played by the crucified people.

Because the crucified people stand in historical continuity with Jesus, they serve as a principle of conversion to the salvific process of the Reign. As those who bear the weight of the world's sins today, the crucified people unmask how distant our present is from the Reign. They interrupt our rationalization and escapism and reveal reality as it is calling forth a *metanoia,* a compassionate change of life that means salvation for the world. In the face of their suffering, responding to it by seeking the removal of those structures or conditions that cause their suffering, Christians are led on a path that carries forward Christ's mission in the present. Ellacuría historicizes Ignatius of Loyola's colloquy at the foot of the cross by inviting Christians to stand before the sufferings of the crucified people, examine their consciences in light of that suffering, and enter into the redemptive process of proclaiming and manifesting the Reign that promises liberation both for the suffering and for themselves.

In the end, Ellacuría's work is about "saving history." The polysemy in the word "saving" reveals a twofold movement at the heart of Ellacuría's theology. On the one hand, Ellacuría directs historical discipleship to the transformation of historical reality so that it more closely resembles the Reign preached by Jesus. The church cannot sit idly by when the majority of the world languishes in poverty. Rather, it is called to follow the example of Jesus in constantly working to remove the sin of the world. On the other hand, in discerning the signs of the times and enacting a historical discipleship that transforms reality, the church is itself saved. By responding to the thrust of historical reality, particularly that noetic, ethical, and praxical challenge of the crucified people, the church finds itself caught up in the incarnational-kenotic dynamic that characterizes the Christian story and so participates in that divinizing grace of the Trinitarian life that we call salvation history.

Perhaps what is most remarkable about Ellacuría's story is that while his theology is characterized by the circularity of saving history, his life was as well. The young Basque priest left the security and privileges of one life and entered into the suffering of a crucified people, taking up the task of transforming Salvadoran society. In doing so, he ultimately took on the fate of so many Salvadorans before him. Yet his death, like the deaths of so many others, was a death in the hope of resurrection. In his last public speech Ellacuría declared, "It is necessary to redirect history, subvert it, and launch it in another direction."[106] In his attempt to launch Salvadoran history in another direction, Ellacuría bore the weight of salvation. Working to transform society, he was transformed; seeking the salvation of the poor, he found his own salvation. This mutuality, which characterizes his biographical and intellectual legacy, invites others to enter into that transformative circle of hope for resurrection that is saving history.

Notes

Introduction

1. There exists a great deal of material on the assassinations of the Jesuits. In English, the best are Martha Doggett, *Death Foretold: The Jesuit Murders in El Salvador* (Washington, DC: Georgetown University Press, 1993), and the broader story in Teresa Whitfield, *Paying the Price: Ignacio Ellacuría and the Murdered Jesuits of El Salvador* (Philadelphia: Temple University Press, 1995). Other materials include Instituto de Estudios Centroamericanos and El Rescate, *The Jesuit Assassinations* (Kansas City: Sheed & Ward, 1990), John Hassett and Hugh Lacey, eds., *Towards a Society That Serves Its People: The Intellectual Contribution of El Salvador's Murdered Jesuits* (Washington, DC: Georgetown University Press, 1991), and Jon Sobrino, Ignacio Ellacuría, and others, *Companions of Jesus: The Jesuit Martyrs of El Salvador* (Maryknoll, NY: Orbis Books, 1990).

2. On the afternoon following the killings, archdiocesan staff workers heard loudspeakers on military vehicles proclaiming, "Ignacio Ellacuría and Martín-Baró are dead. We will continue killing communists." See Phillip Berryman, *Stubborn Hope* (Maryknoll, NY: Orbis Books, 1994), 97. Outrageous claims are not limited to El Salvador. The Spaniard, Ricardo de la Cierva, would later claim that Ellacuría was one of a group of Jesuits whose theology "demolished" the Society of Jesus. See *Jesuitas, Iglesia y Marxismo 1965-1985: La teología de la liberación desenmascarada.*

3. Truth Commission for El Salvador, "From Madness to Hope: The Twelve Year War in El Salvador," April 30, 1993. Reprinted in *The United Nations and El Salvador, 1990-1995*, The United Nations Blue Books Series, vol. 4 (New York: United Nations, 1993). For a vivid portrayal of the plight of the poor in El Salvador and those in the church who attempted to serve them, see the gripping novel of Manlio Argueta, *One Day of Life* (New York: Random House, 1991). A journalist's perspective on the persecution of the church throughout Latin American can be found in Penny Lernoux, *Cry of the People* (New York: Penguin Books, 1980).

4. Research coming from the UCA in San Salvador, including that of his fellow Jesuit and colleague Jon Sobrino, represents the best starting point. In Spanish, see *Ignacio Ellacuría, el hombre y el cristiano: "Bajar de la cruz al pueblo crucificado"* (San Salvador: Centro Monseñor Romero, 2001); Jon Sobrino and Rolando Alvarado, eds. *Ignacio Ellacuría: Aquella libertad esclarecida* (San Salvador: UCA Editores, 1999); and Héctor Samour, *Voluntad de liberación: El pensamiento filosófico de Ignacio Ellacuría* (San Salvador: UCA Editores, 2002). See also the solid collection of essays in José A. Gimbernat and Carlos Gómez, eds., *La pasión por la libertad: homenaje a Ignacio Ellacuría* (Estella: Verbo Divino, 1994). In English,

"Companions of Jesus," in Jon Sobrino, Ignacio Ellacuría, and others, *Companions of Jesus: The Jesuit Martyrs of El Salvador* (Maryknoll, NY: Orbis Books, 1990), 3–56; Jon Sobrino, *Witnesses to the Kingdom: The Martyrs of El Salvador and the Crucified Peoples* (Maryknoll, NY: Orbis Books, 2003).

    5. See Robert Lassalle-Klein, "The Jesuit Martyrs of the University of Central America: An American Christian University and the Historical Reality of the Reign of God" (Ph.D. diss., Graduate Theological Union, Berkeley, CA, 1995), Kevin Burke, "The Ground beneath the Cross: Historical Reality and Salvation in the Theology of Ignacio Ellacuría" (S.T.D. diss., Weston Jesuit School of Theology, Cambridge, MA, 1997), which is published as *The Ground beneath the Cross: The Theology of Ignacio Ellacuría* (Washington, DC: Georgetown University Press, 2000). Lassalle-Klein and Burke edited a collection of essays by prominent scholars entitled *The Love That Produces Hope* (Collegeville, MN: Liturgical Press/Michael Glazier, 2006).

    6. Most, if not all, of the surveys of Latin American liberation theology mention the importance of the concept of praxis. See, for example, David F. Ford, ed., *The Modern Theologians: An Introduction to Christian Theology in the Twentieth Century* (Cambridge: Blackwell, 1987); Rebecca Chopp, *The Praxis of Suffering: An Interpretation of Liberation and Political Theologies* (Maryknoll, NY: Orbis Books, 1986); Christian Smith, *The Emergence of Liberation Theology: Radical Religion and Social Movement Theory* (Chicago: University of Chicago Press, 1991); Alfred T. Hennelly, *Theology for a Liberating Church: The New Praxis of Freedom* (Washington, DC: Georgetown University Press, 1989); Rosino Gibellini, *The Liberation Theology Debate*, trans. John Bowden (London: SCM, 1987).

    7. Yet the only book-length treatment of the theme of praxis in Ellacuría's work is Jose Joaquín Castellón Martín, *Ellacuría y la filosofía de la praxis* (Huelva: Hergué, 2003).

    8. Among the helpful sources, Nicholas Lobkowicz, *Theory and Practice: History of a Concept from Aristotle to Marx* (Notre Dame: University of Notre Dame Press, 1967); Richard Bernstein, *Praxis and Action* (Philadelphia: University of Pennsylvania Press, 1971), and Matthew Lamb, "The Theory-Praxis Relationship in Contemporary Christian Theology," in CTSA Proceedings (1976): 147–78.

    9. For a list of works exploring the assassinations, see note 1 on page 161.

    10. For material on the four U.S. churchwomen, see Ana Carrigan, *Salvador Witness: The Life and Calling of Jean Donovan* (New York: Simon & Schuster, 1984), Cynthia Glavac, *In the Fullness of Life: A Biography of Dorothy Kazel* (Denville, NJ: Dimension Books, 1996), and Judith Noone, *The Same Fate as the Poor* (Maryknoll, NY: Orbis Books, 1994).

    11. For an outstanding exception to this rule, see the thorough examination of Gustavo Gutiérrez's context in Gaspar Martínez, *Confronting the Mystery of God: Political, Liberation, and Public Theologies* (New York: Continuum, 2001).

    12. Sobrino gladly acknowledges the importance of Ellacuría. For example, the first two English-language dissertations on Ellacuría were written by scholars originally intending to study Sobrino, but were directed by Sobrino himself to investigate Ellacuría. His writings on Ellacuría are numerous. Many have been collected in Jon Sobrino, *Witnesses to the Kingdom: The Martyrs of El Salvador and the Crucified Peoples* (Maryknoll, NY: Orbis Books, 2003). Sobrino has also used the anniversary of the martyrdom to write a letter to Ellacuría that reveals both the personal and

theological impact of his close friend. See Jon Sobrino, *Cartas a Ellacuría 1989–2004* (San Salvador: Centro Monseñor Romero, UCA, 2004).

13. See "Hacia una fundamentación filosófica del método teológico Latino-americano," in *Liberación y cautiverio: Debates en torno al método de la teología en America Latina*, ed. Enrique Ruiz Maldonado (Mexico City: Encuentro Latino-americano de Teología, 1975), 609–35; *ET* I: 187–218. For a helpful parsing of this method and terminology, see Kevin F. Burke, *The Ground beneath the Cross* (Washington, DC: Georgetown University Press, 2000).

14. For the sake of consistency in English-language scholarship on Ellacuría, I utilize Kevin Burke's translations of the Spanish forms.

15. These figures include John Milbank, Daniel M. Bell Jr., and William T. Cavanaugh.

16. For an insightful account of these nature-grace debates, see Stephen J. Duffy, *The Graced Horizon: Nature and Grace in Modern Catholic Thought* (Collegeville, MN: Liturgical Press/Michael Glazier, 1992).

17. The homily was given at St. Ignatius Church in New York City, November 22, 1989. It was published as Joseph P. O'Hare, "In Solidarity with the Slain Jesuits of El Salvador," *America* 161, no. 19 (December 16, 1989): 446.

Chapter 1: Liberation Theology

1. The interest in the intersection between theology and practice(s) may be seen in the growing area of the academic study of spirituality. For a magisterial work on the history of Christian mysticism, which includes substantive theological analyses, see the volumes in the series by Bernard McGinn, *The Presence of God: A History of Western Christian Mysticism* (New York: Crossroad, 1998).

2. Examples of the traditional denotation include E. L. Peterman's claim that soteriology "conceives the Incarnate Word in His redemptive role; it is the dynamic and practical aspect of Christology"; see Bernard Marthaler, ed., *New Catholic Encyclopedia*, 2d ed. (Farmington Hills, MI: Thomson Gale, 2002), 329. The *Handbook of Catholic Theology*, ed. Francis Schüssler Fiorenza (New York: Crossroad, 2002), considers soteriology as a "dogmatic treatise" that involves "the doctrine of redemption by atoning death." It identifies soteriology as treating the "objective act of Christ's redemption," with the doctrine of grace as a complement that treats the "subjective reception by believers." The *Encyclopedia of Catholicism*, ed. Richard P. McBrien (New York: HarperCollins, 1995), defines soteriology as a "branch of Christology" that involves "critical reflection upon the salvific activity of Jesus Christ" (1210).

3. The use of the term "liberation theology" should be qualified. In reality, one could speak of liberation theologies, even among the Latin Americans, because of the diverse ways these theologians have articulated their theologies. However, it also seems fair to use a collective singular to indicate the mutual connections and sympathies shared by these theologians. Therefore, the use of the singular "theology" is not mean to homogenize, but rather to indicate, like any label for a "school" of thought, art, etc., the similarities that this group shares.

4. Although it is difficult to identify a precise moment for liberation theology's beginning, the landmark texts include the CELAM documents from Medellín (1968) and the publication of Gustavo Gutiérrez's *Teología de la liberación: Perspectivas* (1971), based, in large part, on the lecture he gave one month prior to Medellín

in Chimbote, Peru. One must acknowledge the pastoral experience of the 1950s as foundational to these texts, as well as noting important theological reflection that preceded Medellín and Gutiérrez's book, e.g., Juan Luis Segundo's work in the late 1950s and early 1960s and the meeting of theologians in Petrópolis, Brazil, in 1964. See Alfred Hennelly, ed., *Liberation Theology: A Documentary History* (Maryknoll, NY: Orbis Books, 1990), 29–47. Of course, precedents for Christian theology in the Americas that involved reflection on behalf of the poor can be traced as far back as the courageous stance of missionaries in the Spanish conquest such as Bartolomé de Las Casas and Antonio de Montesinos.

5. Second General Conference of Latin American Bishops, "The Church in the Present-Day Transformation of Latin America in the Light of the Council" (Washington, DC: Division for Latin America — United States Catholic Conference, 1973).

6. For a helpful summary of this debate and its major figures, see Stephen J. Duffy, *The Graced Horizon: Nature and Grace in Modern Catholic Thought* (Collegeville, MN: Liturgical Press/Michael Glazier, 1992).

7. Henri de Lubac, *Surnaturel* and *Le mystère du surnaturel*. See *The Mystery of the Supernatural,* trans. Rosemary Sheed (New York: Crossroad, 1967, 1998). Though some would describe Karl Rahner's entire theology as one of grace, good examples include: "Concerning the Relationship between Nature and Grace" in *Theological Investigations* 1 (Baltimore: Helicon, 1961), 297–317, and "Nature and Grace" in *Theological Investigations* 4 (Baltimore: Helicon, 1966), 165–88.

8. In making the case for the need of more explicit reflection on salvation itself, Gustavo Gutiérrez cites the following lines from Yves Congar, "It is necessary to ask ourselves again very seriously about our idea of salvation. There is hardly any other theological notion implying immediate consequences — very concrete and very important — which has been left so vague and which calls in a most urgent way for an adequate elaboration." "Christianisme et libération de l'homme," *Masses Ouvrières* 258 (December 1969): 8, as cited in Gustavo Gutiérrez, *A Theology of Liberation: History, Politics, and Salvation,* 15th Anniversary ed. (Maryknoll, NY: Orbis Books, 1988), 217 n. 1.

9. In this respect, the 1975 conference in Detroit, a landmark event for U.S. liberation theologies (e.g., black, feminist, and Latino/a) that stress marginalization due to race and gender, and the 1976 formation of the Ecumenical Association of Third World Theologians, stand out. On the former, see Sergio Torres and John Eagleson, eds., *Theology in the Americas* (Maryknoll, NY: Orbis Books, 1976). For the latter, see Sergio Torres and Virginia Fabella, eds., *The Emergent Gospel: Theology from the Underside of History* (Maryknoll, NY: Orbis Books, 1978).

10. For example, Gustavo Gutiérrez and Leonardo Boff have been personal targets of ecclesial suspicion, though the former never underwent any official inquiry nor censure. See the Vatican's Congregation for the Doctrine of the Faith, "Ten Observations on the Theology of Gustavo Gutiérrez," and "Notification Sent to Fr. Leonardo Boff Regarding Errors in His Book, *Church, Charism, and Power*" in *Liberation Theology: A Documentary History,* 348–50, 425–30.

11. On the shift in ecclesiastical climate, particularly the campaign waged against liberation theology by the head of the Vatican's Congregation for the Doctrine of the Faith, see John L. Allen Jr., *Cardinal Ratzinger: The Vatican's Enforcer of the Faith* (New York: Continuum, 2000). Penny Lernoux, *People of God: The Struggle for World Catholicism* (New York: Viking, 1989) documents the clash with special attention to the rise of Opus Dei in Latin America.

12. This is captured in the title of Gustavo Gutiérrez's reflection, "Criticism Will Deepen, Clarify Liberation Theology," in Hennelly, *Liberation Theology: A Documentary History*, 419–24. Certainly there needs to be a distinction made between serious issues bearing on liberation theology; for example, the demise of socialism as an alternative to capitalism, or the continuing survival of ecclesial base communities without episcopal support, versus superficial considerations having more to do with the rise and fall of faddish intellectual movements in U.S. academic circles.

13. For a clear demonstration of this breadth of thought, consult one of the many collections of essays by liberation theologians. The best include Ignacio Ellacuría and Jon Sobrino, eds., *Mysterium Liberationis: Fundamental Concepts of Liberation Theology* (Maryknoll, NY: Orbis Books, 1993), and Rosino Gibellini, ed., *Frontiers of Theology in Latin America* (Maryknoll, NY: Orbis Books, 1979). A perceptive reading of the soteriological perspective is Dean Brackley, *Divine Revolution: Salvation and Liberation in Catholic Thought* (Maryknoll, NY: Orbis Books, 1996).

14. Certain factors make Gutiérrez and Boff good candidates for comparison. Both men have made significant contributions to liberation theology. They provide interesting similarities (as Roman Catholic priests) and differences (coming from Peru and Brazil, and influenced by the Dominican and Franciscan religious orders, respectively) with Ellacuría (a Jesuit in El Salvador). Thematically, Ellacuría wrestled with similar issues. For an essay in which Ellacuría explicitly debates points in Clodovis Boff's methodology, see Ignacio Ellacuría, "La historicidad de la salvación cristiana," *ET* I, 535–96.

15. One must be careful not to overstate the cautions and warnings found in certain Vatican documents. The Vatican never "condemned" liberation theology, and only one figure, Leonardo Boff, faced official sanctions. That having been said, the intellectual unease expressed in CDF documents is particularly important given the ascendance of Joseph Ratzinger to the papacy as Benedict XVI.

16. Rosino Gibellini, *The Liberation Theology Debate*, trans. John Bowden (London: SCM Press, 1987), 4. To prevent this misinterpretation, Hugo Assmann avoids the nomenclature of "theology of liberation" (*teología de la liberación*), and prefers "theology from the praxis of liberation" (*teología desde la praxis de la liberación*). See Hugo Assmann, *Theology for a Nomad Church*, trans. Paul Burns (Maryknoll, NY: Orbis Books, 1975), whose original Spanish title is in fact, *Teología desde la praxis de la liberación: Ensayo teológico desde la América dependiente*.

17. For example, George V. Pixley, *On Exodus: A Liberation Perspective*, trans. Robert Barr (Maryknoll, NY: Orbis Books, 1987).

18. Prominent examples of liberationist reflection on methodology include Clodovis Boff, *Theology and Praxis: Epistemological Foundations*, trans. Robert Barr (Maryknoll, NY: Orbis Books, 1987), and Juan Luis Segundo, *The Liberation of Theology*, trans. John Drury (Maryknoll, NY: Orbis Books, 1976).

19. Gustavo Gutiérrez, *A Theology of Liberation: History, Politics, and Salvation*, 15th Anniversary ed. (Maryknoll, NY: Orbis Books, 1988), 24. See Hugo Assmann's complete adoption of this formulation in *Theology for a Nomad Church*.

20. While later developments in liberation theologies will explore marginalization at different levels, Gutiérrez stresses death as that fundamental opposite of liberation and, theologically, of the will of God. This can be recognized in the title of one of his later works, *The God of Life*.

21. The language of liberation in Latin American sociopolitical thought of the 1960s and 1970s must be understood in relation to that which it superseded: the concept of development so prevalent in the policies of the 1950s. As the attempts at development during the 1950s failed, primarily in the form of enormous investment-loans, structural analysis gave birth to an alternative diagnosis and vision for Latin America. Rather than viewing themselves as simply "underdeveloped" as compared to the United States and nations of Europe, Latin Americans began to understand their poverty as structural in cause, as the result of dependence. The dependency theory, in figures such as André Gunder Frank and Fernando Henrique Cardoso, emerged as a way to explain the widespread destitution in Latin America that seemed to defy all attempts at relief in development projects. Consequently, in light of a situation diagnosed as oppression, the diagnosis-solution pair "underdeveloped-development" gave way to "dependent-liberation." For a good summary of the theory and its relationship to liberation theology, see Arthur McGovern, *Liberation Theology and Its Critics: Toward an Assessment* (Maryknoll, NY: Orbis Books, 1989).

22. The relative character of this autonomy signals the careful relationship between theology and social science that Gutiérrez attempts to articulate. In acknowledging this relative autonomy, Gutiérrez in no way designates theology a mere subset or servant to the social sciences. As he notes in his introduction to the revised version of *Theology of Liberation* (1988), "We also know that the sciences and, for a number or reasons, the social sciences in particular, are not neutral. They carry with them ideological baggage requiring discernment; for this reason the use of the sciences can never be uncritical." Thus, Gutiérrez calls for the rigorous "discernment, but not fear of the contributions of the human disciplines." *Theology of Liberation*, xxv.

23. Dean Brackley calls attention to Gutiérrez's extensive use of the phrase *el devenir histórico de la humanidad*, which is translated as, "future," "development," "process," and "destiny," in this and later works. Brackley, *Divine Revolution*, 169 n. 22.

24. In the final part of *Theology of Liberation*, "Faith and the New Humanity," Gutiérrez acknowledges the influence of *Gaudium et spes* in using the phrase "new humanity." See *Gaudium et spes*, 55. Additionally, Brackley notes insightfully that the chapters of this part (9–11) are structured along this theme. Brackley, *Divine Revolution*, 75.

25. *Theology of Liberation*, 86. Acknowledging this unity prevents the identification of salvation exclusively with this level of liberation, underlining its historical character as well.

26. Clodovis Boff, *Theology and Praxis: Epistemological Foundations,* trans. Robert Barr (Maryknoll, NY: Orbis Books, 1987), xxviii.

27. That there exist some differences in the way the "theologizing" is carried out should be no surprise. After all, even within "each" theology there are differences based upon the content. For example, within first theology there is consideration of Trinity, Christ, the church, and so on. Yet Trinitarian theology may be carried out in a methodologically distinct manner than Christology or ecclesiology. However, they retain a unity at the level of discipline: they are all theology.

28. For a good summary of how Clodovis Boff understands these mediations, see his essay, "Methodology of the Theology of Liberation," in *Mysterium Liberationis: Fundamental Concepts of Liberation Theology*, ed. Jon Sobrino and Ignacio Ellacuría (Maryknoll, NY: Orbis Books, 1993).

29. See Brackley, *Divine Revolution,* 70.

30. C. Boff, *Theology and Praxis,* 86.

31. "It stays on too general and abstract a level to be able to take account of concrete situations. In virtue of its vague, oversimplifying tenor, it does manage to hold a semantic mix and bilingualism at bay; but it does so in a purely formal, even verbal, fashion." Ibid., 86.

32. He summarizes the process this way, "The process of theological articulation consists in this: to transform, with the help of the properly theological concept of 'salvation' (second generality), the sociological concept of 'liberation' (first generality) in such a way as to produce a theological proposition such as 'liberation is salvation' (third generality)." Ibid., 88.

33. See Brackley, *Divine Revolution,* 82ff.

34. In addition to the conciliar documents, Gustavo Gutiérrez frequently cites the speech given by John XXIII one month prior to the opening of the council in which he exhorts, "As for the underdeveloped countries, the church is, and wants to be, the church of all, and especially the church of the poor." See Gutiérrez, *A Theology of Liberation,* xxvi.

35. *Gaudium et spes,* 1. In *The Documents of Vatican II,* edited by Walter M. Abbott (New York: America Press, 1966), 200–201, italics mine.

36. *Gaudium et spes,* 4, italics mine.

37. Gutiérrez will also point out how this language has made its way into the church's magisterial documents, frequently citing examples including: the CELAM documents of Medellín and Puebla, the Extraordinary Synod of Bishops of 1985, and several writings of John Paul II. An example of the latter comes from *Sollicitudo rei socialis,* 42, that identifies the option for the poor as a "special form of primacy in the exercise of Christian charity to which the whole tradition of the church bears witness."

38. Gustavo Gutiérrez, *We Drink from Our Own Wells: The Spiritual Journey of a People* (Maryknoll, NY: Orbis Books, 1984), 104.

39. One of the great lessons taken from that work locates the preferential option as a *theocentric* option. Divine love, not bound by human justice, embraces the poor because their situation goes contrary to the divine will for life. "The ultimate basis for the privileged position of the poor is not in the poor themselves but in God, in the gratuitousness and universality of God's *agapeic* love." Gustavo Gutiérrez, *On Job: God-Talk and the Suffering of the Innocent* (Maryknoll, NY: Orbis Books, 1987), 94.

40. Gustavo Gutiérrez, *Las Casas: In Search of the Poor of Jesus Christ,* trans. Robert Barr (Maryknoll, NY: Orbis Books, 1993).

41. Brackley, *Divine Revolution,* 91. By invoking the language of "sacrament of salvation," Boff clearly references one of the great titles given to the church in *Lumen gentium.* See *Lumen gentium,* 1, 9.

42. For an excellent schema of contemporary theological use of praxis, see Matthew Lamb, "The Theory-Praxis Relationship in Contemporary Christian Theology," in *CTSA Proceedings* (1976): 147–78. For a more extensive bibliography on the notion of praxis, see the notes in chapter 4.

43. For a good summary, see Rebecca Chopp, *The Praxis of Suffering: An Interpretation of Liberation and Political Theologies* (Maryknoll, NY: Orbis Books, 1986). See also Enrique Dussel, *Philosophy of Liberation* (Maryknoll, NY: Orbis Books, 1985).

44. C. Boff, *Theology and Praxis,* 229.

45. "Methodology of the Theology of Liberation," in *Mysterium Liberationis: Fundamental Concepts of Liberation Theology,* ed. Ignacio Ellacuría and Jon Sobrino (Maryknoll, NY: Orbis Books, 1990), 6.

46. Juan Luis Segundo underscores the hermeneutic importance of praxis in his description of liberation theology's "hermeneutic circle," a phrase associated with Rudolf Bultmann, but given new meaning by Segundo. He describes the circle as possessing four steps, the first of which begins with the experience of reality. The experience of a problem leads to a suspicion that questions. This suspicion is then directed to larger superstructures, including theology. The third step consists in a "new manner of experiencing theological reality, which leads . . . to the suspicion that current biblical interpretation does not take into account important data." Finally, a new hermeneutic is born that emerges both from the initial commitment and provides a new place for further commitment to initiate the circle once again. Thus, praxis provides a "liberation of theology." Juan Luis Segundo, *The Liberation of Theology,* trans. John Drury (Maryknoll, NY: Orbis Books, 1976). An exploration of Segundo's work is Alfred Hennelly, *Theologies in Conflict: The Challenge of Juan Luis Segundo* (Maryknoll, NY: Orbis Books, 1979).

47. See Gutiérrez, *On Job,* 39ff.

48. Though it appears in several places, one of the most developed readings of the Beatitudes occurs in a chapter entitled, "The Ethics of the Kingdom," in *The God of Life* (Maryknoll, NY: Orbis Books, 1991), 118–28.

49. "Option for the Poor," in *Mysterium Liberationis,* ed. Ellacuría and Sobrino, 247. Italics in the text.

50. *God of Life,* 128.

51. For a summary of the major positions, see Paul Sigmund, *Liberation Theology at the Crossroads* (New York: Oxford University Press, 1990). His schema of those opposed to liberation theology includes American Catholic, Evangelical, Niebuhrian, and neoconservative critics, as well as those in the Vatican.

52. In the United States, the most vocal opposition has come from neoconservative critics centering on liberation theologians' criticism of capitalism and preference for socialism. Commentator Michael Novak stands out as preeminent among these voices. Typical of his position is an early editorial in which he states, "The Marxist vulgate of so much Latin American intellectual life obliges them to think in terms of Marxist analysis." For his most complete assessment, see Michael Novak, *Will It Liberate? Questions about Liberation Theology* (New York: Paulist Press, 1986).

53. For example, the novelist Walker Percy claims, "Liberation theology is a perversion of Christianity." *National Catholic Register,* January 6, 1986. While Richard John Neuhaus perceives the soteriological import of liberation theology's interpretation of praxis, his characterization of it as "unbridled Pelagianism" might reveal more about this Lutheran-turned-Catholic than it does liberation theology. *The Catholic Moment* (San Francisco: Harper & Row, 1987), 177.

54. See several articles in Sergio Torres and John Eagleson, eds., *Theology in the Americas* (Maryknoll, NY: Orbis, 1976). As U.S. Latino/a theology has turned to the importance of aesthetics, there has been a concomitant critique of the Latin American emphasis on praxis as too materialist. See Roberto Goizueta, *Caminemos con Jesús: Toward a Hispanic/Latino Theology of Accompaniment* (Maryknoll, NY: Orbis Books, 1995), 77–100.

55. These include a declaration from the International Theological Commission (ITC) and documents from the Congregation for the Doctrine of the Faith (CDF) and its prefect, Cardinal Joseph Ratzinger. One of the finest collections of documents relating to liberation theology is Alfred T. Hennelly, ed., *Liberation Theology: A Documentary History* (Maryknoll, NY: Orbis Books, 1990).

Understanding those Vatican texts requires knowledge of three key figures involved in Latin American ecclesial politics who possess influence in Vatican circles. The first is the Brazilian Franciscan Bonaventura Kloppenburg. A member of the ITC, Kloppenburg focuses his opposition to liberation theology on the ecclesiology coming from the base communities, particularly the work of his countryman, Leonardo Boff. See Kloppenburg, *Temptations for a Theology of Liberation* (Chicago: Franciscan Herald Press, 1974), *The People's Church: A Defense of My Church* (Chicago: Franciscan Herald Press, 1978), and *Christian Salvation and Human Temporal Progress* (Chicago: Franciscan Herald Press, 1979).

The second, Belgian Jesuit Roger Vekemans, views liberation theology as inextricably linked to Marxist thought and has battled against it vociferously, both in the political and ecclesial spheres. For an example of this opposition, see *Teología de la Liberación y Cristianos por el Socialismo* (Bogota: CEDIAL, 1976). An early example of his opposition to theology that is politicized "horizontalism" can be found in *God and Caesar: The Priesthood in Politics* (Maryknoll, NY: Orbis Books, 1972). In *De Medellín a Puebla* (Mexico City: Editorial Edicol, 1979), Enrique Dussel talks about the access to money that Vekemans had, including the DeRance Foundation (a conduit for CIA funds of which he was later accused of misspending) and the Adveniat fund of the German bishops. On the latter, see Gregory Baum, "German Theologians and Liberation Theology," in *Liberation Theology: A Documentary History*, ed. Alfred Hennelly, 220–24. See also Penny Lernoux, "The Long Path to Puebla," in *Puebla and Beyond*, ed. John Eagleson and Philip Scharper (Maryknoll, NY: Orbis Books, 1979), 3–27.

Vekemans influenced the purging of liberation theologians from positions in CELAM conducted by the third critic, and perhaps the most recognizable opponent to liberation theology in Latin America, the Colombian cardinal Alfonso López Trujillo. While his early criticism retained a strident character, his later work is the more subtle form of opposition by replacement. He uses the language of liberation, but argues against its "politicization" by liberation theologians. López Trujillo's most thorough statement on liberation theology is *De Medellín a Puebla* (Madrid: Biblioteca de Autores Cristianos, 1980). For an earlier, less subtle attack on liberation theology, see his *Liberation or Revolution?* (Huntington, IN: Our Sunday Visitor, 1977).

56. Sadly, in the ecclesial documents, the term, "Marxist," functions not to describe a nuanced reading of Marx and subsequent schools of Marxist thought, but rather a blanket accusation that is pejorative without exception. While this negative evaluation needs to be read against the political backdrop of fear of Soviet communism, criteria of intellectual accuracy call for a more sophisticated exposition.

57. It must be noted that even though this study focuses on the Vatican criticism of liberation theology during the 1980s, the same years (and sometimes even the same documents) reflect a profound agreement with many of the central concerns of liberation theologians. The significant, and continuing, use of liberation theology's discourse in ecclesial documents — use of the language of integral liberation, the preferential option for the poor, attention to the social dimensions of sin, focus on

the plight of the poor as integral to the church's calling — constitutes one of the great legacies of liberation theology from this period.

58. These include the 1977 ITC *Declaration on Human Development and Christian Salvation,* and the 1984 CDF *Instruction on Certain Aspects of the "Theology of Liberation."* Joseph Ratzinger's preparatory notes on that instruction help illumine its content. Other important sources include: the CDF's "Ten Observations on the Theology of Gustavo Gutiérrez (1983)," and "Notification Sent to Fr. Leonardo Boff regarding Errors in His Book, *Church: Charism and Power"* (New York: Crossroad, 1985). These may all be found in Hennelly, *Liberation Theology: A Documentary History.*

59. In 1974, the commission, whose members included Joseph Ratzinger and Bonaventura Kloppenburg, decided to set up a subcommittee, presided over by Karl Lehmann, to study liberation theology. Two years later, members of that subcommittee presented four reports on different theological concerns of the commission: methodological and hermeneutical by Karl Lehmann, biblical by Heinz Schürmann, ecclesiological by Olegario González de Cardedal, and systematic by Hans Urs von Balthasar.

60. *Declaration,* 207.

61. Ibid., 216.

62. Ibid., 207. Unfortunately, the commission never cites a single author or text to identify these theological movements or its expositors.

63. Ibid., 208.

64. Ibid. The document comfortably affirms distinguishing between the orders of divine grace and human activity, what it designates as divinization and humanization, but does not spell out how to make said distinction.

65. Ibid., 217. Two years after the ITC's *Declaration,* John Paul II's opening speech at the Third CELAM conference in Puebla, Mexico, echoes a similar concern with salvation declaring that Jesus' mission "has to do with complete and integral salvation through a love that brings transformation, peace, pardon, and reconciliation." John Paul II, "Opening Address at the Puebla Conference," in *Puebla and Beyond,* ed. John Eagleson and Philip Scharper (Maryknoll, NY: Orbis Books, 1979), 57–71.

66. Joseph Ratzinger, "Vi spiego la teología della liberazione," *30 Giorni* (1984): 48–55. In English, this would appear as a chapter entitled, "A Certain 'Liberation,' " in *The Ratzinger Report* (San Francisco: Ignatius Press, 1985), 169–90.

67. Ratzinger, *Ratzinger Report,* 174. "In what follows, the concept of liberation theology will be understood in a narrower sense: it will refer only to those theologies which, in one way or another, have embraced the Marxist fundamental option."

68. Ibid., 175.

69. Ibid., 172. The "they" to which Ratzinger refers were previously, and vaguely, identified as "theologians from South America."

70. In light of the intellectual sources he cites (e.g., Bultmann, Bloch, Frankfurt school) and the dangers they represent, Ratzinger could be characterized as reading Latin American liberation theology from the situation of the European church, and specifically, the situation in Germany. This might explain the ferocity of his attacks. Revealingly, he disputes the notion of liberation theology as Latin American. He

remarks, "Behind the Spanish or Portuguese language of their preaching one senses German, French, and Anglo-American ideas." Ibid., 173.

71. Ibid., 173.

72. Ibid., 184.

73. Ibid., 188. Ratzinger laments that in the "tangible vacuum of meaning" between the Second World War and the Second Vatican Council the movements associated with revisionary Marxist and Frankfurt school thinkers such as Bloch, Adorno, Horkheimer, Habermas, and Marcuse "offered models of action by which people believed they could respond to the moral challenge of misery in the world." Ibid., 178.

74. CDF, *Instruction on Certain Aspects of the "Theology of Liberation,"* 411.

75. Ibid., 393.

76. Ibid., 400.

77. Ibid.

78. Ibid., 406.

79. Ibid., 408.

80. Ibid., 404.

81. Christian Smith identifies Ellacuría with this "second generation" of liberation theologians in his *The Emergence of Liberation Theology* (Chicago: University of Chicago Press, 1991), 201.

82. For example, Teresa Whitfield, *Paying the Price: Ignacio Ellacuría and the Murdered Jesuits of El Salvador* (Philadelphia: Temple University Press, 1994), 15–40; Kevin F. Burke and Robert Lassalle-Klein, eds., *Love That Produces Hope: The Thought of Ignacio Ellacuría* (Collegeville, MN: Liturgical Press, 2006), xii–xxxv: Rodolfo Cardenal, "De Portugalete a San Salvador: De la mano de cinco maestros," in *Ignacio Ellacuría: Aquella libertad esclarecida* (San Salvador: UCA Editores, 1999), 43–58; and José Sols Lucia, *La teología histórica de Ignacio Ellacuría* (Madrid: Editorial Trotta, 1999), 19–71.

83. Whitfield, *Paying the Price*. Miguel Elizondo often reminded the novices, "We're not in Spain now. Just because something is one way in Spain, it does not have to be the same in El Salvador."

84. For insight into Ellacuría's respect for Espinosa, see the essay from 1963, "El P. Aurelio Espinosa Pólit, S.J." *EF* I, 525–33.

85. The report on Ellacuría's four years in Innsbruck reveals a bit of his personality. It rated him *eximia* (excellent) for intelligence, but *mediocris* for *virtus* (behavior). "While he is highly talented, his character is one that is potentially difficult; his own spirit of critical judgment is persistent and not open to others; he separates himself from the community in small groups among whom he exercises a strong influence." For a personality and intellect that some found acerbic and arrogant, it is reported that Ellacuría was nicknamed, 'the Sun King.' " See Whitfield, *Paying the Price*.

86. On this influence, see Martin Maier, "La influencia de Karl Rahner en la teología de Ignacio Ellacuría I y II" in *Revista Latinoamericana de Teología* 39 (1996): 233–55; 44 (1998): 163–87. These articles are distilled and reworked in "Karl Rahner, el maestro," in *Ignacio Ellacuría, "Aquella libertad esclarecida,"* ed. Jon Sobrino and Rolando Alvarado (San Salvador: UCA Editores, 1999), 171–93.

87. In one essay, Ellacuría suggests his attempt to understand the terms "salvation history" and "salvation in history" as synonymous with earlier theologians' work on grace and nature. See "Historia de la salvación y salvación en la historia,"

ET I, 519ff. For a fine summary of the issues surrounding these nature-grace debates, see Stephen J. Duffy, *The Graced Horizon: Nature and Grace in Modern Catholic Thought* (Collegeville, MN: Liturgical Press/Michael Glazier, 1992).

88. Among his many works, see Karl Rahner, *Hearer of the Word,* trans. Joseph Donceel (New York: Continuum, 1994); "Concerning the Relationship between Nature and Grace," *Theological Investigations* 1 (Baltimore: Helicon, 1961), 297–317; and "Nature and Grace," *Theological Investigations* 4 (Baltimore: Helicon, 1966), 165–88.

89. Juan Bautista Arríen, as cited in Whitfield, *Paying the Price,* 30.

90. Certainly, one finds one of the great reflections on the significance of the council in Karl Rahner, "Basic Theological Interpretation of the Second Vatican Council," in *Concern for the Church* (New York: Crossroad, 1981), 77–89.

91. From its opening lines of solidarity and the call to scrutinize the signs of the times to its concluding sections that deal with socioeconomic life and peace, *Gaudium et spes* represents one of the most important documents in the Roman Catholic Church's social teaching tradition. Yet one cannot exclude the power of statements from *Lumen gentium* such as "the Church recognizes in those who are poor and who suffer, the image of her poor and suffering founder. She does all in her power to relieve their need and in them she strives to serve Christ." *Lumen gentium,* 8.

92. Of these *cursos,* Robert Caponigri writes, "The *cursos,* even more than the treatise or essay, must be recognized as Zubiri's personal and original mode of expression and communication. In them . . . is to be found the living movement, the vital rhythm as well as the weighty insights of his thought." A. Robert Caponigri, introduction to Xavier Zubiri, *On Essence* (Washington, DC: Catholic University of America Press, 1980), 18.

93. More material on their personal relationship can be found in those conversations and correspondence that have been published. See "Conversaciones con Zubiri," and "Correspondencia con Zubiri," in *EF* II, 19–70.

94. Diego Gracia identifies the generations of Zubiri's disciples in the following manner: Zubiri himself he places in the "Generation of '27," philosophers in Spain who immediately followed Ortega y Gasset. The first generation of Zubiri's disciples (1945–60) runs from the beginning of his *cursos* to the publication of *Naturaleza, historia, Dios.* He places Ellacuría and himself in the next generation, influenced primarily by *Sobre la esencia.* See Diego Gracia, "Actualidad de Zubiri: La filosofía como profesión de verdad," in *Zubiri: 1898–1983,* ed. I. Tellechea (Vitoria: Departmento de Cultura del Gobierno Vasco, 1984), 73–137.

95. In fact, he entitles the final third (over four hundred pages) of *Sobre la esencia,* "La esencia, momento estructural de lo real." The most recent edition is *Sobre la esencia* (Madrid: Alianza Editorial, Fundación Xavier Zubiri, 1985).

96. The title of Ellacuría's one significant philosophical monograph is *Filosofía de la realidad histórica.* The influence of *Sobre la esencia* can be seen in both his 1965 doctoral dissertation, "Principalidad de la esencia en Xavier Zubiri" (doctoral thesis, Universidad Complutense, Madrid, 1965), and his publication of *Indices de Sobre la esencia* (Madrid: Sociedad de Estudios y Publicaciones, 1965).

97. On the crucial nature of the Salvadoran reality and Ignatian spirituality shaping Ellacuría, see Jon Sobrino and Ignacio Ellacuría, "Companions of Jesus," in *Companions of Jesus: The Jesuit Martyrs of El Salvador* (Maryknoll, NY: Orbis Books, 1990), 3–56. A more detailed analysis of Ellacuría's Ignatian spirituality can

be found in J. Matthew Ashley, "Ignacio Ellacuría and the *Spiritual Exercises* of Ignatius of Loyola," *Theological Studies* 61 (2000): 16–39.

98. The text for this talk is Ignacio Ellacuría, "Nuestra situación colectiva vista desde la primera semana," *ET* IV, 178. Other talks given at this retreat include "El problema del traslado del espíritu de los *Ejercicios* a la Viceprovincia," and "El tercer mundo como lugar óptimo de la vivencia cristiana de los *Ejercicios*." There is also an unedited reflection from the same year, "Misión de la Compañía de Jesús en Centroamérica." All of these may be found in *ET* IV. For an in-depth analysis of this retreat, see Robert Lassalle-Klein, "The Jesuit Martyrs of the University of Central America: An American Christian University and the Historical Reality of the Reign of God" (Ph.D. dissertation, Graduate Theological Union, Berkeley, CA, 1995).

99. On structural sin, see the Second General Conference of Latin American Bishops, document on Justice, par. 2. For Ellacuría, the reality of structural sin shapes new answers to the classic Ignatian questions regarding what it means to follow Christ today. See "Nuestra situación," *ET* IV, 189–91.

100. His reflections on Arrupe include Ignacio Ellacuría, "Pedro Arrupe, renovador de la vida religiosa," in *Pedro Arrupe: Así lo vieron* (Santander, 1986), 141–71; *ET* IV, 262–87, and the previously unpublished "El segundo general de los jesuitas vasco," *ET* IV, 257–61.

101. See "Jesuits Today," 2.2, 2.9 in *Documents of the 32nd General Congregation of the Society of Jesus: An English Translation* (Washington, DC: Jesuit Conference, 1975), 7. Note that this mission is defined in contrast to two opposing extremes of either a "distorted emphasis upon the transcendence of the Christian religion," or an " 'immanentism' which runs counter to the Gospel message." See "Introductory Decree," 1.2–1.4, in *Documents*, 1–2.

102. Ellacuría's writings on the university are collected in *Escritos universitarios* (San Salvador: UCA Editores, 1999).

103. This is a gross simplification of a complex argument that treats violence under the category of sin. While not dismissing the violence advocated by a Camilo Torres, he also acknowledges other approaches to violence embodied by figures such as Charles de Foucauld and Martin Luther King Jr. For Ellacuría's writings on the subject of violence, see *ET* III, 427–512.

104. *ECA* 337 (1976): 637–43; *EP* I, 649–56.

105. The phrase attributed to Ellacuría in Jon Sobrino, *Ignacio Ellacuría, el hombre y el cristiano: "Bajar de la cruz al pueblo crucificado"* (San Salvador: Centro Monseñor Romero, 2001), 33.

106. As auxiliary bishop in 1973, Romero published an article in the diocesan weekly, *Orientación*, entitled, "Educación liberadora, pero cristiana y sin demagogia" ("Liberative education, but Christian and without demagoguery"), which criticized the work of the Jesuits at the Externado San José. For a fuller account of the "Externado affair," see Whitfield, *Paying the Price*, 52–55.

107. For example, see Jon Sobrino, "Archbishop Romero — Some Personal Recollections," in Jon Sobrino, *Witnesses to the Kingdom* (Maryknoll, NY: Orbis Books, 2003), 11–53.

108. The collection of his homilies and writings utilize this nickname. See Jon Sobrino, Ignacio Martín-Baró, and Rodolfo Cardenal, eds., *La voz de los sin voz: La palabra viva de Monseñor Romero*, 2d ed. (San Salvador: UCA Editores, 1986). In English, *Voice of the Voiceless* (Maryknoll, NY: Orbis Books, 1985).

109. Oscar Romero, "Homilia en Aguilares (19.6.1977)," in *La voz de los sin voz*, 208.

110. Jon Sobrino, "Mi recuerdo de Monseñor Romero," in *Monseñor Romero* (San Salvador: UCA Editores, 1990), 35. In English, "Archbishop Romero: Some Personal Recollections," in Sobrino, *Witnesses to the Kingdom*, 29.

111. Cited in *Monseñor Romero*, 64. In English, Sobrino, *Witnesses to the Kingdom*, 53.

112. For example, in 1980, military aid to El Salvador totaled $5.9 million. By 1982, that increased to $82 million, and in 1984, military aid reached $243.5 million, a sum that equaled the combined total of the three previous years. Thomas Carothers, "The Reagan Years: The 1980s," in *Exporting Democracy: The United States and Latin America*, ed. Abraham F. Lowenthal (Baltimore: John Hopkins Univerity Press, 1991), 93.

113. "La responsabilidad de las 'terceras fuerzas' " *ECA* 394 (1981): 745ff. See also "Replanteamiento de soluciones para el problema de El Salvador," *EP* II, 1105–38. This volume of the *Escritos políticos* has a wealth of articles on topics including agrarian reform, popular organizations, and proposals for dialogue and a solution to the war.

114. Phillip Berryman, *Stubborn Hope: Religion, Politics, and Revolution in Central America* (Maryknoll, NY: Orbis Books, 1994), 82. See also Jeffrey Klaiber, *The Church, Dictatorships, and Democracy in Latin America* (Maryknoll, NY: Orbis Books, 1998), 181ff.

115. Rodolfo Cardenal, *Biografías: Mártires de la UCA*, 2d ed. (San Salvador: UCA Editores, 2001), 24.

116. His explicit response to the CDF *Instruction* is "Estudio teológico-pastoral de la 'Instrucción sobre algunos aspectos de la teología de la liberación,'" *Revista Latinoamericana de Teología* 2 (1984): 145–78; *ET* I, 397–448. Ellacuría, like other liberation theologians, criticizes much of the document, but does recognize how much the language of liberation theology has entered into magisterial documents.

117. A title given by some commentators of Ellacuría's work. Note the claim that his "historical soteriology leads to a historical theology" in José Sols Lucia, *La teología histórica de Ignacio Ellacuría* (Madrid: Editorial Trotta, 1999).

118. Ignacio Ellacuría, "La Iglesia de los pobres, sacramento histórico de la liberación," *ECA* 348–49 (1977): 707–22; *ET* II, 453–85.

119. This event also marks a dramatic shift in Archbishop Oscar Romero's ecclesial praxis, a shift that influences Ellacuría profoundly. For more on this, see the relevant sections in chapter 4.

120. "Iglesia," 453. Ellacuría acknowledges that "liberation theology" actually denotes a diversity of currents, but uses the singular collective to differentiate it from other theological schools of thought.

121. Ibid., 464.

122. Ibid., 467.

123. In a posthumously published piece, Ellacuría comments, "Liberation theology takes with great seriousness that there has been and is salvation history, and that this salvation has a personal dimension, but also a structural one; a transcendent dimension, but also an immanent one," in "Conclusiones sobre la teología de la liberación," *ET* IV, 291–93.

124. "Iglesia," 468.

125. Ibid., 470. Here he defines the "political order" as "global institutional-ization of social relations, the institutional objectification of human actions, which comprises the public venue of their personal and interpersonal actions."

126. Ibid., 471.

127. Ibid., 473. This notion will be developed in the analysis of Ellacuría's account of ecclesial discipleship in chapter 4.

128. Ibid., 471.

129. Ibid., 472.

130. See "El pueblo crucificado: Un ensayo de soteriología histórica," in Ignacio Ellacuría et al., *Cruz y resurrección: Anuncio de una Iglesia nueva* (Mexico City: CRT, 1978), 49–82; *ET* II, 137–70. For a fuller discussion of this article and its significance, see chapter 3.

131. Ignacio Ellacuría's direct response may be found in "Estudio teológico-pastoral de la 'Instrucción sobre algunos aspectos de la teología de la liberación,' " *Revista Latinoamericana de Teología* 2 (1984): 145–78; *ET* I, 397–448. The major article of 1984 that also mentions the CDF document is "Historicidad de la salvación cristiana," *Revista Latinoamericana de Teología* 1 (1984): 5–45; *ET* I, 535–96. It is also worth consulting the 1987 lecture transcribed as "El desafío cristiano de la teología de la liberación," *Cartas a las Iglesias,* no. 263 (1992): 12–15; no. 264 (1992): 11–13; no. 265 (1992): 14–16; *ET* I, 19–33.

132. "Estudio teológico-pastoral," *ET* I, 403.

133. *Instruction,* III, *ET* I, 4.

134. "Estudio teológico-pastoral," *ET* I, 407–8.

135. "Estudio teológico-pastoral," *ET* I, 411. Even while noting that no other theology has performed this task like liberation theology, he adds that liberation theology has "not reached its fullness, nor has it been able to overcome its proper limitations in a perfect way."

136. "Estudio teológico-pastoral," *ET* I, 414.

137. Evaluating the CDF's method as "much is affirmed, but little is proven," Ellacuría ponders, "If instead of following this method, the *Instruction* would have contented itself with discovering the best possible concrete examples of authors in whom the imputed theological errors are found, how Marxism is the determinant source of their discourse, and how in particular, the principle of class struggle oper-ates at the moment of giving a determined significance to one or other theological affirmations, this would have been a more scientific, and definitely more useful, task." "Estudio teológico-pastoral," *ET* I, 429.

138. "Estudio teológico-pastoral," *ET* I, 434.

139. In English, see "New Evangelization, Human Development, Christian Cul-ture: Fourth General Conference of Latin American Bishops, Santo Domingo, Dominican Republic, October 12–28, 1992" (Washington, DC: United States Catholic Conference, 1993).

140. "Historicidad de la salvación cristiana," *Revista Latinoamericana de Teo-logía* 1 (1984): 5–45; *ET* I, 537. Ellacuría also sees as his objective "to respond to critics of the liberation theologians' efforts to rethink the whole revelation and the life of the church in the search for the salvation-liberation of the poor, but also in the search for a profound renewal of the thinking, the spirituality, the pastoral practice, and even the institutionality of the universal church."

141. "Historicidad," *ET* I, 538.

142. Ibid., I, 541.

143. This issue will be dealt with at greater length in chapter 2.
144. "Historicidad," *ET* I, 539.
145. Ibid., I, 560.
146. Ibid.
147. Ibid., I, 555–56.
148. Ibid., I, 557.
149. Mark 10:17. See also Matt. 19:16; Luke 18:18.
150. Mark 10:21. See also Matt. 19:21; Luke 18:22.
    151. For example, the 1975 Encuentro Latinoamericano de Teología in Mexico City, which included figures such as Enrique Dussel, Hugo Assmann, Leonardo Boff, and Juan Luis Segundo published as *Liberación y cautiverio* (Mexico City: Comité Organizador, 1975); his inclusion and editing of *Mysterium liberationis: Conceptos fundamentales de la teología de la liberación* (Madrid: Editorial Trotta, 1990).

Chapter 2: Principle and Foundation of Ellacuría's Soteriology

    1. John W. O'Malley, *The First Jesuits* (Cambridge, MA: Harvard University Press, 1993), 39. It also underscores the soteriological bent of the *Exercises*. Thus, Ignatius's opening remarks that the *Exercises* are for the "preparing and disposing our soul to rid itself of all its disordered affections and then, after their removal, of seeking and finding God's will in the ordering of our life for the salvation of our soul." Ignatius of Loyola, *The Spiritual Exercises of Saint Ignatius,* trans. George Ganss (New York: Doubleday, 1992), no. 1.
    2. It is important to note that while Zubiri speaks of reality, Ellacuría qualifies it as historical reality. Héctor Samour describes Ellacuría's philosophy as a "radicalization of Zubirian metaphysics, most of all in reference to the dynamic structural character of reality and the metaphysical importance of the historical." Héctor Samour, "Introducción a la filosofía de la liberación de Ignacio Ellacuría," in *El compromiso político de la filosofía en America Latina*, ed. Ignacio Ellacuría (Santafé de Bogotá: Editorial El Buho, 1994), 15. Samour fleshes out this thesis in his monograph, *Voluntad de liberación: El pensamiento filosófico de Ignacio Ellacuría* (San Salvador: UCA Editores, 2002).
    3. See Antonio Gonzalez, *La novedad teológica de la filosofía de Zubiri,* (Madrid: Fundación Xavier Zubiri, 1994).
    4. Though discussed in many of his works, Zubiri develops the notion of *religación* most fully in Xavier Zubiri, *El hombre y Dios,* ed. Ignacio Ellacuría (Madrid: Alianza Editorial, Fundación Xavier Zubiri, 1984).
    5. I find Kathryn Tanner's nomenclature of "non-contrastive discourse" a useful way to describe this coherence. For her insightful exploration of these issues see Kathryn Tanner, *God and Creation in Christian Theology* (New York: Blackwell, 1988), 36–80.
    6. Identifying this similarity of movement (from a statement of the fundamentally graced nature of the world to an analysis of sin) does not overlook the many questions raised by liberation theologians concerning the principle and foundation's formulation. Ellacuría himself points to "the ambiguous formalism" and "danger of de-historicization" in the principle and foundation. See "Lectura latinoamericana de los *Ejercicios Espirituales* de san Ignacio," *ET* IV, 65.

7. That Ellacuría possesses both mystical and prophetic dimensions in his thought challenges those who might identify liberation theologians exclusively with the latter while neglecting the former. For a helpful morphology that identifies and organizes these as fundamental Christian impulses see David Tracy's morphology in *The Analogical Imagination: Christian Theology and the Culture of Pluralism* (New York: Crossroad, 1981).

8. Ellacuría states, "As a consequence [of the separation and opposition of sense and intellect], humans and reality itself are left inevitably broken and dual. Humans, divided into sensibility and intelligence; and reality, divided into sensible and supra-sensible." Ignacio Ellacuría, "La nueva obra de Zubiri," *EF* III, 309.

9. Personal reflections by Ellacuría on Zubiri's importance and influence can be found in the reviews of Zubiri's *Inteligencia sentiente*, and especially in the pieces honoring him after his death in 1983. Selected examples include "La nueva obra filosófica del vasco Xavier Zubiri," "Zubiri, el filósofo más importante de España," "Zubiri, filósofo teologal," "Zubiri, vasco universal," and "Zubiri, cuatro años después." All of these may be found in *EF* III.

10. Ignacio Ellacuría, "La superación del reduccionismo idealista en Zubiri," *Estudios Centroamericanos* 477 (1988): 643; *EF* III, 419.

11. The Spanish terms here are "anchored" (*anclados*), "held" (*retenidos*), and "impelled" (*impulsados*).

12. This sense of modernity's great failure as constituting separations resonates in David Tracy's identification of three great separations of modernity as feeling and thought, form and content, and theory and practice. See "Traditions of Spiritual Practice and the Practice of Theology," *Theology Today* 55, no. 2 (1998): 235–41.

13. For Ellacuría's understanding of these basic categories, see his *Filosofía de la realidad histórica,* ed. Antonio González (Madrid: Editorial Trotta & Fundación Xavier Zubiri, 1991), 43–103.

14. Though traces of this influence may be found in nearly all of Ellacuría's work, it is directly alluded to in Ellacuría's reviews of Zubiri's massive trilogy and especially in his most significant critical reflection on Zubiri's work, "The Overcoming of Idealistic Reductionism in Zubiri." See "La nueva obra de Zubiri: *Inteligencia sentiente*" (1981) in *EF* III, 297–317; "La obra de Xavier Zubiri sobre la inteligencia humana" (1983) in *EF* III, 333–42; "Aproximación a la obra completa de Xavier Zubiri" (1983) in *EF* III, 365–94; and "La superación del reduccionismo idealista en Zubiri" (1988) in *EF* III, 403–30.

15. The imposing list of disciplines and scholars include: mathematics with De la Valée-Poussin and Zermelo, biology with von Geluchten and Goldschmidt, physics with Schrödinger, philology with W. Jaeger, and philosophy, having attended lectures of both Husserl and Heidegger. While in Berlin, he also interacted with Max Planck and Werner Heisenberg and lived with Albert Einstein at the "Harnack House." The best source for biographical information on Zubiri is the *Fundación Xavier Zubiri* located in Madrid. For published biographies, see Carmen Castro de Zubiri, *Biografía de Xavier Zubiri* (Málaga: Ediciones Edinford, 1992); Fannie A. Simonpietri, "Un filósofo para el siglo XXI. Biografía intelectual en el centenario del natalicio de Xavier Zubiri 1898–1983," in *La Torre: Revista de la Universidad de Puerto Rico,* tercera época, no. 11 (1999): 147–61.

16. For an example of Zubiri reflecting on the developments in physics, see Xavier Zubiri, "La nueva física: Un problema de filosofía" (1934) which was later published as "La idea de naturaleza: La nueva física," in *NHD*, 243–304.

17. This work was published as three volumes: *Inteligencia sentiente: Inteligencia y realidad* (Madrid: Alianza Editorial, 1980), *IRE; Inteligencia y logos* (Madrid: Alianza Editorial, 1982), *IL;* and *Inteligencia y razón* (Madrid: Alianza Editorial, 1983), *IRA.*

18. Xavier Zubiri, *Sobre la esencia* (Madrid: Sociedad de Estudios y Publicaciones, 1962), henceforth *SE.*

19. I will quote from English translations whenever possible and give the parallel Spanish citations as well. Xavier Zubiri, *Sentient Intelligence,* trans. Thomas B. Fowler (Washington, DC: Xavier Zubiri Foundation of North America, 1999), henceforth *SI* 3; *IRE,* 10.

20. *SI,* 44; *IRE,* 116.

21. *SI,* 4; *IRE,* 13. I translate the Spanish verb *inteligir* as "act of intelligence" or "intellection" in an attempt to convey the verbal aspect of the word without resorting to terms such as "conceiving," "thinking," or the neologism, "intelligizing," which seem to obfuscate the meaning more than clarify.

22. *SI,* 4; *IRE,* 13. Lest there be any doubt of its importance, Zubiri follows this definition by affirming that it is "the only idea that there is in this entire book, throughout its hundreds of pages."

23. Diego Gracia (echoed by Thomas Fowler) links these three terms to the ancient Greek division of *Nous* into three moments: the noetic (intellection), noematic (reality), and noergic (actualization). See Diego Gracia, "Xavier Zubiri," in *Dictionary of Fundamental Theology,* ed. René Latourelle (New York: Crossroad, 1995), 1166.

24. *SI,* 35; *IRE,* 86.

25. Diego Gracia notes, "Zubiri transfers phenomenological investigation from 'awareness' (Husserl), 'life' (Ortega), and 'understanding' (Heidegger) to 'apprehension' in such a way that the primary object of philosophy would be the analysis of 'human apprehension.' " Diego Gracia, "Xavier Zubiri," 1165.

26. For the fullest statement of this critique see Jacque Derrida, *Of Grammatology* (Baltimore: Johns Hopkins University Press, 1976).

27. Rather than use awkward English phrases, the Spanish will be retained.

28. Here one can note the influence, and critique, of Husserl's distinction between "content" and "reality" as aspects of objects that are made present to the consciousness. Zubiri is unwilling to "bracket" the question of reality. For more on this critique, see Robert Lassalle-Klein, "Ignacio Ellacuría's Debt to Xavier Zubiri: Critical Principles for a Latin American Philosophy and Theology of Liberation," in *Love That Produces Hope: The Thought of Ignacio Ellacuría,* ed. Kevin Burke and Robert Lassalle-Klein (Collegeville, MN: Liturgical Press, 2006), 88–127.

29. Here Zubiri's language ventures perilously close to what George Lindbeck has labeled an "experiential-expressivist" model of religious experience. However, Zubiri does not posit an "experience" of reality that is subsequently thematized. His proposition of the (formal) apprehension of reality asserts that there can be no human knowing or sensing outside of or prior to the inherent immersion in reality. By identifying this as one moment along with logos and reason, Zubiri leaves open the possibility of assigning a constitutive role to culture and language in human experience. For the contrasting categories "experiential-expressivist" and "cultural-linguistic," see George A. Lindbeck, *The Nature of Doctrine: Religion and Theology in a Postliberal Age* (Philadelphia: Westminster Press, 1984), 30–45.

30. Zubiri describes the three moments of this apprehension as affection (*afección*), in which the person is affected by the thing perceived; alterity (*alteridad*), in which the perceived is perceived as other; and the force (*fuerza*) of reality in which the perceived maintains an autonomy in relation to the apprehension.

31. Thomas B. Fowler, introduction to Xavier Zubiri, *Sentient Intelligence* (Washington, DC: Xavier Zubiri Foundation of North America, 1999), xii.

32. For more on this idea of structure, see Ellacuría's "La idea de estructura en la filosofía de Zubiri," in *EF* II, 445–513.

33. *IRE,* 258.

34. This language of "field" indicates a close connection to the field concept of physics. Fowler likens it to the gravitational field, "where a body may exist 'by itself' in an individual moment, but by virtue of its existence, the body creates a field around itself through which it interacts with other bodies, its field moment." *Sentient Intelligence,* xiii. David Gandolfo prefers to translate *campo* as "region" and the adjectival *campal* as "regional" to preserve the hierarchical link (as smaller) to the realm of reason, which he calls "world." See his "Human Essence, History and Liberation: Karl Marx and Ignacio Ellacuría on Being Human" (Ph.D. dissertation, Loyola University of Chicago, 2003), 255–56 n. 80.

35. *IL,* 77–78. Zubiri notes that as "re-actualization," logos is still a mode of intellection and must be understood as such. Thus, one has an "intelligization of the logos."

36. Given Zubiri's studies in quantum physics and personal acquaintance with Heisenberg, one might see the relation of this modesty to the notions of wave-particle duality and the uncertainty principle.

37. See *IRA,* 12.

38. See *IRE,* 267.

39. "La nueva obra de Zubiri," *EF* III, 312.

40. "Hacia una fundamentación," *ET* I, 207. Note how this threefold characterization of human intelligence bears the influence of Zubiri's formulation of sentient intelligence as primordial apprehension, logos, and reason.

41. As Ellacuría states, "The totality of intramundane reality constitutes a single physical unity that is complex and differentiated in such a way that the unity does not nullify the differences and the differences do not nullify the unity." *Filosofía de la realidad histórica,* ed. Antonio González (San Salvador: UCA Editores, 1999), 31. For a helpful summary of how Ellacuría views the structure of reality, see Kevin Burke, *The Ground beneath the Cross* (Washington, DC: Georgetown University Press, 2000), 53–60.

42. Héctor Samour describes Ellacuría's position as an "open material realism." He notes that reality always maintains a primacy; that human reality involves that which is material; and yet that human reality, as a constitutive principle, possesses an openness and transcendence that makes it irreducible to any closed system. See *Voluntad de liberación,* 45–154.

43. For a fuller investigation of Zubiri's concept of entification, including his genealogy of the concept from Aristotle through Thomas and Scotus, and finally to the moderns, see *IRE,* 225ff.

44. Claiming something greater than Heidegger's insight that "being" is often reduced to a thing or entity, Zubiri argues that once what is intellectively known equals being (because of "logification"), then reality is but a mode of being.

45. "Superación," *EF* III, 409.

46. "Hacia una fundamentación," *ET* I, 207.

47. For this terminology and the translations of the phrases involving forms of *cargar,* I rely on Burke, *The Ground beneath the Cross,* 100–108. These three dimensions bear a close relationship to that set which Zubiri defines as the three essential moments of personal human self-realization: religation, intellective march or progress (*marcha intelectiva*), and experience. See Zubiri, "El problema teologal del hombre," 61ff.

48. "Hacia una fundamentación," *ET* I, 208. The translation "realizing" is not without its problems. David Gandolfo prefers "becoming aware" because of the technical meaning that "realizing" and "realization" carry in Ellacuría's philosophy. See Gandolfo, "Human Essence, History and Liberation," 226–27 n. 11.

49. So the importance of Zubiri's overcoming the separation of sense and intellect begins to take on more weight. As Kevin Burke notes, "The more destructive moments of this latter division [between sensibility and intelligence] represent not only an epistemological error but a historical injustice." He also notes how the epistemological-metaphysical split is not just academic, but has concrete effects such as "the division of society into educated ruling elites and an illiterate peasantry." Burke, *The Ground beneath the Cross,* 49–50.

50. Theologically, Ellacuría will describe the vision for what reality should be as the Christian utopia; the vision of the anticipated Reign of God that prophecy contrasts with the present situation.

51. Though Ellacuría never writes a formal treatise on the Trinity, his references to God, and, in particular, to God's presence in the world utilize Trinitarian language. This will be explored in more depth when we consider his use of the term *plasmación.*

52. "Superación," *EF* III, 403.

53. "Few authors merit such serious consideration, so that Zubiri's realism should certainly be considered post-Kantian, but in the sense of being a critical overcoming of Kant's critique; a positive overcoming rather than a dogmatic forgetting." "Superación," *EF* III, 407.

54. "La nueva obra de Zubiri," *EF* III, 307. See "Filosofía, ¿para qué?" *EF* III, 123.

55. Ignacio Ellacuría, "Zubiri, filósofo teologal," *Vida Nueva* 1249 (1980): 45; *EF* III, 271–73.

56. "Zubiri, filósofo teologal," *EF* III, 273.

57. Exceptions include Kevin Burke's brief treatment of the "theologal." *The Ground beneath the Cross,* 48–49, and Antonio Gonzalez, *La novedad teológica de la filosofía de Zubiri* (Madrid: Fundación Xavier Zubiri, 1994).

58. In no way does this negate or even diminish the importance of Zubiri's philosophical writings. It merely suggests that because Zubiri's major philosophical works, *Sobre la esencia* and the massive *Inteligencia sentiente,* focus on intra-mundane reality, it is easy to restrict his influence on Ellacuría solely to those terms. However, examination of other key texts, most importantly *Naturaleza, Historia, Dios* and *El hombre y Dios,* reveals crucial categories and terminology that find their way into Ellacuría's descriptions of God's transcendence, creation, and God's salvific relationship to humanity.

59. This claim and a preliminary version of the argument in the following section are based on my study, "Liberation Theology's Transcendent Moment: The Work of Xavier Zubiri and Ignacio Ellacuría as Non-Contrastive Discourse," *Journal of Religion* 83, no. 2 (April 2003): 226–43. For a helpful study on the proper grammar

of God-language, see Kathryn Tanner, *God and Creation in Christian Theology* (New York: Blackwell, 1988). In it, she claims, "Far from appearing to be incompatible with it, a non-contrastive transcendence of God suggests an extreme of divine involvement with the world," provided that in speaking of God, theologians adhere to two rules: "avoid both a simple univocal attribution of predicates to God and world and a simple contrast of divine and non-divine predicates," and "avoid in talk about God's creative agency all suggestions of limitation in scope or manner" (46–47).

60. For a detailed chronology of Zubiri's work on God, see Ellacuría's introduction to *El hombre y Dios*, ed. Ignacio Ellacuría (Madrid: Alianza Editorial, 1984), i–x. Helpful secondary works include: Jesús Sáez Cruz, *La accesibilidad de Dios: Su mundanidad y transcendencia en Xavier Zubiri* (Salamanca: Publicaciones Universidad Pontificia, 1995), and José D. Millás, *La realidad de Dios: Su justificación y sentido en Xavier Zubiri y Javier Monserrat* (Rome: Gregorian University, 2004).

61. Originally published as "En torno al problema de Dios," *Revista de Occidente* 149 (1935): 129–59.

62. Besides the early "The Problem of God" (Thirty-three lectures, 1948), these *cursos* include "The Philosophical Problem of the History of Religions" (1965), "Philosophical Reflections on Various Theological Problems" (Ten lectures in 1967), and "The Human and the Problem of God" (Six lectures in 1968). These are noted by Ellacuría in his introduction of *El hombre y Dios*.

63. The Fundación Xavier Zubiri has published the other two volumes unfinished by Zubiri: *El problema filosófico de la historia de los religiones*, ed. Antonio González (Madrid: La Alianza, 1993), and *El problema teologal del hombre: Cristianismo*, ed. Antonio González (Madrid: La Alianza, 1997). Zubiri's process of composing his books consisted of putting together notes from his cursos and editing the texts to produce a final product. Though these two volumes had not reached the stage of a completed draft (as is the case for *El hombre y Dios*), they can still be considered Zubiri's authentic work.

64. Among them: "Historicidad de la salvación cristiana" (1984), "Voluntad de fundamentalidad y voluntad de verdad: conocimiento-fe y su Configuración histórica" (1986), "Historia de la salvación" (1987), and "Utopía y profetismo desde América Latina: Un ensayo concreto de soteriología histórica." (1989).

65. As Diego Gracia asserts, "Ellacuría understood his theology of liberation as the natural consequence of the assertions that Zubiri makes in *El hombre y Dios*, but that he, for various reasons, was not able to develop." "Filosofía práctica," in *La pasión por la libertad: Homenaje a Ignacio Ellacuría*, ed. José A. Gimbernat and Carlos Gómez (Estella: Editorial Verbo Divino, 1994), 346.

66. Xavier Zubiri, *NHD*, 363ff. Though originally published in 1942, cited texts will come from the subsequently revised and expanded fifth edition. The English translation is *Nature History God*, trans. Thomas B. Fowler (Washington, DC: University Press of America, 1981); henceforth, *NHG*.

67. There is an implicit play on the Spanish verb *hacer*. Its nominal form, *un hecho*, means "a fact," while its past participial form, *hecho*, means "made, created." Thus, Zubiri suggests a contrast between the view of the existence of the world as *hecho* (fact) with the view of it as *hecho* (made, created). The world as given stands in contrast to the world as gift, as gracious creation.

68. Note the similarity of this position with Ellacuría's critique of "ahistorical soteriology" that construes the world and history as extrinsic additions to the human. "Historia de la salvación," *ET* I, 527–28.

69. However, Zubiri's notion differentiates itself from idealist positions that would tie the objectivity of the world to its position vis-à-vis the subject. For Zubiri, humans are embedded in a reality in which they realize themselves through the power of the real, what he later terms *apoderamiento*. This will be developed further in *El hombre y Dios*.

70. *HD*, 52.

71. "El problema teologal del hombre," in *Teología y mundo contemporáneo: Homenaje a Karl Rahner en su 70 cumpleaños*, ed. A. Vargas-Machuca (Madrid: Universidad Pontificia Comillas y Ediciones Cristiandad, 1975), 57. Zubiri describes reality-as-fundament as possessing three characteristics for persons: "ultimacy" (*ultimidad*), "making possible" (*posibilitante*), and impelling (*impelente*). *HD*, 82ff.

72. One should note that in Spanish *optar* has more of a sense of long-term commitment and aspiration than its English cognate, "opt." Recalling Ellacuría's method for Latin American theology, one can see the seeds of the optative/ethical moment (*cargar con la realidad*). The next chapter will demonstrate how Ellacuría interprets the preferential option for the poor as that location of Christian option, of Christian adoption of a new form of reality.

73. "Problema teologal," 58. See also *HD*, 138ff.

74. Along with terms like "power" (*poder*) and "force" (*fuerza*), Zubiri also uses "domination" (*dominación*) to indicate this dynamic in which "something" beyond reality as apprehended plays a constitutive role in human realization as person. "Domination is a real and physical character;... the reality that makes us personal realities is dominating." *HD*, 86–87.

75. Here one might note the influence, and Zubiri's modification, of Heidegger's *Geworfenheit*.

76. "Problema teologal," 58. See also *HD*, 307ff.

77. For further investigation into Zubiri's use of the term, see M. L. Rovaletti, *La dimensión teologal del hombre: Apuntes en torno al tema de la religación en Zubiri* (Buenos Aires: Editorial Universitaria, 1979); Candido Aniz Iriarte, "Punto de partida en el acceso a Dios: Vía de la religación, de Zubiri," *Estudios filosóficos* 35 (1986): 237–68; and José L. Martín García-Alós, "Dios como realidad religante del hombre," *Arbor*, 116:57–81.

78. *HD*, 98. Unlike English, Spanish uses a definite article before abstract nouns like reality. Hence, Zubiri uses this to distinguish *"esta" realidad* (this reality or real thing) from *"la" realidad* (reality itself).

79. *HD*, 307–8. The verb *probación* is associated with reason, an ulterior mode of sentient intellection. This will be significant when Zubiri attempts to locate the experience of God.

80. See *HD*, 96–97. For Ellacuría, this ambiguity manifests itself in trying to articulate the difference between pure or nude (*nuda*) reality and the power of the real. See "La religación, actitud radical," *Asclepio* 16 (1966): 97–155; *ET* I, 39–109.

81. *HD*, 133.

82. "Problema teologal," 56. In *HD*, 149, he claims, "God is formally and precisely constituting the reality of each thing. Because of this, God is the fundament of the reality of each thing and the power of the real in it."

83. For more on the problem of God in Zubiri, see Antonio Pintor-Ramos, "Dios como problema en Zubiri," *Universitas Philosophica* 2 (June 1985): 29–44; Urbano Gil Ortega, "Dios en el pensamiento de Xavier Zubiri," *Lumen* 38

(1989): 158–82; and Jesús Sáez Cruz, *La accesibilidad de Dios: Su mundanidad y transcendencia en X. Zubiri* (Salamanca: Universidad Pontifica, 1995).

84. Note the resemblance that these bear to the previously cited "grammatical rules" of Kathryn Tanner in *God and Creation in Christian Theology* (New York: Blackwell, 1988).

85. *NHG,* 322. Though not mentioned explicitly, Zubiri's mention of feeling (*sentimiento*) appears to be directed to Schleiermacher's fundamental claim about the referent and scope of meaning of our God-talk.

86. Kevin Burke notes, "Zubiri does not locate a conceptual foundation for philosophy in the apprehension of reality as fundament. Hence, Zubirian fundamentality should not be confused with philosophical foundationalism.... In his view, the fundament predominates in reality." Burke, *The Ground beneath the Cross,* 48–49.

87. For example, in Aquinas, created *esse* is an *esse ad Creatorem.*

88. Zubiri, "Problema teologal," 59

89. *NHG,* 330.

90. Ibid., 333. See Zubiri's emphasis on considering God as "reality-fundament" and not "reality-object." *HD,* 81–108.

91. *NHG,* 337.

92. Ibid., 338.

93. Ibid., 349.

94. "Problema teologal," 59. "God's transcendence is not one of identity nor of distance, but transcendence in things." *HD,* 176.

95. "Problema teologal," 61. See Rahner, for whom the human is formally the "event" of God's self-communication. Since this essay appears in a festschrift to Karl Rahner, the overtones to his work do not seem accidental.

96. On "theologal" as indicating "existential God-centeredness" see Edward Schillebeeckx, *Christ the Sacrament of the Encounter with God* (New York: Sheed & Ward, 1963), 16.

97. Difficult to translate, *plasmación* is the nominal form of the verb *plasmar,* which has a range of meanings including "giving form to something," and "reflecting or representing an idea or feeling in a physical form." *Diccionario de la lengua española* (Madrid: Editorial Espasa Calpe, 1999), 1035.

98. "Problema teologal," 61. The use of *plasmación* here seems directly related to the notion of actualization in Zubiri's account of sentient intelligence and what Ellacuría will come to describe as "historicization."

99. Ignacio Ellacuría, "Historicidad de la salvación cristiana," *Revista Latino-americana de Teología* 1 (1984): 5–84; *ET* I, 541.

100. "Historicidad," *ET* I, 540. Practically, Ellacuría sees this problem in Latin America in the paradox of some Christians being responsible for great evil and suffering, while some non-believers exemplifying heroic commitment to the liberation of the poor and oppressed. "Before this terrible paradox they [believers] ask themselves how it can be this way, and what they should do with their faith and their works to put an end to this scandal." "Historicidad," *ET* I, 541.

101. For example, he cites Balthasar's admitting that "the theology of liberation has its specific place in a theology of the Reign of God." "Historicidad," *ET* I, 538.

102. The danger of this dualism is that it, and not a unity, becomes the point of departure for reflection on and analysis of reality. That conceptual separation, which is abstract and ahistorical, then "is placed ideologically and uncritically at the service of institutionalized interests." Ellacuría recognizes this danger even within

some liberation theologies. For example, the previous chapter's demonstration of how he criticizes Clodovis Boff's distinction between a theology that deals with the classical themes God and Christ (T1), and a theology that deals with political themes (T2) as perpetuating the separation of what he will argue as unified in a theology of the Reign of God. "Historicidad," *ET* I, 540.

103. Ibid., I, 539–40.

104. Ibid., I, 541.

105. Ibid., I, 542.

106. Ellacuría refers directly to Zubiri's *El hombre y Dios* as an influence in this section of the essay.

107. It is in the interpretation of the Scriptures that Ellacuría specifically criticizes Hans Urs von Balthasar. He identifies as "a distortion of the problem," Balthasar's assertion that "in Israel the religious is always political, and political religious.... This monism of religion and politics, which constitutes the essence of Israel, has been and remain entirely detrimental for the church." "Historicidad," *ET* I, 542.

108. Ibid., I, 578.

109. Ibid. Because it is difficult to translate, and it draws significance from Zubiri's work, I chose to leave *plasmación* in the quote and not translate it. Margaret Wilde renders it "grafting," but it may also be rendered as "forming," "shaping," "molding," and "creating." See ibid., 276.

110. Along with his reworking of Zubirian concepts, Ellacuría also elaborates insights learned from Karl Rahner's theology of grace, but in a way that attempts to overcome perceived weaknesses in Rahner's theoretical-philosophical conceptuality.

111. "Historicidad," *ET* I, 578.

112. On the significance of holding on to this distinction, see Robert Sokolowski, *The God of Faith and Reason: Foundations of Christian Theology* (Washington, DC: Catholic University of America Press, 1982, 1995).

113. "Historicidad," *ET* I, 579.

114. Recall that Zubiri does not take "experience" dualistically/empiricistically as the impingement of one independently existing thing on another.

115. Ibid. Here Ellacuría footnotes Zubiri's *El hombre y Dios* as the place to read more about these ideas. For Zubiri's use of the term *probación*, see n. 79 above.

116. "Historia," *ET* I, 604. The essay, published posthumously in 1993, was originally composed in 1987. One sees clearly Rahner's theological influence here as well.

117. Thus Ellacuría continues rethinking the tremendous advancements made by theologians such as de Lubac and Rahner, broadening the "human subject" to the human person in historical reality.

118. "Historia," *ET* I, 605. Parenthetical comments are his.

119. Ibid., I, 605.

120. Ibid., I, 606. In this language, not only does he reflect a deep-seated humility characteristic of Zubiri's writings, but he also mirrors the thrust of Rahner's later theological work and its emphasis on God as "Incomprehensible Mystery." See Karl Rahner, *Foundations of Christian Faith*, trans. William Dych (New York: Crossroad, 1978), 44–71.

121. "Historia," *ET* I, 608. He alludes to the biblical examples of Isaiah 48, identifying the pagan Cyrus of Persia as a "messiah" sent by God, and Matthew 7:21–23, in which those who say "Lord, Lord," prophesy, cast out demons, and

do mighty works are contrasted with simply doing the will of the Father (See Luke 13:25–27).

122. Ibid., I, 601.

123. For example, ibid., I, 535ff.

124. Ibid., I, 540.

125. Antonio González, "Aproximación a la obra filosófica de Ignacio Ellacuría," *Estudios Centroamericanos* 505–6 (1990): 980.

126. This was subsequently published as Xavier Zubiri, *Estructura dinámica de la realidad*, ed. Diego Gracia (Madrid: Alianza Editorial, 1989).

127. Ibid., 272.

128. Ignacio Ellacuría, *FRH*, 591. By "respectivity," Ellacuría utilizes the Zubirian neologism that refers to the foundational intraconnectedness of reality.

129. González, "Aproximación," 317. *Imbricación* indicates an overlap or partial layering without a loss of character on the part of the items, like the scales of a fish or the tiles on a roof.

130. Ellacuría, "Filosofía y política," *EP* I, 51.

131. Of course, mention of history in philosophy signals an engagement with the thought of Karl Marx. To date, the best analysis in English comparing Ellacuría and Marx, including the crucial terminology of history as *transmisión tradente* is Gandolfo, "Human Essence, History, and Liberation."

132. "Historicidad," *ET* I, 541.

133. An article with the title "Historia de la salvación y salvación en la historia" was published as a chapter in Ellacuría's first book, *Teología política* (San Salvador: Ediciones del Secretariado Social Interdiocesano, 1973). See *ET* I, 519–33. In English, *Freedom Made Flesh*, trans. John Drury (Maryknoll, NY: Orbis Books, 1976), 3–19.

134. "Historia de la salvación y salvación en la historia," *ET* I, 519.

135. For bibliographical references on both the broad nature-grace debates and specifically Rahner's contributions, see notes 6 and 7 in chapter 1.

136. Yet Ellacuría evaluates even this parallelism as misleading because it still tends to accept a certain dualism. For this, he lashes out at modern European political theology as an "equivocating bait" at best, or equally an "equivocal purgative," in attempting to take seriously the notion of these histories as one. Unfortunately, Ellacuría does not cite any specific political theologian at this point in the text. So one cannot be sure against whom this invective is directed. That he evaluates positively the enterprise of a political theology may be seen in the title of the book, *Teología política*, and his claim, "In these pages we will not talk about political theology as much as *do* it." "Historia de la salvación y salvación en la historia," *ET* I, 521.

137. Ibid., I, 527–28.

138. Ibid., I, 597.

139. Ibid., I, 598.

140. Ibid., I, 598–99.

141. Ibid., I, 600–601. This "historicized" view of Jesus will be developed further in the subsequent chapter.

142. Ibid., I, 602. The mentioning of Zubiri in brackets without citation is in the text.

143. It is paramount to see how Ellacuría views the human being, not as a subject in a "neutral" or given world, but within a graced creation. "It is in historical reality,

where revelation and salvation can be viewed as a second grace to the fundamental grace of creation." Ibid., I, 602.

144. In noting this human openness to transcendence, Ellacuría makes a direct allusion to Rahner. "This openness which in each human is the elevated transcendental openness of a 'supernatural existential,' is, in the totality of history, the elevated transcendental openness of a gratuitous historicity." Ibid., I, 604.

145. Ibid., I, 604–5.

146. "History, which is the place, by antonomasia, of the revelation and glorification of God, is also the place of obfuscation and perdition." See ibid., I, 609.

147. José Sols Lucia correctly notes that while Ellacuría uses a variety of adjectives with the term "sin," including personal, social, structural, and historical, the latter three can be considered basically synonymous. *La teología histórica de Ignacio Ellacuría* (Madrid: Editorial Trotta, 1999), 152. For another analysis of sin that has great affinities with Ellacuría's thought, even invoking the language of the theologal, see José Ignacio González-Faus, "Sin" in *Mysterium Liberationis: Fundamental Concepts of Liberation Theology,* ed. Ignacio Ellacuría and Jon Sobrino (Maryknoll, NY: Orbis Books, 1990).

148. For example, he refers to the Third World "not just as the historical location of the objectivization of domination, but the theological location of the objectivization of sin." "Teorías económicas y relación entre cristianismo y socialismo," as cited in Sols, *La teología histórica,* 150.

149. Ibid., 151.

150. "Historicidad," *ET* I, 576. Drawing on Zubiri, Ellacuría distinguishes between "considering sin not just as *opus operantis,* the action committed by the person, but also as *opus operatum,* the objectified action." "En torno al concepto y a la idea de liberación," in *Implicaciones sociales y políticas de la teología de la liberación* (Seville: Instituto de Filosofía, 1989); *ET* I, 635.

151. Ellacuría considers this particularly important because even though "social and historical sin is not directly or immediately attributable to any person in particular, it does not cease being the active covering over of the truth of God and the positive intention to annul the fullness of life that God wishes to communicate to human beings." "Liberación," *ET* I, 636.

152. "Historicidad," *ET* I, 577. italics mine.

153. Ellacuría also moves against a pervasive "modern" tendency, found in eighteenth-century deists, in Kant (by and large), and in nineteenth century "liberal" theologians (even socially conscious ones such as Rauschenbusch) to reduce religion to morality.

154. "Historicidad," *ET* I, 577. Thus, this claim is not just a rhetorical flourish or an arbitrary "allegorical" reading of Scripture, but is grounded in his philosophy and fundamental theology. For example, see how this notion will be critical when analyzing Ellacuría's well-known description of the poor as the "crucified peoples," a concept to be analyzed in the next chapter.

155. Ibid., I, 580. Ellacuría sounds an apocalyptic note as he describes the widespread blinding of the collective conscience by this absolutization as a participation in the eschatological final days. See "Historia," *ET* I, 608–9. Thus, Ellacuría repeatedly argues for de-ideologization, the unmasking of idols, as a primary function of philosophy. See "Filosofía, ¿para qué?" *EF* III, 125.

156. For example, Oscar Romero, "The Church's Mission amid the National Crisis" (Fourth Pastoral Letter) in *Voice of the Voiceless* (Maryknoll, NY: Orbis Books, 2001), 133–36.

157. "Historicidad," *ET* I, 581–82.

158. "Historia," *ET* I, 611–12. In discussing the relationship between liberation and freedom, Ellacuría states, "The liberation of unjust structures and the creation of new structures that promote dignity and freedom are constituted by the movement toward freedom" "Liberación," 642.

159. "Nuestra situación colectiva vista desde la primera semana," a paper given at a meeting of the Central American Jesuits in Madrid, June 1969. *ET* IV, 195.

160. "Nuestra situación," *ET* IV, 196.

161. Ellacuría's writings on the Society of Jesus and Ignatian spirituality may be found in *ET* IV, 173–290. See also J. Matthew Ashley, "Ignacio Ellacuría and the *Spiritual Exercises* of Ignatius of Loyola," *Theological Studies* 61 (2000): 16–39.

162. "Nuestra situación," *ET* IV, 188–89.

163. Ibid., IV, 178.

164. "Liberación," *ET* I, 637.

Chapter 3: Locus Salvificus

1. Though not explored here, the legacy of the other martyrs: Ignacio Martín-Baró, Segundo Montes, Amando López, Juan Moreno, Joaquín López y López, Celina and Elba Ramos deserves attention as well. In English, selections from the important scholarly work of Martín-Baró and Montes (as well as Ellacuría) may be found in John Hassett and Hugh Lacey, eds., *Towards a Society That Serves Its People: The Intellectual Contribution of El Salvador's Murdered Jesuits* (Washington, DC: Georgetown University Press, 1991). Biographical information on all of the martyrs may be found in Jon Sobrino, Ignacio Ellacuría, and others, *Companions of Jesus: The Jesuit Martyrs of El Salvador* (Maryknoll, NY: Orbis Books, 1990).

2. Orbis Books used this painting as the cover to Jon Sobrino, *Witnesses to the Kingdom: The Martyrs of El Salvador and the Crucified Peoples* (Maryknoll, NY: Orbis Books, 2003).

3. Dean Brackley, S.J., conversation with author, San Salvador, November 13, 2005.

4. Ignatius of Loyola, *Spiritual Exercises*, no. 53.

5. "Las iglesias latinoamericanas interpelan a la Iglesia de España," *Sal Terrae* 826 (1982): 219–30; *ET* II, 602.

6. A survey of just the titles of his most significant essays confirms this interest. For example, "Historia de la salvación y salvación en la historia" (1973); "El pueblo crucificado: Ensayo de soteriología histórica" (1978); "Historicidad de la salvación cristiana" (1984); "Historia de la salvación" (1987); and "Utopía y profetismo desde América Latina: Un ensayo concreto de soteriología histórica" (1989).

7. The quotes signal the key elements of Ellacuría's method for Latin American theology: *el hacerse cargo de la realidad, el cargar con la realidad,* and *el encargarse de la realidad.* See the discussion of these terms in the preceding chapter.

8. Albert Schweitzer's classic book on the first quest starts with Reimarus, whose texts were published by Lessing in the 1780s. See *Geschichte der Leben-Jesu-Forschung, The Quest of the Historical Jesus,* trans. W. Montgomery (New York: Macmillan, 1910). Indeed, its original title was *Von Reimarus zu Wrede* (Tübingen:

Mohr, 1906). For a magisterial treatment of the so-called quest for the historical Jesus, both in its history and as a constructive proposal, see the multivolume
work of John P. Meier, *A Marginal Jew: Rethinking the Historical Jesus* (New York:
Doubleday, 1991).

9. Ignacio Ellacuría, *Teología política* (San Salvador: Ediciones del Secretariado Social Interdiocesano, 1973). The English translation curiously bears the title,
Freedom Made Flesh, trans. John Drury (Maryknoll, NY: Orbis Books, 1976).
The essays, under their own titles, appear separately in the *Escritos teológicos*. All
citations and pagination will come from these *Escritos*.

10. One should note that important christological work was being done by
Ellacuría's colleague at the UCA, the Jesuit Jon Sobrino. Major works of Sobrino
published during Ellacuría's life include: *Cristología desde América Latina: Esbozo
a partir del seguimiento del Jesús histórico* (Río Hondo, Guatemala: Centro de Re-
flexión Teológica, 1976), and *Jesús en América Latina: Su significado para la fe y
la cristología* (Santander: Sal Terrae, 1982). For an example of Ellacuría's regard
for this work, see his 1982 review, "Contraportada de J. Sobrino *Jesús en América
Latina*," *ET* II, 125–26.

11. See the discussion in the previous chapter.

12. Ignacio Ellacuría, "Carácter político de la misión de Jesús," *ET* II, 16.

13. Ibid., *ET* II, 16–17.

14. A prime example can be found in John P. Meier, "The Bible as a Source for
Theology," *CTSA Proceedings* 43 (1988): 1–14. Although he directs his criticisms
specifically at Jon Sobrino and Juan Luis Segundo many of the same criticisms would
apply to Ellacuría, particularly in the case of Sobrino, whose work is in dialogue with
Ellacuría's intellectual framework.

15. Ellacuría accepts the insights of historical-critical investigation into the
scriptural texts and the character of the Greco-Roman and Jewish milieu in which
these texts were composed. He indicates his interest in this research by citing biblical scholars such as: Joachim Jeremias, S. G. F. Brandon, Heinrich Schlier, and
Oscar Cullmann. Indeed, Ellacuría indicates that in understanding this milieu, one
can better appreciate the sociopolitical significance of Jesus' ministry and preaching
as portrayed in the Gospels.

16. If Ellacuría's philosophical and theological anthropology portray human
existence embedded in reality in a complex and dynamic manner, then his hermeneutic approach may be suggested by asking, "According to the Gospels, how did
Jesus confront reality (*enfrentarse con la realidad*)?"

17. "Carácter político," *ET* II, 15.

18. Meier, *A Marginal Jew*, 21–22.

19. "Carácter politico," *ET* II, 18. It is interesting to note that in providing
examples of *a priori* Christologies, Ellacuría identifies modern, not classical sources.
Among them he names Vogtle, Rahner, Gutwenger, and Schnackenburg.

20. For example, before Peter's confession at Caesarea Philippi, the people are
said to have called him: John the Baptist, Elijah, Jeremiah, or "one of the prophets"
(Matt. 16:14; see also Mark 8:28; Luke 9:19).

21. While on the surface Ellacuría does not differentiate clearly whether he
speaks of the so-called historical Jesus or the historical reality of the Jesus portrayed
in the Gospels, the fact that his evidence comes exclusively from biblical texts warrants the latter. Whether Jesus himself or his contemporaries identified him with the

prophetic tradition may be a matter of debate; the notion that the Gospels portray him as such can hardly be denied.

22. See Matthew 19:16–22; Mark 10:17–31; Luke 18:18–30.

23. "Carácter político," *ET* II, 27.

24. He notes that Jesus was killed with two *lestai* (rebels), and that the *titulus* on the cross stated a political crime, a fact that Ellacuría learns from "Oscar Cullmann, an interpreter seldom suspicious of politicization." "Dimensión política del mesianismo de Jesús," *Estudios sociales* 7 (1972): 81–105; *ET* II, 39.

25. Given the tragic history of anti-Semitism that has arisen from claims that "the Jews" killed Jesus, it is important to note that Ellacuría states directly that Jesus suffered a Roman execution under Pilate. His implication of Jewish authorities has less to do with their being "Jewish" than their being "authorities." Again, reference to the Salvadoran situation in which priests, nuns, and lay church workers were tortured and killed by authorities who considered themselves "good Catholics" (and indeed had bishop-generals blessing their work) underscores why Ellacuría clearly perceives the connection between religious and social authority.

26. On this danger of resembling a rebel, Ellacuría ominously quips in a later lecture, "If one day they find me killed, it will not be because they mistook me for an astronaut." The lecture, originally delivered on January 19, 1982, has recently been published as "La muerte de Jesús: Realidad y teologización," *Revista Latinoamericana de Teología* 58 (2003): 117–34.

27. "Dimensión política," *ET* II, 41. Later on in the essay, noting a direct parallel with the Chalcedonian claim of Jesus' two distinct natures in the unity of one person, Ellacuría asserts, "It is one thing to assert an intrinsic connection between the reign of this world and the reign of God, between salvation history and salvation in history, and another to make an unqualified identification between both extremes." *ET* II, 52.

28. "Dimensión política," *ET* II, 57.

29. "Carácter político," *ET* II, 20.

30. "¿Por qué muere Jesús y por qué lo matan?" *Misión Abierta* 10 (1977): 176–86; *ET* II, 67–88. It should be noted that the year this article appeared coincides with the year in which a brutal campaign of priests' assassinations commenced with the killing of the Jesuit Rutilio Grande.

31. This represents another example of Ellacuría's "historicization," the demonstrating of certain concepts' impact within a particular context. Jesus' historical incarnation serves as a paradigm of what the historicization of salvation should be.

32. Elsewhere, Ellacuría differentiates the former question, "Why did he die?" as a theologization (*teologización*) of Jesus' death and the latter, "Why was he killed?" as the reality (*realidad*) of Jesus' death. "La muerte de Jesús," 118.

33. In his lecture on why Jesus was killed, Ellacuría adds, "Then perhaps you will understand why priests are killed in Latin America, some of them our very close companions." "La Muerte de Jesús," 120.

34. Indeed, relying on Von Rad, Ellacuría claims that "Israel did not arrive at the idea of a creator God through rational reflection on the course of nature, but through theological reflection on what had happened to the chosen people [in history]." "Pueblo crucificado," *ET* II, 144.

35. "Pueblo crucificado," *ET* II, 147.

36. In identifying the two reigns, Ellacuría echoes the language from the "Meditation on Two Standards" in Ignatius of Loyola's *Spiritual Exercises*.

37. "Pueblo crucificado," *ET* II, 148.

38. In a U.S. context, Dr. Martin Luther King Jr.'s comments about the possibility/imminence of his own death, expressed in the "I See the Promised Land" speech delivered the night before his assassination, provide a powerful parallel. *A Testament of Hope: The Essential Writings of Martin Luther King Jr.*, ed. James M. Washington (San Francisco: Harper & Row, 1986), 279–86.

39. Romero's comment to the editor of the Mexican magazine *Excelsior* indicates a manner in which one might even tie the notion of resurrection to Jesus' death without stripping it of its historical weight: "I have often been threatened with death. I must tell you, as a Christian, I do not believe in a death without resurrection. If they kill me, I will rise again in the Salvadoran people.... A bishop may die, but God's church, which is the people, will never perish." Cited in María López Vigil, *Oscar Romero: Memories in Mosaic* (Washington, DC: EPICA, 2000), 396.

40. "¿Por qué muere Jesús y por qué lo matan?" *ET* II, 78.

41. In order to substantiate this claim, Ellacuría contends with the moment in the Gospels that seems closest to an expiatory theology: the accounts of the Last Supper. He acknowledges that the accounts of the Last Supper represent a complex weaving of historical, theological, and liturgical reflection. A danger lies in the complexity of this scriptural moment: one may take from the Last Supper a perspective that de-emphasizes the reason Jesus was killed; therefore, "what becomes important for Christianity is the cultic celebration in faith of the passion and resurrection of Jesus leaving aside the real and historical celebration of the real and historical following [*seguimiento*] of his life." "¿Por qué muere Jesús?," *ET* II, 79–80.

42. With this as the background, Ellacuría states bluntly, "Jesus knows why he dies. He dies for the Reign of God, and because God desires to establish it on earth. That is why he dies." "La Muerte de Jesús," 126.

43. Ibid., 128.

44. These texts include "La Iglesia de los pobres, sacramento histórico de la liberación," *ECA* 348–49 (1977): 707–22; *ET* II, 453–86; "El pueblo crucificado: Ensayo de soteriología histórica," in Ignacio Ellacuría et al., *Cruz y resurrección: Anuncio de una Iglesia nueva* (Mexico City: CRT, 1978), 49–82; *ET* II, 137–70; "Los pobres, 'lugar teológico' en América Latina," *Misión Abierta* 4–5 (1981): 225–40; *ET* I, 139–62; and "Pobres," in *Conceptos fundamentales del cristianismo*, ed. Casiano Floristán and Juan José Tamayo (Madrid: Editorial Trotta, 1983), 1043–57; *ET* II, 171–92.

45. Recalling Ellacuría's method for Latin American theology, the second moment, carrying the weight of reality (*el cargar con la realidad*) involves that option of place in which what one knows and becomes depends on the location in reality. Kevin Burke notes it as the "ethical dimension that has to do with taking upon ourselves what things really are and what they really demand." Burke, *The Ground beneath the Cross*, 127. The poor then as theological locus (*lugar teológico*) signal this place of ethical commitment and ultimate access to the real.

46. "Los pobres, lugar teológico," *ET* I, 148.

47. This assertion leaves Ellacuría vulnerable to critics who fault Latin American liberation theologians for an emphasis on the socioeconomic that overlooks marginalization on the basis of race, gender, or culture. Yet to the degree that these forms of poverty ultimately mean death, often involving socioeconomic factors, they are not obviated from Ellacuría's thought. Moreover, Ellacuría's position calls for a more complex analysis of the "poverty" claimed by those of a marginalized group

who enjoy economic privilege. See the criticism of feminist theologians by their womanist and mujerista counterparts.

48. For example, in one essay, Ellacuría notes that some would include in the category "poor" the sick or even wealthy widows who suffer. While not wishing to dismiss them, because all suffering is important, Ellacuría draws from the Medellín and Puebla documents to define the poor as dispossessed. "One is poor, not just because, but because they have taken away your things." "Las iglesias interpelan," *ET* II, 592.

49. This conclusion echoes that which Ellacuría in his analysis of the socio-political dimensions of Jesus' ministry, in whose preaching he sees an identification of this dialectic. Reflecting on the Christian appropriation of Jesus' teaching, Ellacuría claims, "Christianity does not consist in abstract praise of poverty as if it were an indispensable condition for accepting the Christian God; nor reciprocally, is it abstract condemnation of wealth.... It involves a dialectic relation in which wealth produces poverty in such a way that one's alternative is either being with the oppressors or being with the oppressed." "Carácter político," *ET* II, 25.

50. "Los pobres, lugar teológico," 144. Ellacuría denies that this dialectical analysis of poverty necessarily stems from Marxist categories, noting that even the Old Testament prophets and Early Church Fathers denounced the fact that there are poor because there are rich. Aware that this is a common accusation against liberation theologians, Ellacuría repeats this claim in several places. For example, see "Los pobres, lugar teológico," *ET* I, 142–43; "Pobres," *ET* II, 175.

51. Though he does not specify who may fall into this group, it appears certain that he would place himself in this category. Ellacuría never naïvely equates his, or any of his Jesuit companions', suffering with that of the poor of El Salvador. The call to solidarity with them never carried this delusion of historical reality.

52. For more on the "theologal," particularly its meaning in the work of Xavier Zubiri, see the previous chapter.

53. "Pobres," *ET* II, 177–78.

54. This moment provides an interesting resemblance to the dark moments of apophatic mystics, such as Eckhart or Juan de la Cruz. See the Cloud of Unknowing and its invitation to "shoot arrows of longing love" into the cloud.

55. "Los pobres, lugar teológico," *ET* I, 149.

56. *Lumen gentium,* 8, in Walter M. Abbott, ed., *The Documents of Vatican II* (New York: America Press, 1966), 23. Ellacuría cites this very passage, along with citations of Medellín and Puebla. See "Pobres," *ET* II, 185.

57. Scholars of "Jesus research" might object to the call for implanting rights and justice by claiming that Jesus did not seek a structural transformation of society, however much he performed certain acts which he took to be signs of the imminence of the Reign. This criticism might be valid if Ellacuría were interested only in a kind of analogous reconstruction of Jesus' ministry in the present. However, his soteriology demands a discipleship that engages historical reality (and sin within that reality) in all its complexity. Ironically then, these critics seem to substantiate Ellacuría's claim to the importance of the poor, in the way they illuminate the complexity of living Jesus' example and message today, as a theological locus that helps guide discernment of proper discipleship.

58. "Pobres," *ET* II, 187.

59. Of whom Ellacuría cites Gustavo Gutiérrez, Leonardo Boff, Ronaldo Muñoz, Jon Sobrino, and Raúl Vidales as examples.

60. "Pobres," *ET* II, 189.

61. "Pueblo crucificado," *ET* II, 137–70.

62. Ibid., II, 138–39. This choice serves as a correlate to both his preference for a "historical" logos over a "Greek" or "natural" logos for theology, and the philosophical suspicions of Western thought inherited from Zubiri. See the previous section.

63. "Pueblo crucificado," *ET* II, 138.

64. Here Ellacuría echoes the meditation on the "Two Standards" from Week Two of Ignatius of Loyola's *Spiritual Exercises* by identifying the opposing realities of the Reign of God and reign of sin. See "Pueblo crucificado," *ET* II, 147.

65. A viewpoint Ellacuría associates with the framework of Anselm of Canterbury's *Cur Deus homo?* Yet because he alludes to Anselm only occasionally as an exemplar of this thinking, never engaging Anselm's texts directly, it seems clear that Anselm serves a rhetorical function in Ellacuría's writing. In essence, Ellacuría argues not so much against Anselm, but rather against an expiatory view of Jesus' crucifixion, one entirely consistent with the legacy of Spanish Catholicism in the Americas, which ignores the historical character of that crucifixion and the historical demands of discipleship flowing from that insight.

66. "Pueblo crucificado," *ET* II, 151.

67. Ibid., II, 152–53.

68. "Función liberadora de la filosofía," *Estudios Centroamericanos* 435–36 (1985); *EP* I, 119–20.

69. He cites Joachim Jeremias as the source behind this evaluation of Isaian theology.

70. For example, Isaiah 53:12 states, "He shall take away the sins of many and win pardon for their offenses."

71. "Pueblo crucificado," *ET* II, 162–63.

72. In a similar way, Ellacuría reads Matthew's parable of the Last Judgment as applying to those "who suffer unaware that their suffering is connected to the name of Jesus and the proclamation of the Reign." "Pueblo crucificado," *ET* II, 169–70.

73. Ellacuría notes the frequency of the term *basileia* in the Gospels and draws from biblical scholars such as J. Jeremias and K. L. Schmidt to assert that the "Reign" is the central theme of Jesus' preaching. See "Recuperar el reino de Dios: Desmundanización e historización de la Iglesia," *Sal Terrae* 5 (1978): 335–43; *ET* II, 312.

74. "Aporte de la teología de la liberación a las religiones abrahámicas en la superación del individualismo y del positivismo," *Revista Latinoamericana de Teología* 10 (1987): 3–28; *ET* II, 202–3.

75. He notes, "What Jesus came to announce and began to realize (*realizar*) is that specific presence of God in history which is reflected above all in his way of being, the words and actions of Jesus. The Reign is not something abstract, nor is it deductible from our idea of God." "Aporte de la teología," *ET* II, 203.

76. "El reino de Dios y el paro del tercer mundo," *Concilium* 180 (1982): 588–96; *ET* II, 302.

77. These five points are taken from "Recuperar el reino de Dios," *ET* II, 313–16.

78. "Recuperar el reino de Dios," *ET* II, 314.

79. Ibid.

80. Ibid., II, 315.

81. Elsewhere, Ellacuría claims that the Reign indicates the "indissoluble connection between God and history" so that what can be said of the Incarnation must be said of the Reign as well. "Aporte de la teología," *ET* II, 203.

82. "Recuperar el reino de Dios," *ET* II, 315.

83. Ibid., II, 315–16.

84. Ibid., II, 316.

85. "Utopía y profetismo desde América Latina: Un ensayo concreto de soteriología histórica," *Revista Latinoamericana de Teología* 17 (1989): 141–84; *ET* II, 233–93.

86. I follow Kevin Burke in translating the Spanish *profetismo*, as "propheticism" to differentiate it from *profecía*, which is rendered "prophecy." As Burke notes, the former term "comes very close to the meaning Ellacuría intends: a prophetic way of life, a life imbued with a prophetic vision, option, and praxis." Kevin Burke, *The Ground beneath the Cross* (Washington, DC: Georgetown University Press, 2000), 146, n. 26.

87. "Utopía," *ET* II, 233.

88. For an analysis of Ellacuría's use of utopia in relation to its historical use by figures ranging from Thomas More to Karl Marx, see José Sols Lucia, *La teología histórica de Ignacio Ellacuría* (Madrid: Editorial Trotta, 1999), 169–210. Sols, whose text explores Ellacuría's terminology in sociological/political-theological pairs (e.g., liberation-salvation, injustice-sin, praxis-discipleship), insists that Ellacuría does not utilize the correlate utopia-Reign without including the notion of prophecy as well.

89. Indeed, he claims, "up to a point, Christian utopia and the Reign of God can be considered equivalent." "Utopía," *ET* II, 236.

90. Ibid.

91. For a utopia to be Christian, Ellacuría asserts that it cannot put aside "the prophecy of the Old Testament (prophets and non-prophets), the Sermon on the Mount, the Last Supper discourse, the Book of Revelation, the primitive Christian community, the Fathers of the Church, the great saints, or certain conciliar and papal documents, to cite a few sources by way of example." Ibid., II, 235.

92. Ibid., II, 237.

93. This movement echoes Zubiri's language for the power of the real that impels humans. See the relevant discussion in chapter 2.

94. Again, this language demonstrates the importance of Ellacuría's philosophical framework (and particularly Zubiri's language and concepts) on Ellacuría's theology. See the discussion in chapter 2.

95. However, to the degree that utopia may be concretized, Ellacuría evades Marx's critique of religion. "If utopia were not realizable at all, it would run the almost insuperable risk of becoming an evasive opium, but if it must achieve a high degree of realization and is put into close relation to prophetic contradiction, it can be what animates correct action." "Utopía," *ET* II, 237.

96. Ellacuría invokes this term as Zubiri's without citing any particular text. In function, the term appears to operate as a synonym for "historicization."

97. "Utopía," *ET* II, 239–40.

98. To that end, this discussion of utopia and prophecy reiterates his contention that salvation history is a salvation in history. Moreover, it indicates the manner in which God's transcendence in history, a *plasmación ad extra* of the Trinitarian life, is

something in which humans may participate, but cannot be restricted to that human activity as such.

99. See above the material on the crucified people, pp. 89ff.

100. In that final year of his life, Ellacuría was asked to write an essay on the five hundredth anniversary of the so-called "discovery" of the Americas. Though he would not complete it because of his assassination, a lecture he gave on the topic was transcribed. It echoes much of the international analysis found in the "Utopía" essay. See "Quinto centenario de América Latina ¿descubrimiento o encubrimiento?" *Revista Latinoamericana de Teología* 21 (1990): 271–82; *ET* II, 525–39.

101. Ellacuría notes the problems of socialist regimes in Cuba and Nicaragua and even identifies the Shining Path in Peru as a case that could be considered as evil as capitalism.

102. "Utopía," *ET* II, 252–53. The phrase *negación superadora* suggests that prophecy's "no" leads to an overcoming of present ills, injustice, sin, etc.

103. In using the language of the universal, Ellacuría employs the Kantian sense of the term. So a "maxim" or principle of action (whether individual or social) cannot be moral if it cannot be universalized; that is, if in choosing it I cannot at the same time choose (will) that everyone else in the world choose it too. This indicates that though Ellacuría (through Zubiri) often criticizes modern thought, particularly in forms inherited from German idealism, he retains an appreciation for its genuine contributions.

104. "Utopía," *ET* II, 256–57. Note Zubiri's language and concepts (God as fundament, the force of reality that throws humans forward) that shapes this description.

105. Ellacuría speaks about the ability of the poor to find joy, to possess a spirit of fiesta, themes that liberation theologians have often been criticized for ignoring.

106. "Utopía," *ET* II, 264.

107. Ibid., II, 266.

108. Ibid., II, 268.

109. Once again, he reveals the influence of John Paul II's *Sollicitudo rei socialis* and *Laborem exercens* in his naming the civilization of poverty a civilization of work, a theme present in those documents.

110. "Utopía," *ET* II, 289. Here rather than use the term from his philosophical work, *plasmación*, he chooses historical presence (*presencia histórica*).

111. Ibid., II, 293.

Chapter 4: Ecclesial Praxis as Real Discipleship

1. This "turn" consists of both an analysis of the relationship between theory and praxis, and between praxis and poiesis. Among the standard references, Nicholas Lobkowicz, *Theory and Practice: History of a Concept from Aristotle to Marx* (Notre Dame, IN: University of Notre Dame Press, 1967); Richard Bernstein, *Praxis and Action: Contemporary Philosophies of Human Activity* (Philadelphia: University of Pennsylvania Press, 1971); and Matthew Lamb, "The Theory-Praxis Relationship in Contemporary Christian Theologies," *CTSA Proceedings* 31 (1976): 149–78.

2. While this negative proposal seems sanguine to most theologies of praxis, finding a generally accepted positive proposal is more complex a problem. David Tracy suggests, "Any proper understanding of praxis involves some form of authentic personal involvement and/or commitment." *The Analogical Imagination* (New

York: Crossroad, 1989), 69. For Rebecca Chopp, "Praxis is, positively stated, the realization that humans make history and, negatively stated, the realization that humans cannot rely on any ahistorical, universal truths to guide life." Rebecca Chopp, *The Praxis of Suffering* (Maryknoll, NY: Orbis Books, 1986), 36.

3. Of course, liberation theologians' use of Marxist theory is a much more complex phenomenon. For works by liberation theologians on this question see José Míguez Bonino, *Christians and Marxists: The Mutual Challenge to Revolution* (Grand Rapids: Eerdmans, 1976); or Juan Luis Segundo, *Faith and Ideologies*, trans. John Drury (Maryknoll, NY: Orbis Books, 1984). Among commentators, see Chopp, *The Praxis of Suffering*.

4. See the discussion in chapter 1, p. 168 170, notes 52, 53, and 55. See also Arthur McGovern, *Marxism: An American Christian Perspective* (Maryknoll, NY: Orbis Books, 1981).

5. Once again, for the sake of consistency, I follow Kevin Burke's translations found in *The Ground beneath the Cross*. Indeed, he refers to this final moment as "praxical" in contrast to the "noetic" (realizing) and "ethical" (shouldering).

6. In his introduction to Ellacuría's only full-length philosophical monograph, *Filosofía de la realidad histórica,* editor (and Ellacuría's most prominent student) Antonio González claims, "It can be said that the book constitutes a true attempt to lay the foundation for the theoretical concept of historical praxis." *FRH*, 10. For further elaboration of the place of praxis in Ellacuría's philosophy, see Héctor Samour, *Voluntad de liberación* (San Salvador: UCA Editores, 2002), 11–20. For an analysis of the relationship between praxis, understood as a philosophical term, and discipleship (*seguimiento*) as its theological cognate, see José Sols Lucia, *La teología histórica de Ignacio Ellacuría* (Madrid: Editorial Trotta, 1999).

7. Though this engagement points to a profoundly modern vocabulary in Ellacuría's thought, his critical view of the moderns leads many commentators, including Samour and Lassalle-Klein, to describe Ellacuría's work as "postmodern" in nature. See Senent's claim that Ellacuría, "without renouncing their emancipative interest, presents a 'postmodern' alternative to the 'developmental' categories with which the moderns understood historical reality." Juan Antonio Senent de Frutos, *Ellacuría y los derechos humanos* (Bilbao: Desclée de Brouwer, 1998), 126.

8. For example, Sols, *La teología histórica;* Samour, *Voluntad de liberación;* or Gracia, "Filosofía práctica," in *La pasión por la libertad: Homenaje a Ignacio Ellacuría,* ed. José Gimbernat and Carlos Gómez (Estella [Navarra]: Editorial Verbo Divino, 1994).

9. José Joaquín Castellón Martín, *Ellacuría y la filosofía de la praxis* (Huelva, Spain: Hergué, 2003). Ellacuría's first publications include a trio of essays on Ortega y Gasset: "Ortega y Gasset: Hombre de nuestro ayer," *Estudios Centroamericanos* 104 (1956): 198–203; "Ortega y Gasset, desde dentro," *Estudios Centroamericanos* 105 (1956): 278–83; and "¿Quién es Ortega y Gasset?" *Estudios Centroamericanos* 110 (1956): 595–601. They can all be found in *EF* I, 15–46.

10. One can see this attempt in Ortega y Gasset's concept of "life" (*la vida*) and Zubiri's notion of "reality" (*la realidad*). See Ortega y Gasset, *Unas lecciones de metafísica* (Madrid, 1993), 151–61, and Xavier Zubiri, *Inteligencia sentiente.*

11. Diego Gracia, "Filosofía práctica," 332.

12. Ibid. Other students in this "second generation" include Carlos Baciero, Alfonso López Quintás, Antonio Ferraz, and Antonio Pintor Ramos; however, Gracia

adds that "without doubt, the principal figure among the members of this generation has been Ignacio Ellacuría."

13. "Das Wahre muss gegenwärtig, wirklich, sinnlich, anschaulich, menschlich sein . . . nur das Wirkliche, Sinnliche, Menschliche ist das Wahre." Ludwig Feuerbach, "Aus dem Vorwort zur ersten Gesammtaugsgabe" (1846) in *Sämtliche Werke*, ed. Bolin-Jodl (Stuttgart: Frommann Holzboog, 1959), 2:410.

14. See Richard Bernstein, *Praxis and Action*, 42–55.

15. Gracia, "Filosofía práctica," 338.

16. Commenting on Ellacuría's *Filosofía*, Diego Gracia claims, "the entire book is an attempt to overcome the classical dichotomy [between history understood simply as the collection of individuals' actions vs. history as social structures]." Ibid., 342.

17. Ellacuría would quickly add that the admission of relative autonomy does not mean an "ab-solutizing" from historical reality. See "Función liberadora de la filosofía," *EP* I, 119.

18. *FRH*, 591–96. The following summary draws from the helpful analysis of Héctor Samour in *Voluntad de liberación*, 234–45.

19. *FRH*, 564ff. See also Xavier Zubiri, *Estructura dinámica de la realidad*, 107–99.

20. Samour rightly emphasizes that while variation is the most elemental dynamism, it is also the most truly radical; any more complex dynamism is rooted in variation.

21. In the more pithy Spanish phrase, "La vida es un dinamismo para poder seguir siendo *el* mismo precisamente no siendo *lo* mismo." Italics are Ellacuría's. *FRH*, 591. It is a phrase that he will later use to describe the nature of the church.

22. Ibid., 592.

23. Ibid., 594.

24. Domínguez Miranda emphasizes that while historical praxis, as a structural unity, diversifies in a plurality of relatively autonomous dynamisms, it must be remembered that these are "notes-of," moments or substructures of that radical unity which is praxis. See M. Domínguez Miranda, "Aproximaciones al concepto de praxis en Ignacio Ellacuría," *Universitas Philosophica* 21 (1993): 50ff.

25. *FRH*, 594. Ellacuría emphasizes the dynamic nature of praxis elsewhere. "Praxis should be understood as historical reality's dynamism in its entirety. This praxis is an active, immanent totality because its action and result remain within the same totality in process. . . . The activity of historical reality is praxis, understood as dynamic totality." "Función liberadora," *EP* I, 119.

26. This provides a response to Roberto Goizueta's criticism of Latin American liberation theologians' understanding of praxis in *Caminemos con Jesús*. There, Goizueta accuses the Latin Americans of "too materialistic" an understanding of praxis that eschews "activities done for their own sake," such as celebration. In reality, Goizueta claims, the Latin American emphasis on sociopolitical transformation properly indicates *poiesis*, and thus, he argues for a recognition of *praxical* aesthetics and fiesta as a U.S. Latino/a corrective to Latin American overemphasis on social-transformative (poietic) praxis.

27. *FRH*, 594.

28. Ibid., 595. As he reflects on personal spirituality, Ellacuría will utilize this sense of contemplation to interpret Ignatius of Loyola's "Contemplation to attain

love" in the *Spiritual Exercises* as a "contemplation-in-action-for-justice." See the concluding section of this chapter.

29. "Función liberadora," *EP* I, 110–11.

30. *FRH*, 596.

31. For one example of a wider view of praxis, see Ada María Isasi-Díaz, *En La Lucha = In the Struggle: Elaborating a Mujerista Theology*, tenth anniversary ed. (Minneapolis: Fortress Press, 2004), 176–95, and María Pilar Aquino, *Our Cry for Life: Feminist Theology from Latin America* (Maryknoll, NY: Orbis Books, 1993), who emphasize daily existence (*lo cotidiano*) as an essential component of praxis.

32. "Función liberadora," 111.

33. Though one might be tempted to associate this language with the type that Lamb describes as "primacy of praxis," the interrelated nature of theory and praxis in Ellacuría's thought better fits the "critical praxis correlation" type (that type that Lamb associates with other Latin American liberation theologians). See Lamb, "The Theory-Praxis Relationship," 171–78.

34. "Función liberadora," *EP* I, 111. Héctor Samour observes that Ellacuría prefers to speak of "theoretical moments of praxis" and not of "theoretical praxis" because the latter, in overextending the realm of praxis, can give way to two equally dangerous positions he wishes to overcome: one that negates any autonomy to the theoretical and another that proposes an absolute autonomy such that criteria of validation may be found outside of historical praxis. See *Voluntad de liberación*, 378–82.

35. For Matthew Lamb, this insight is characteristic of that type he describes as "critical praxis correlations." "When dealing with human activity one cannot isolate 'fields of activity' not dynamically interrelated (for all their relative autonomy) with the others. Christian praxis is authentically incarnational and eschatological when its very commitment to a particular praxis critically opens it to all other authentic praxis." "Theory-Praxis Relationship," 172 n. 75. See also Bernard Lonergan, *Method in Theology* (New York: Herder and Herder, 1972), 101–24; Hugo Assmann, *Theology for a Nomad Church* (Maryknoll, NY: Orbis Books, 1976), 111–25.

36. "Función liberadora," *EP* I, 112.

37. Ellacuría alludes to this moment as including discernment and judgment, but does not develop a full-fledged theory. In vocabulary, he demonstrates tantalizing proximity to that of Bernard Lonergan, but never cites his work. For more on Lonergan's development of the notions of discernment and judgment, see his magisterial work, *Insight: A Study of Human Understanding* (New York: Philosophical Library, 1957).

38. "Función liberadora," *EP* I, 112.

39. He states, "The necessity of the ideological for social change is clear, but that should not lead one to fall into the illusion of thinking that a change of ideas is a change of reality, or that a change of intention — the purity of intention — is sufficient to change reality." "Función liberadora," *EP* I, 114. Here Ellacuría reveals the influence of Marx's critique of Feuerbach.

40. José Sols mentions the notion of "reflective separation" in which theory constitutes an order in which the person takes distance with respect to action, precisely to understand it better. *La Teología histórica*, 225.

41. "Función liberadora," *EP* I, 113.

42. Ellacuría states that a Christian philosophy would not begin its task necessarily from conformity to dogma nor submission to ecclesiastical hierarchy (though not necessarily in opposition either), but "be that which places its autonomous philosophizing in the privileged location of the truth in history, which is the cross as hope and liberation." "Función liberadora," *EP* I, 116.

43. "Función liberadora," *EP* I, 115. Ellacuría cites this as a discernment of the "injustice that suppresses the truth" (Rom. 1:18).

44. José Sols notes the multiple adjectives that Ellacuría uses with praxis including: historical, social, biographical, ecclesial, and pastoral. José Sols Lucia, *La teología histórica*, 219.

45. "La teología como momento ideológico de la praxis ecclesial," *Estudios Eclesiásticos* (1978); *ET* I, 167–68. This follows an earlier definition of ecclesial praxis as "an action that surges from that totality that we call the Church and that affects [*incide sobre*] that totality that we call society, or if one prefers, the political world." "La cuestión fundamental de la pastoral Latinoamericana," *Sal Terrae* 8–9 (1976); *ET* II, 543.

46. "Cuestión fundamental," *ET* II, 544.

47. An indication of this historical role emerges in the titles Ellacuría uses for the church, including: visible sign, efficacious sacrament, prophetic community, eschatological sign, leaven in the world, credible sign, sacrament of liberation, and church of the poor.

48. "La teología como momento ideológico," *ET* I, 169. Elsewhere he claims, "The Church is, in the first place, that people of God that carries forward [*prosigue*] in history that which Jesus sealed definitively as the presence of God among humans." "Iglesia de los pobres," *ET* II, 454.

49. "Liberación: misión y carisma de la iglesia latinoamericana," *ECA* 268 (1971); *ET* II, 556.

50. "Iglesia y realidad histórica," *ECA* 331 (1976); *ET* II, 501ff. See "Recuperar el reino de Dios: desmundanización e historización de la Iglesia," *Sal Terrae* 5 (1978); *ET* II, 307, where Ellacuría attempts to demonstrate "the necessity that the Church retrieve the notion of the Reign of God so that the latter not be 'spiritualized' and the former 'made worldly' ('*mundanizada*')."

51. "Misión y carisma," *ET* II, 558.

52. Although he does not note any source for this formulation, the language strongly resembles that of his mentor of theological studies in Innsbruck, Karl Rahner. Indeed, the thread of this argument comes from early in Ellacuría's career, a time that he demonstrated Rahner's influence more explicitly. On the language of humans as "hearers of the Word," see Karl Rahner, *Hörer des Wortes: Zur Grundlegung einer Religionsphilosophie* (Munich: Kösel, 1941). On the influence of Karl Rahner on Ignacio Ellacuría, see Martin Maier, "La influencia de Karl Rahner en la teología de Ignacio Ellacuría I y II," *Revista Latinoamericana de Teología* 39 (1996): 233–55; 44 (1998): 163–87. An edited version of these articles appeared as "Karl Rahner, el maestro," in *Ignacio Ellacuría: Aquella libertad esclarecida*, ed. Jon Sobrino and Rolando Alvarado (San Salvador: UCA Editores, 1999), 171–93. This language also reflects the influence of the *Spiritual Exercises* as Ellacuría learned them from Miguel Elizondo. See "Lectura latinoamericana de los *Ejercicios Espirituales* de san Ignacio," *ET* IV, 62, which includes a reference to Rahner's own interpretation of the *Exercises*.

53. "Misión y carisma," *ET* II, 559.

54. Ibid., II, 565. This view corresponds to the language of "objectivization" he uses elsewhere. "Historical acts, all of them, although in distinct grades, are either the objectification of grace, in which divine donation and human action are in accord, or the objectification of sin, where human action remains supported by the evil it objectivizes, denying the offer of grace." "Historia de la salvación," *ET* II, 604–5. Elsewhere, he avers, "The church makes real its historic, salvific sacramentality by announcing and fulfilling the Reign of God in history. Its fundamental praxis consists in the fulfillment of the Reign of God in history, in action that leads to the fulfillment of the Reign of God in history." "Iglesia de los pobres," *ET* II, 548.

55. Unfortunately, Ellacuría does not footnote any scholarship in taking this reading. While much of Ellacuría's exegesis here (and elsewhere) often includes broad statements that would come under scrutiny of current biblical scholars, the importance of his argument here lies in how the views of salvation that he identifies with the early Hebrew Bible and a certain reading of the New Testament serve to justify attitudes that he wishes to correct.

56. Actually, the language that Ellacuría cites is much more severe. Marx's criticism is that Feuerbach considers praxis *"in ihrer schmutzigjüdischen Erscheinungform."*

57. "Just as Marx sees a distinct alternative to Jewish praxis and Christian interiorization (as understood by Feuerbach), so does the contemporary Christian have the right and obligation to search for a fourth option that overcomes "Jewish" politicization, purely contemplative interiorization, and Marxist praxis." "Misión y carisma," *ET* II, 564. For a good summary of Feuerbach and Marx and the role they play in Ellacuría's formulation of praxis, see José Sols Lucia, *La teología histórica,* 215ff. In using the phrase, "Jewish politicization," Ellacuría does not accept Marx's characterization of Judaism at large. Rather, he seems to assign this politicization to the early strata of the Hebrew Bible's composition that in his mind was corrected by the prophetic tradition. Thus, Ellacuría can put forth the (Jewish) prophets and Jesus as the models for his (fourth) alternative. This strategy has been criticized more recently by Jon D. Levenson as a typical one that goes back to "liberal Protestant theology" of the nineteenth century, with its preference for the prophetic strand in the Hebrew Bible over the cultic, temple-oriented strand, caricaturing the latter in the process and overlooking its own distinctive transformative potential. See *Sinai and Zion: An Entry into the Jewish Bible* (San Francisco: Harper & Row, 1987).

58. "Historia de la salvación," *ET* II, 621, 623.

59. "Iglesia y realidad histórica," *ET* II, 505.

60. Compare this to the language of the church as "sacrament" and its relationship to the Reign in *Lumen gentium,* 1, 5.

61. "Misión y carisma," *ET* II, 564. Ellacuría often uses the terms "sign" (*signo*) and "sacrament" (*sacramento*) interchangeably. To expand on the depth of meaning Ellacuría attaches to "sign," he claims, "The sign permits and demands that we transform the worldly because only in the worldly is the sign given to us; it demands that we search for that sign that makes present the truth that God has revealed to us in Jesus Christ; it demands that we do not stop at its immanence because the sign by the power of its intrinsic immanence throws us beyond itself, if it is truly the sign put by Christ in his historical revelation."

62. "Misión y carisma," *ET* II, 564–65. This distinctive role includes that function of overcoming extremes that Ellacuría attaches to his theology. "If Christian

action is established in the line of a sign, it is possible to overcome both naturalism and supernaturalism, secularism and pietism; it is possible to overcome many forms of schizophrenia, many misinterpretations, of Christianity in the world" (565).

63. "Iglesia y realidad histórica," *ET* II, 509.

64. For example, "Every ecclesial practice should be realized in order to carry forward [*proseguimiento*] [the mission] of the historical Jesus." "La teología como momento ideológico," *ET* I, 175. "In order to be a sign of credibility, the church must, in everything it says and does, manifest the visible and historical presence of Jesus." "Iglesia y realidad histórica," *ET* II, 508.

65. In particular, I would argue that Ellacuría's notion of ecclesial praxis here bolsters my claim that what he means by "historical Jesus" is best represented as the "historicized Jesus."

66. See my treatment of his article "¿Por qué muere Jesús y por qué le matan?" in chapter 3, p. 82 above. Ellacuría cites this very text to argue that Paul's call to Christians to death and resurrection in baptism should be seen as historical rather than "mystical," or at least to see the mystical element as the gracious invitation to take up "the way of death that leads to life" in history. "Iglesia de los pobres," *ET* II, 459–60.

67. "If the Church wishes, as it should, to be a sign of credibility, it must manifest in everything it does and says the visible and historical presence of Jesus." "Iglesia y realidad histórica," *ET* II, 508. "If the world and society should be the mediation of God, the church should be the sign par excellence, of the redemptive presence of Christ among human beings." "Misión y carisma," *ET* II, 578.

68. Among the many places where this formulation appears, see "Misión y carisma," *ET* II, 571ff.; "Iglesia y realidad histórica," *ET* II, 511ff.; "Cuestión fundamental," *ET* II, 550.

69. "Misión y carisma," *ET* II, 575. See also "Misión y carisma," 580. Elsewhere he refers to the removal of sin in necessary relation to the construction of a new earth. See "Cuestión fundamental," *ET* II, 550. "Utopía y profetismo," *ET* II, 271–72.

70. "Misión," 573. Note that the language of God as *fundamento* recalls Ellacuría's acknowledgment of God as creator of reality, including the important concepts of *religación* and of reality as the *plasmación ad extra* of the Trinity. See the material in chapter 2.

71. Ellacuría reads this drive to historicization even in the work of someone like Augustine in whose "interiorization" of the concept of sin he sees a genuine incarnational drive. "Augustinian thought, which demands that one not go outside, but rather enter into oneself [*sí mismo*] to find the truth, has a greater importance and exactitude if that self [*sí mismo*] is human history in which the Son of God was incarnated." "Cuestión fundamental," *ET* II, 546.

72. So Ellacuría will insist on the profoundly personal and specific nature of salvation, "Faith is a personal relation that comes from a personal God and is directed personally to a person conditioned by her or his time and place, by her or his people and history. . . . In that faith, salvation is communicated." Yet he will go on to assert that the complex reality of personal existence includes a sense much wider than the personal. "The true universality of salvation may be achieved only by extending to the totality of historical variation of human existences [*existencias humanas*]." "Misión y carisma," *ET* II, 566.

73. For Ellacuría, this identification of social or structural sin has its immediate ecclesial precedent in the documents of the Latin American Bishops' Conference (CELAM) meetings of Medellín and Puebla.

74. See the previous chapter's discussion of Ellacuría's contrast of the sinful "civilization of wealth/capital" and the utopic "civilization of work/poverty" in one of his definitive articles, "Utopia y profetismo." This emphasis also echoes Ignatius of Loyola's characterization of wealth as the primary sin in his "Meditation on Two Kingdoms" in the Second Week of the *Spiritual Exercises*.

75. These are found primarily in the three-volume set *Veinte años de historia en El Salvador (1969–1989): Escritos políticos.* For a moving personal summary of the situation of El Salvador and the reasons that he (and the others) chose the particular praxis at the UCA, see Ellacuría's lecture, "El compromiso político de la Iglesia en América Latina," *Corintios XIII* 4 (1977): 143–62; *ET* II, 667–82.

76. This indicates a complex relationship between the church and the poor. Ellacuría suggests, "It is not that the poor are necessary for there to be a Church or for the Church to be holy … however, if there are poor, then the Church can be holy and salvific only from, with, and for the poor." "Misión y carisma," *ET* II, 569.

77. "Iglesia de los pobres," *ET* II, 473–74.

78. "Ecclesial praxis has its center in the Reign of God and in the realization of this Reign in history, a Reign that presents itself in the Gospel parable as the leaven in bread, as salt in food, etc., not the bread-dough nor the food." "La teología como momento ideológico," *ET* I, 171.

79. Even though he is sympathetic to theological statements of the church's priority, Ellacuría does not confuse these with reality. "What ecclesial praxis wants to be and to claim for itself — the source of all-embracing meaning and the final critical moment — does not confer to it the ability to 'really' be that. To think otherwise is a purely idealistic illusion that confuses the fabrications of feeling with the operative reality of history." "La teología como momento ideológico," *ET* I, 170.

80. "Iglesia y realidad histórica," *ET* II, 511.

81. "La teología como momento ideológico," *ET* I, 184.

82. Ibid., I, 185.

83. For an example of this pastoral side, see "Carta a un ordenando vacilante," *Hechos y dichos* 385 (1968): 355–62; *ET* IV, 163–72.

84. In this vein, Ellacuría represents an important current in appropriating and reinterpreting the creative vision of Ignatius of Loyola. Ellacuría reflects on Ignatian spirituality in three main periods. In 1969, Ellacuría prepared talks for meetings of the Central American Jesuits, which occurred both in Madrid and San Salvador. See "Nuestra situación colectiva vista desde la primera semana," "El problema del traslado del espíritu de los *Ejercicios* a la Viceprovincia," and "El tercer mundo como lugar óptimo de la vivencia cristiana de los *Ejercicios*," *ET* IV, 173–234. The outline of a 1974 course also provides important reflections. See "Lectura latinoamericana de los *Ejercicios Espirituales* de san Ignacio," *ET* IV, 59–106. In 1977, Ellacurí gave a presentation at a meeting of Jesuit educators in Lima. He elaborated and published his central points in two parts as "Fe y justicia," *Christus* (August 1977): 23–33, and (October 1977): 19–34; *ET* III, 307–73. Another set of writings comes in response to the Jesuit's General Congregation XXXIII of 1983. See "Misión actual de la Compañía de Jesús," and "Congregación General XXXIII como hecho teológico," *ET* IV, 235–56. In addition, this period brought some reflection on the significance

of the great superior general, Pedro Arrupe. See "El segundo general de los jesuitas vasco," and "Pedro Arrupe, renovador de la vida religiosa," *ET* IV, 257–63.

85. The central insights here come from an important contribution that Ellacuría made to the theological dictionary *Conceptos fundamentales de pastoral,* ed. C. Floristán and J. . Tamayo (Madrid: Trotta, 1983). Along with "pobres" and "pueblo de Dios," Ellacuría defined "espiritualidad." For these entries, see pages 786–802, 840–59, and 304–9 respectively.

86. "Espiritualidad," *ET* IV, 51.

87. For example, in another article, Ellacuría describes matrimony as "offering the best conditions to arrive, through the second commandment, at the perfection of the great commandment. Matrimony is the ideal place to express in its highest form the loving of another as you love yourself, and from this love, to love God above all else." See "El seglar cristiano en el tercer mundo," *Búsqueda* 2 (1973): 15–20; *ET* IV, 123–32.

88. "Espiritualidad," *ET* IV, 53.

89. Ellacuría stresses that the institutional church be differentiated from the Reign. "Desiring to replace the spirituality of the Reign with a spirituality of the institutional church is a betrayal of the Reign of God and the church." "Espiritualidad," *ET* IV, 55.

90. Ellacuría admits, "Certainly, the Sermon on the Mount and the Beatitudes do not express the entire richness of Jesus' life and message, but they provide very specific models (*pautas*) that cannot be ignored without being in danger of abandoning something essential in Christian spirituality." "Espiritualidad," *ET* IV, 56. For more of Ellacuría's reflections on the Beatitudes, see "Las bienaventuranzas, carta fundacional de la Iglesia de los pobres," in *Iglesia de los pobres y organizaciones populares* (San Salvador: UCA Editores, 1979), 105–18; *ET* II, 417–38.

91. "Las bienaventuranzas," *ET* II, 435.

92. As was noted in chapter 3, the contrast between the civilization of poverty or work and the civilization of wealth or profit occupies a central place in Ellacuría's thought, particularly in the last few years of his life. See "Utopía y profetismo desde América Latina: Un ensayo concreto de soteriología histórica," *Revista Latinoamericana de Teología* 17 (1989): 141–84; *ET* II, 233–94.

93. "Fe y justicia," *ET* III, 313.

94. Ibid., III, 316.

95. As the next chapter will demonstrate, the failure to do this is a criticism levied against liberation theologians by contemporary thinkers such as Stanley Hauerwas and Daniel Bell Jr.

96. "Fe y justicia," *ET* III, 316.

97. Ibid., III, 325.

98. The "Contemplation to Attain Love" is the last "exercise" given for the Fourth Week and considered by many to be the climax of the spiritual experience of the *Exercises.* Ganss notes how even though a few early commentators (e.g., Miró and Hoffaeus) thought that the contemplation could be given in one of the other Weeks, "consensus soon arose that this Contemplation pertains to the unitive way and is part of the Fourth Week." George Ganss, ed., *The Spiritual Exercises,* 183.

99. "Fe y justicia," *ET* III, 366. In making this claim, Ellacuría notes that Ignatius's phrase possesses a purely formal character.

100. Ellacuría admits that he uses the phrase as a kind of "straw man" to represent "an extreme that needs to be avoided and a negative reference to demonstrate

what is positive in the opposed scheme." He often uses this rhetorical strategy. For example, see his treatment of Clodovis Boff's theological method in "Hacia una fundamentación," and Anselm's theory of atonement in "Historicidad."

101. "Fe y justicia," *ET* III, 367.

102. Ibid., III, 368.

103. Ibid., III, 369.

104. Ibid., III, 368, 372.

105. Ibid., III, 370. Note again the use of the visual metaphor.

106. "[Contemplation] recognizes an initial movement of God present in salvation history and that consequently there is the desire to find this God, not for the mere caprice of finding God, but by the conscious acceptance that without God there is no salvation." Ibid., III, 371.

107. Ibid., III, 372. Italics his.

108. Ibid.

109. Ibid. The general outline of the Exercises divides into four "weeks." The first week's meditations on sin correspond roughly to what is traditionally called the purgative way. The second and third weeks' meditations focus on the public ministry and passion of Christ respectively. Finally, the fourth week focuses on the risen Christ, culminating in the contemplation to attain love. Ellacuría's emphasis on action for justice does not exclude other components of contemplation. He mentions the explicit exercise of faith in proclamation and even celebration of the faith.

110. Ibid.

111. As José Sols puts it, "Archbishop Romero's influence on Ellacuría was not through the transmission of ideas, but as the visible configuration of the Christian personality, integrated in the Catholic hierarchy and profoundly committed, until death, to the cause of the great popular majorities who suffered the consequences of an unjust socioeconomic structure and of a military-political repression that was increasingly violent and inhumane." *La teología histórica de Ignacio Ellacuría,* (Madrid: Editorial Trotta, 1999), 41. For an example of Ellacuría's interpretation, see "Monseñor Romero, un enviado de Dios para salvar a su pueblo," *Sal Terrae* 811 (1980): 825–32; *ECA* 497 (1990): 141–46; *ET* III, 93–100.

112. In making this theological interpretation of a saint's life (and surely to Ellacuría Romero was a saint), Ellacuría stands in a long Christian tradition. Perhaps the most best-known and most apt comparison involves the role of Francis of Assisi in the theology of Bonaventure of Bagnoregio. In Bonaventure's writings on Francis, including homilies and the *Legendas,* we see more than merely a great figure. Francis represents the ideal of "exemplarity," the perfect man of action and contemplation, who embodies the theological principles laid out in Bonaventure's *Itinerarium mentis in Deum.* Examples from an extensive bibliography include Ewert Cousins, "Francis of Assisi and Bonaventure: Mysticism and Theological Interpretation," in *The Other Side of God: A Polarity in World Religion,* ed. Peter Berger (Garden City, NY: Anchor/Doubleday, 1981), 74–103; and Bernard McGinn, "The Influence of St. Francis on the Theology of the High Middle Ages: The Testimony of St. Bonaventure"; in *Bonaventuriana: Miscellanea in onore di Jacques Guy Bougerol, OFM,* ed. Francisco de Asis Chavero Blanco (Rome: Edizioni Antonianum, 1988), 97–117.

113. In her compilation of stories and anecdotes, *Oscar Romero: Memories in Mosaic* (Washington, DC: EPICA, 2000), María López Vigil illustrates this circular movement of being confronted by the reality of the poor, responding, and then being

led to a deeper realization. Examples include Romero's listening to the Mother's Committee for the Disappeared and Political Prisoners and his support for the archdiocesan agencies Caritas and Socorro Jurídico. Even Romero's episcopal motto, "Sentir con la Iglesia," conveys this dynamic.

114. Ellacuría, "Romero, un enviado," *ET* III, 96.

115. Though it is an oversimplification to ascribe Romero's development to a single conversion experience, there is no doubt that Grande's assassination profoundly affected Romero and catalyzed a significant change in his style of leadership. For moving personal accounts of Romero's leadership, see López Vigil, *Memories in Mosaic.* For other secondary material on Romero, see James Brockman, *Romero: A Life* (Maryknoll, NY: Orbis Books, 1989); Dean Brackley, "Rutilio and Romero: Martyrs for Our Time," Annual Archbishop Romero Lecture (Notre Dame, IN: LANACC, Kellogg Institute, 1997); and Jon Sobrino, *Witnesses to the Kingdom: The Martyrs of El Salvador and the Crucified Peoples* (Maryknoll, NY: Orbis Books, 2003).

116. This corresponds with the centrality of "mission" for Ellacuría's understanding of spirituality. See "Espiritualidad," *ET* IV, 54ff.

117. Ellacuría, "Romero, un enviado," *ET* III, 97.

118. Romero thus demonstrates the necessity of the Scriptures and preaching to proper Christian action that transforms the world. For a fuller statement on the importance of preaching, see Ellacuría, "Predicación, palabra, comunidad," originally published as, "La predicación ha de poner en contacto vivificante la palabra de Dios y la comunidad," *Sal Terrae* 3 (1978): 167–76; *ET* IV, 17–28. See Romero's assertion in the lecture he gave at the University of Louvain upon receiving an honorary doctorate: "The course taken by the archdiocese has clearly issued from its faith conviction. The transcendence of the gospel has guided us in our judgment and in our action." "The Political Dimension of the Faith from the Perspective of the Option for the Poor," in *Voice of the Voiceless: The Four Pastoral Letters and Other Statements* (Maryknoll, NY: Orbis Books, 1985), 183.

119. In the previous chapter, we noted that Ellacuría emphasized the proper understanding of Jesus' crucifixion comes through asking not, "Why did he die?" (¿Por qué murió?), but "Why was he killed?" (¿Por qué lo mataron?). Here his blunt phrase describing Romero, "Así murió, por eso lo mataron," echoes that very language. Ellacuría, "Romero, un enviado," *ET* III, 100.

120. Ibid.

121. Ellacuría identifies these pillars in a larger essay reflecting on the legacy of Romero in relation to the work of the UCA. See "La UCA ante el doctorado concedido a Monseñor Romero," *Estudios Centroamericanos* 437 (1985): 167–76; *ET* III, 112.

Chapter 5: Transforming Realities and Contesting Orthodoxies

1. For a brief narrative of its development see editor Laurence Paul Hemming's introduction of *Radical Orthodoxy? A Catholic Enquiry* (Aldershot: Ashgate, 2000), 3–20. A good variety of authors who make up this group may be found in John Milbank, Catherine Pickstock, and Graham Ward, eds., *Radical Orthodoxy: A New Theology* (New York: Routledge, 1999).

2. John Milbank, *Theology and Social Theory: Beyond Secular Reason* (Oxford: Blackwell, 1990).

3. Ibid., 4.

4. In this respect, the "and" in the title *Theology and Social Theory* functions as oppositional, as in Gadamer's *Theology and Method*. As Anthony Godzieba observes, "*and* really does become *or* when theology confronts modernity, because for him there is no overlapping of these narratives." Anthony J. Godzieba, "Fear and Loathing in Modernity: The Voyages of Capt. John Milbank," *Philosophy and Theology* 9, nos. 3–4 (1996): 432.

5. Milbank, *Theology and Social Theory*, 148. As David Burrell points out, Hegel's critical instinct is done in by a reliance on Fichte and Schelling, "whose combined influence led him in effect to base his transcendental logic on 'the Cartesian subject.' " See David B. Burrell, "An Introduction to *Theology and Social Theory: Beyond Secular Reason,*" in *Modern Theology* 8, no. 4 (October 1992): 321. See also *Theology and Social Theory*, 153ff.

6. Milbank, *Theology and Social Theory*, 157.

7. Ibid., 160–61. Indeed, Milbank will go on to argue that there is no "true *Sittlichkeit*" in Hegel because, "it is undermined by negative dialectics, which turns out to be a blend of political economy and Kantian or Fichtean deontology, mediated by Boehme's gnostic trinitarianism" (170).

8. Ibid., 171.

9. Ibid., 177.

10. Ibid., 189.

11. David B. Burrell, "An Introduction to *Theology and Social Theory: Beyond Secular Reason,*" *Modern Theology* 8, no. 4 (October 1992): 322–23.

12. Despite a footnote referencing texts in Gutiérrez, Segundo, and Clodovis Boff, Milbank cannot substantiate his statement that these three claim that "liberation theology alone is to be considered the authentic outworking of post-conciliar Catholic thought." *Theology and Social Theory*, 206.

13. Ibid., 207.

14. These "main proponents" are Gustavo Gutiérrez, Juan Luis Segundo, and Clodovis Boff. He does not mention Ignacio Ellacuría, nor any other significant figures across Latin America.

15. Ibid., 208. Italics are his.

16. Ibid., 209.

17. Ibid., 210.

18. See ibid., 232ff.

19. In particular, Milbank spends most of his time criticizing the work of Clodovis Boff, but often applies these critiques to liberation theology at large. Note his claim that "it is Clodovis Boff who most clearly articulates what they all, less consistently, maintain: namely, that salvation is a properly theological concept, belonging to a specifically theological discourse," or subsequently, "In common with all the liberation theologians, [Boff] makes ethics the mediating term between political commitment and theological interpretation." Ibid., 234, 236.

20. Ibid., 236.

21. See ibid. One should note that Milbank argues with liberationist exegesis at a theoretical level. Unlike many liberation theologians, he does not engage in analysis of biblical texts as part of his theological method.

22. Ibid., 237.

23. Ibid.

24. Ibid.

25. Ibid., 245.

26. Ibid., 244.

27. Daniel Bell Jr., *Liberation Theology after the End of History: The Refusal to Cease Suffering* (London and New York: Routledge, 2001), and William T. Cavanaugh, *Torture and Eucharist: Theology, Politics, and the Body of Christ* (Malden, MA: Blackwell, 1998).

28. For a critical account of Stanley Hauerwas's development, and particularly the manner in which he appropriates important figures such as Alisdair MacIntyre and John Howard Yoder, see the chapter entitled, "The New Traditionalism," in Jeffrey Stout, *Democracy and Tradition* (Princeton, NJ: Princeton University Press, 2004), 118–39.

29. Bell, *Liberation Theology after the End of History*, 3.

30. Ibid., 4.

31. Francis Fukuyama, *The End of History and the Last Man* (New York: Free Press, 1992). See also his "The End of History?" *National Interest* 16 (Summer 1989): 3–18.

32. The phrase "savage capitalism" comes from the liberation theologian-economist Franz Hinkelammert. See his *Cultura de la esperanza y sociedad sin exclusión* (San José, Costa Rica: DEI, 1995), 92.

33. Beyond sympathetic, the following lines from his introduction suggest that Bell could be characterized as once self-identifying with liberation theology. "At times I assumed I was engaged with the liberationists in a common effort to answer the question, how do we proclaim God as savior in the midst of a world suffering from the madness of capitalism? While capitalism has created a certain bond between us, the legitimacy of this assumption rested on the presumption on my part that we shared a common faith. . . . Yet I have come to see the error in this too." *Liberation Theology after the End of History*, 6.

34. William Cavanaugh and Daniel Bell Jr. adopt the same analysis from Foucault's writings. Since they utilize it mainly to make an ecclesiological point, more extended analysis of their use of Foucault will appear in the subsequent section of this chapter.

35. Bell, *Liberation Theology after the End of History*, 72.

36. Ibid., 73.

37. Bell cites this line from Ellacuría (the English translation, *Mysterium Liberationis: Fundamental Concepts of Liberation Theology*, ed. Ignacio Ellacuría and Jon Sobrino [Maryknoll, NY: Orbis Books, 1993], 548) with no reference to its context nor even to its central point. In fact, this line appears in a paragraph talking about the temptation of the church to consider itself an end in itself.

38. Bell, *Liberation Theology after the End of History*, 96.

39. Ibid., 97.

40. Nowhere does Bell clarify how the mendicant Aquinas's vision "was most clearly displayed in medieval monastic communities, like the Cistercians." Ibid., 103.

41. The dismissal of justice language in liberation theology echoes the argument made by Stanley Hauerwas that, "the current emphasis on justice and rights as the primary norms guiding the social witness of Christians is in fact a mistake." *After Christendom? How the Church Is to Behave If Freedom, Justice, and a Christian Nation Are Bad Ideas* (Nashville: Abingdon Press, 1991), 46.

42. Bell, *Liberation Theology after the End of History,* 101. Bell asserts this even while citing Ellacuría's own claim that not every conception of justice is commensurable with Christianity. "The Church of the Poor: Historical Sacrament of Liberation," *Mysterium Liberationis,* 556.

43. Bell, *Liberation Theology after the End of History,* 100. He makes this claim footnoting Ellacuría's *Fe y justicia,* 21.

44. Gustavo Gutiérrez, *Las Casas,* trans. Robert Barr (Maryknoll, NY: Orbis Books, 1993), 235.

45. Bell, *Liberation Theology after the End of History,* 130.

46. See D. Bentley Hart, "A Gift Exceeding Every Debt: An Eastern Orthodox Appreciation of Anselm's *Cur Deus Homo?*" *Pro Ecclesia* 7 (1993): 333–49.

47. Bell, *Liberation Theology after the End of History,* 146.

48. Ibid., 147.

49. Ibid., 148.

50. This claim demands a question that Bell never addresses: Is the hypothetical claim by a liberation theologian that forgiveness is incomplete without reparations, or indeed whether salvation is complete without justice, the same as making the identity statements that Bell assumes, forgiveness = reparations; salvation = justice?

51. Bell, *Liberation Theology after the End of History,* 144.

52. Ibid., 186.

53. In particular, he praises Elsa Tamez for consistently carrying through with this conception of justice, though he will also cite Jon Sobrino, José González Faus, Leonardo Boff, and Gustavo Gutiérrez. See Bell, *Liberation Theology after the End of History,* 186–95.

54. Ibid., 187.

55. William T. Cavanaugh, *Torture and Eucharist: Theology, Politics, and the Body of Christ* (Malden, MA: Blackwell, 1998).

56. Examples include "The Ecclesiologies of Medellín and the Lessons of the Base Communities," *Cross Currents* 44, no. 1 (Spring 1994): 67–84; "The World in a Wafer: A Geography of the Eucharist as Resistance to Globalization," *Modern Theology* 15, no. 2 (April 1999): 181–96; "Dying for the Eucharist or Being Killed by It? Romero's Challenge to First-World Christians," *Theology Today* 58, no. 2 (July 2001): 177–90.

57. Cavanaugh's *Torture and Eucharist* represents the book version of his Hauerwas-directed dissertation and belongs to the "Challenges in Contemporary Theology" series that presents "Radical Orthodoxy" titles. His "The City: Beyond Secular Parodies" appears in *Radical Orthodoxy: A New Theology,* ed. John Milbank, Catherine Pickstock, and Graham Ward (London & New York: Routledge, 1999), 182–200.

58. Cavanaugh explicitly contrasts the "alternative soteriologies" of the modern state and the Christian church. "The City," 182.

59. Particularly powerful is the manner in which Cavanaugh utilizes Foucault's invocation of Bentham's "Panopticon," *Torture and Eucharist,* 47–48. See Michel Foucault, *Discipline and Punish: The Birth of the Prison,* trans. Alan Sheridan (New York: Vintage Books, 1977), 200ff. It should be noted that Cavanaugh's *Torture and Eucharist* was published three years prior to Bell's *Liberation Theology at the End of History.*

60. Here the manner in which he locates the church's problem in modern liberal thought reveals his reliance on Stanley Hauerwas, as influenced by Alisdair MacIntyre, more than the post-Constantinian objections of John Howard Yoder that marked Hauerwas's earlier work. On this distinction, see Jeffrey Stout, *Democracy and Tradition,* 141ff.

61. One must be attentive to the ways that Cavanaugh distinguishes between the "New Christendom" ecclesiology and the liberationist one.

62. William T. Cavanaugh, "The City: Beyond Secular Parodies," in *Radical Orthodoxy: A New Theology,* ed. John Milbank, Catherine Pickstock, and Graham Ward (London and New York: Routledge, 1999), 182.

63. Ibid.

64. Ibid., 184. See Henri de Lubac, *Catholicism: Christ and the Common Destiny of Man,* trans. Lancelot C. Sheppard and Sister Elizabeth Englund (San Francisco: Ignatius Press, 1988).

65. Cavanaugh, "The City," 185.

66. Ibid., 186. See John Milbank, *Theology and Social Theory,* 12–15.

67. Cavanaugh, "The City," 191.

68. Ibid., 190.

69. Cavanaugh, *Torture and Eucharist,* 142.

70. Ibid. While Cavanaugh's assertion seems valid in relation to the thought of Clodovis Boff, this comment clearly misunderstands Gustavo Gutiérrez's assertion of theology as a critical reflection on praxis; a second moment to the church's life of faith, preaching, and historical commitment. See Gustavo Gutiérrez, *A Theology of Liberation: History, Politics, and Salvation,* fifteenth anniversary ed. (Maryknoll, NY: Orbis Books, 1988).

71. Cavanaugh, *Torture and Eucharist,* 180. See also John Milbank, *Theology and Social Theory,* 208.

72. In making this accusation, Cavanaugh acknowledges that Maritain carefully distinguishes between the natural *telos* of political action and the supernatural *telos* of the person. However, Cavanaugh maintains that Maritain's vision ultimately distorts Thomas Aquinas's teaching on virtue. In Aquinas, more than "taking into account" the absolute end, the supernatural virtues transform the natural virtues to direct them to their proper end. Cavanaugh, *Torture and Eucharist,* 182ff.

73. Ibid., 206.

74. Ibid.

75. In this notion, Cavanaugh relies on de Lubac. See Henri de Lubac, *The Motherhood of the Church,* trans. Sr. Sergia Englund (San Francisco: Ignatius Press, 1982), 174.

76. William T. Cavanaugh, "The World in a Wafer: The Eucharist as Resistance to Globalization," *Modern Theology* 15, no. 2 (April 1999): 191.

77. Ibid., 191. Cavanaugh apparently equates "City of God" with the Eucharistic community.

78. Cavanaugh, *Torture and Eucharist,* 234. See also "World in a Wafer," 192.

79. Cavanaugh, "World in a Wafer," 192.

80. Cavanaugh, *Torture and Eucharist,* 60. Jon Sobrino's quote comes from *Jesus the Liberator: A Historical-Theological Reading of Jesus of Nazareth,* trans. Paul Burns and Francis McDonagh (Maryknoll, NY: Orbis Books, 1993), 270.

81. Cavanaugh, *Torture and Eucharist,* 62. Elsewhere, Cavanaugh lauds the Salvadoran link between a Jesus who "was killed because he defended the dignity of

the poor and marginalized against their exploiters" and martyrs "who are killed for similar reasons today." See "Dying for the Eucharist or Being Killed by It? Romero's Challenge to First-World Christians," *Theology Today* (July 2001): 179.

82. Cavanaugh, *Torture and Eucharist*, 64. Elsewhere, Cavanaugh adds, "Not everyone who is killed is a martyr; some are merely victims. To be a martyr one must be recognized as such by the discernment of the community." See "Dying for the Eucharist or Being Killed by It?" 179.

83. Cavanaugh, *Torture and Eucharist*, 65.

84. Indeed, it must be stated at the outset that one of the most serious methodological weaknesses in the radical orthodoxy authors involves the lack of sustained focus on the work of a singular liberation theologian. Too often, generalizations take the place of accurate, contextualized citations that do justice to that particular theologian, much less "liberation theology."

85. This warning may be directed to Latin American liberation theology, but it is relevant also for others such as feminist, U.S. Latino/a, and black/womanist theologies that take engagement with the social sciences as a methodological presupposition.

86. Ellacuría's reliance on Zubiri represents another instance in which Milbank's "French-German" dichotomy, with its claim to exhaust the genealogical possibilities of modern theology, does not fit the circumstances. Note Marie-Dominique Chenu's deep appreciation for the work of Gustavo Gutiérrez.

87. This debate also underscores the notion that liberation theology, even Latin American liberation theology, is not a monolithic position such that claims, assumptions, and arguments of one can be assigned without qualification to the others. For more on Ellacuría's critique of Boff's dividing theology into a T1 concerned with classical themes and a T2 with social-scientific mediations, see "La historicidad de la salvación cristiana," *ET* I, 535–96.

88. This could prevent misinterpretation and provide a fuller accounting of Zubiri's "primordial apprehension" of reality.

89. "By 'hermeticism' I mean the enclosure of Christian discourse and practice within a wholly separate universe of thought and action, a universe constituted by the prior 'mythos' of Christianity — that is (I take it, the word is never explained) an overarching, supra-rational, vision of the world, within which alone particular truths can be set forth, particular exemplars of action set up for imitation." Aidan Nichols, "*Non tali auxilio*: John Milbank's Suasion to Orthodoxy," *New Blackfriars* 73, no. 861 (June 1992): 326–32. Parenthetical comment his.

90. As William P. Loewe notes, "When Milbank opposes the persuasiveness of the Christian logos, which he is for, to any apologetic mediation of a universal human reason, which he is against, warning bells began to ring." "Beyond Secular Reason? Reflections in Response to John Milbank's Theology and Social Theory," *Philosophy and Theology* 9, no. 2 (1995): 450.

91. Outstanding examples of the UCA's engagement with these dimensions include its opinion-polling institute, El Instituto Universitario de Opinión Pública, the Institute for Human Rights (El Instituto de Derechos Humanos), and the many editorials and studies in the journal *Estudios Centroamericanos* dedicated to the historical reality of El Salvador.

92. For Miroslav Volf, an ecclesiology of community suffices to substantiate resistance, not one in which the church is a full fledged *polis*. His reading of the New Testament stresses, "Persons are called out of their polities. Strangely, however,

they always remain in them. More precisely, they are called out so as to be able properly to be in. Christians are pilgrims, never fully at home in any political order and never fully at home in the church either." *"Liberation Theology after the End of History:* An Exchange," *Modern Theology* 19, no. 2 (April 2003): 263.

93. An excellent example of this line of thought can be found in Oscar Romero's Third Pastoral Letter, *The Church and the Popular Political Organizations,* in *Voice of the Voiceless: The Four Pastoral Letters and Other Statements,* trans. Michael J. Walsh (Maryknoll, NY: Orbis Books, 1985), 85–114.

94. He does this, for example, when he grapples with the problem of how the Society of Jesus can maintain, on the one hand, its commitment to having the "best institutions," which seems to follow the standard of Satan in the Ignatian meditation, while also advocating distinctively Christian values. See "El problema del traslado del espíritu de los *Ejercicios* a la Viceprovincia," *ET* IV, 197–213. For more on *mundanización,* see "Recuperar el reino de Dios: desmundanización e historización de la Iglesia," *ET* II, 307–16.

95. See the prior discussion, in chapter 4, of justice precisely as more than "what one is due" from "Fe y Justicia," *ET* III, 316ff. Consider also Ellacuría's critique of an unconditional assertion of the "right to private property," or even of "human rights" in general in El Salvador in "La historización del concepto de propiedad como principio de desideologización," *Estudios Centroamericanos* 335–36 (1976): 425–50; *EP* I, 587–628.

96. Despite his rhetoric against the language of justice, Bell himself eventually feels the need to explicate a "biblical" notion of justice that appears closer to what Ellacuría and other liberation theologians propose. See Bell, *Liberation Theology after the End of History,* 187.

97. These terms possess a theological density in Ellacuría's theology. For more on the twofold process, see the discussion in chapter 2.

98. For T. Howland Sanks, "Cavanaugh has an exaggerated expectation of the liturgy. By placing so much burden on the Eucharist, the original referent for *corpus mysticum,* he winds up with an ecclesiology at least as ethereal and unable to resist a dictatorship as that New Christendom ecclesiology he faults.... In the end his argument leads not to a contrast society but to a disjunction between church and world that we thought was overcome at Vatican II." Review of *Torture and Eucharist, Theological Studies* 61, no. 1 (March 2000): 165–66.

99. Jaroslav Pelikan, *The Christian Tradition: A History of the Development of Doctrine,* vol. 1: *The Emergence of the Catholic Tradition (100–600)* (Chicago: University of Chicago Press, 1971), 143.

100. Jon Sobrino warns against two dangers: "mutilating the totality" and "manipulating the deeper truth" of Ellacuría. The first would separate and compartmentalize either Ellacuría's intellectual work or his exemplary life, and in doing so, elevate him in a way that absolves one from imitating him. The second danger would focus merely on that aspect of Ellacuría that could further one's own ideological agenda. *Ignacio Ellacuría, el hombre y el cristiano: "Bajar de la cruz al pueblo crucificado"* (San Salvador: Centro Monseñor Romero, 2001), 9.

101. Kevin Burke, *The Ground beneath the Cross* (Washington, DC: Georgetown University Press, 2000), 204ff.

102. Of course, the theological essays alone fill four volumes and 2,517 pages.

103. Examples of these polished essays include "Historicidad," *ET* I, 535–96; "Superación," *EF* III, 403–30; and "Utopía," *ET* II, 233–94.

104. See his arguments against the Dominican motto *contemplata aliis tradere* in "Fe y justicia," or against Anselmian atonement theory in "Pueblo crucificado."

105. Kevin Burke, José Sols Lucía, and Hector Samour have produced full-length monographs on Ellacuría's thought.

106. "El desafío de las mayorías pobres," *Estudios Centroamericanos* 493–94 (1989): 1075–80; *ET* I, 359.

Bibliography

Works by Ignacio Ellacuría

Books and Collected Essays

Conversión de la Iglesia al Reino de Dios: Para anunciarlo y realizarlo en la historia. Santander: Editorial Sal Terrae, 1984. Also published in San Salvador: UCA Editores.

Escritos filosóficos. Vol. 1. Edited by R. Valdés and H. Vargas. San Salvador: UCA Editores, 1996.

Escritos filosóficos. Vols. 2 and 3. Edited by Carlos Molina Velásquez. San Salvador: UCA Editores, 1999, 2001.

Escritos teológicos. Vols. 1 and 2. Edited by Rolando Alvarado and Aída Estela Sánchez. San Salvador: UCA Editores, 2000.

Escritos teológicos. Vols. 3 and 4. Edited by Aída Estela Sánchez. San Salvador: UCA Editores, 2001.

Escritos universitarios. Edited by Erasmo Ayala. San Salvador: UCA Editores, 1999.

Filosofía de la realidad histórica. Edited by Antonio González. Madrid: Editorial Trotta, 1990.

Mysterium liberationis: Conceptos fundamentales de la teología de la liberación. Vols. I and II. Edited by Ignacio Ellacuría and Jon Sobrino. Madrid: Editorial Trotta, 1990. In English, *Mysterium liberationis: Fundamental Concepts of Liberation Theology.* Edited by Ignacio Ellacuría and Jon Sobrino. Maryknoll, NY: Orbis Books, 1993.

Systematic Theology: Perspectives from Liberation Theology. Readings from *Mysterium Liberationis.* Edited by Ignacio Ellacuría and Jon Sobrino. Maryknoll, NY: Orbis Books, 1996.

Teología política. San Salvador: Ediciones del Secretariado Social Interdiocesano, 1973. In English, *Freedom Made Flesh: The Mission of Christ and His Church.* Translated by John Drury. Maryknoll, NY: Orbis Books, 1976.

Towards a Society That Serves Its People: The Intellectual Contribution of El Salvador's Murdered Jesuits. Edited by John Hassett and Hugh Lacey. Washington, DC: Georgetown University Press, 1991.

Veinte años de historia en El Salvador (1969–1989): Escritos políticos. Vols. 1–3. San Salvador: UCA Editores, 1993.

Articles

"El anuncio del Evangelio y la misión de la Iglesia." *TP*: 44–69. Also published as "Anuncio del Reino y credibilidad de la Iglesia." *Conversion de la Iglesia al*

Reino de Dios (Santander, Spain: Sal Terrae, 1984), 219–63; *ET* I: 659–98. In English, *FMF*: 87–126.

"Aporte de la teología de la liberación a las religiones Abráhamicas en la superación del individualismo y del positivismo." *Revista Latinoamericana de Teología* 10 (1987): 3–28; *ET* II: 193–232.

"Aproximación a la obra completa de Xavier Zubiri." *ECA* 421–22 (1983): 965–83; *EF* III: 365–98.

"El auténtico lugar social de la Iglesia." *Misión Abierta* 1 (1982): 98–106; *ET* II: 439–51. In English, "The True Social Place of the Church." In *Towards a Society That Serves Its People: The Intellectual Contribution of El Salvador's Murdered Jesuits*, translated by Phillip Berryman, ed. John Hassett and Hugh Lacey, 283–92 (Washington, DC: Georgetown University Press, 1991).

"Las bienaventuranzas como carta fundamental de la Iglesia de los pobres." *Iglesia de los pobres y organizaciones populares*. O. Romero, A. Rivera y Damas, I. Ellacuría, J. Sobrino, and T. Campos. San Salvador: UCA Editores, 1979, 105–18; *ET* II: 417–37.

"En busca de la 'cuestión fundamental' de la pastoral latinoamericana." *Sal Terrae* 759–60 (1976): 563–72. Also published as "La 'cuestión fundamental' de la pastoral latinoamericana." *Diakonía* 6 (1978): 20–28; *ET* II: 541–52.

"El compromiso político de la iglesia en América Latina." *Corintios XIII* 4 (1977): 143–62; *ET* II: 667–82.

"El desafío cristiano de la teología de la liberación." *Cartas a las Iglesias* 263 (1992): 12–15; 264 (1992): 11–13; 265 (1992): 14–16. *ET* I: 19–33. Transcript of a paper originally entitled, "Lo religioso y lo temporal en la teología de la liberación," given at a seminar organized by the Fundación Banco Exterior, Madrid, 1987.

"La desmitificación del marxismo." *ECA* 421–22 (1983): 921–30.

"Dios, el gran tema de Zubiri." *Ya*, September 23, 1983, 3; *EF* III: 357–58.

"Discernir 'el signo' de los tiempos." *Diakonía* 17 (1981), 57–59; *ET* II: 133–35.

"Espiritualidad," In *Conceptos fundamentales de pastoral*. Edited by C. Floristán and J. J. Tamayo. Madrid: Trotta, 1983, 304–9. Also published as "La espiritualidad cristiana." *Diakonía* 30 (1984): 123–32.

"Estudio teológico-pastoral de la 'Instrucción sobre algunos aspectos de la teología de la liberación.'" *Revista Latinoamericana de Teología* 2 (1984): 145–78; *ET* I: 397–448.

"Fe y justicia." *Christus* (August 1977): 26–33, and (October 1977): 19–34. See also *Fe y justicia*. Bilbao: Editorial Desclée de Brouwer, 1999.

"Filosofía ¿para qué?" *Abra* 11 (1976): 42–48; *EF* III: 115–31. In English, "What Is the Point of Philosophy?" Translated by T. Michael McNulty. *Philosophy and Theology* 10, no. 1 (1998): 3–18.

"Hacia una fundamentación filosófica del método teológico Latinoamericano." In *Liberación y cautiverio: Debates en torno al método de la teología en América Latina*, ed. Enrique Ruiz Maldonado. Mexico City: Encuentro Latinoamericano de Teología, 1975, 609–35; *ET* I: 187–218.

"Historia de la salvación." In *Revista Latinoamericana de Teología* 28 (1993): 3–25; *ET* I: 597–628. From a previously unpublished manuscript dated 1987.

"Historia de la salvación y salvación en la historia." *TP*: 1–10; *ET* I: 519–33. In English, *FMF*: 3–19.

"La historicidad del hombre en Xavier Zubiri." *Estudios de Deusto* 40, no. 14 (1966): 245–85, 523–47.

"Historicidad de la salvación cristiana."*Revista Latinoamericana de Teología* 1 (1984): 5–45; *ML* I: 323–72; *ET* I: 535–96. In English, "The Historicity of Christian Salvation." Translated by Margaret D. Wilde. *MLT:* 251–89.

"La Iglesia de los pobres, sacramento histórico de la liberación." *ECA* 348–49 (1977): 707–22; *Conversion de la Iglesia al Reino de Dios*, 179–216; *ML* II: 127–54; *ET* II: 453–85. In English, "The Church of the Poor, Historical Sacrament of Liberation." Translated by Margaret D. Wilde. *MLT:* 543–64.

"La Iglesia en El Salvador: la salvación se realiza en la historia." *Aportes* (1981): 34–35; *ET* II: 767–72.

"La Iglesia que nace del pueblo por el Espíritu." *Misión Abierta* 1 (1978): 150–58; *ET* II: 343–55.

"La Iglesia, signo de contradicción." Unpublished manuscript from 1973; *ET* II: 397–416.

"Iglesia y realidad histórica." *ECA* 331 (1976): 213–20; *ET* II: 501–15.

"Las iglesias latinoamericanas interpelan a la iglesia de España." *Sal Terrae* 826 (1982): 219–30; *ET* II: 589–602.

"Lectura latinoamericana de los *Ejercicios Espirituales* de san Ignacio." *Revista Latinoamericana de Teología* 23 (1991): 111–48; *ET* IV: 59–106. Based on previously unpublished notes from a 1974 course at the UCA.

"Liberación: misión y carisma de la iglesia latinoamericana." *ECA* 268 (1971): 61–80; *TP:* 70–90; *ET* II: 553–84. In English, *FMF:* 127–66.

"El método en la teología latinoamericana." Previously unpublished paper written in 1978. *ET* I: 219–34.

"Misión actual de la Compañía de Jesús." *Revista Latinoamericana de Teología* 29 (1993): 115–26. See also *Diakonía* 68 (1993): 33–42. Written in preparation for the 33rd General Congregation of the Society of Jesus, 1983.

"Monseñor Romero, un enviado de Dios para salvar a su pueblo." *Sal Terrae* 811 (1980): 825–32; *ECA* 497 (1990): 141–46.

"Nuestra situación colectiva vista desde la primera semana." Paper given at a meeting of the Central American Jesuits in Madrid, June 1969. *ET* IV: 177–96.

"La nueva obra de Zubiri: *Inteligencia sentiente*." *Razón y fe* 995 (1981): 126–39; *EF* III: 297–317.

"Una nueva obra filosófica del vasco Xavier Zubiri." *Deia* (December 27, 1980): 2; *EF* III: 291–95.

"La obra de Xavier Zubiri sobre la inteligencia humana: Inteligencia y razón." *El País*, March 13, 1983, 4; *EF* III: 333–42.

"Pedro Arrupe, renovador de la vida religiosa." In *Pedro Arrupe: Así lo vieron*, ed. M. Alcala. Santander: Sal Terrae, 1986, 141–72. See also *Revista Latinoamericana de Teología* 22 (1991): 5–23.

"Persecución." *ECA* 259 (1970): 189–90; *ET* II: 585–87.

"Pobres." In *Conceptos fundamentales de pastoral*. Edited by C. Floristán and J. J. Tamayo. Madrid: Trotta, 1983, 786–802; *ET* II: 171–92.

"Los pobres, 'lugar teológico' en América Latina." *Misión Abierta* 4–5 (1981): 225–40; *ET* I: 139–61.

"¿Por qué muere Jesús y por qué le matan?" *Misión Abierta* 2 (1977): 17–26; *ET* II: 67–88.

"Presentación." Introduction to *El Hombre y Dios*, by Xavier Zubiri. Madrid: Alianza Editorial, 1984, i–x.

"El pueblo crucificado, ensayo de soteriología histórica." In *Cruz y resurrección: anuncio de una Iglesia nueva*. Mexico City: CRT, 1978, 49–82; *ML* II, 189–216; *ET* II: 137–70. In English, "The Crucified People." Translated by Phillip Berryman and Robert R. Barr. *MLT*: 580–603.

"Pueblo de Dios," In *Conceptos fundamentales de pastoral*. Edited by C. Floristán and J. J. Tamayo. Madrid: Trotta, 1983, 840–59; *ET* II: 317–42.

"Recuperar el Reino de Dios: Des-mundanización e historización de la Iglesia." *Sal Terrae* 780 (1978): 335–44; *ET* II: 307–16.

"El Reino de Dios y el paro en el tercer mundo." *Concilium* 180 (1982): 588–96; *ET* II: 295–305. In English, "The Kingdom of God and Unemployment in the Third World." In *Unemployment and the Right to Work*. Edited by J. Pohier and D. Mieth. New York: Seabury, 91–96.

"Relación teoría y praxis en la teología de la liberación." Previously unpublished outline written in 1985. *ET* I: 235–45.

"La religación, actitud radical del hombre." *Asclepio* 16 (1966): 97–155; *ET* I: 39–105.

"La superación del reduccionismo idealista en Zubiri." *ECA* 477 (1988): 633–50; *EF* III: 403–30. Lecture given at the Congreso de Filosofía, Ética y Religión in Donostia-San Sebastián, September 28–October 3, 1987.

"La teología como momento ideológico de la praxis eclesial." *Estudios Eclesiásticos* 53, no. 207 (1978): 457–76; *ET* I: 163–85.

"La teología de la liberación frente al cambio socio-histórico de América Latina." *Revista Latinoamericana de Teología* 4, no. 12 (1987): 241–64; *ET* I: 313–45. In English, "Liberation Theology and Socio-historical Change in Latin America." In *Towards a Society That Serves Its People: The Intellectual Contribution of El Salvador's Murdered Jesuits*, trans. James Brockman, ed. John Hassett and Hugh Lacey, 19–43 (Washington, DC: Georgetown University Press, 1991).

"Teología de la liberación y marxismo." *Revista Latinoamericana de Teología* 20 (1990): 109–35; *ET* I: 461–97. Posthumously published notes of a lecture, "Teología de la liberación y marxismo," given at the UCA in November 1985.

"Tesis sobre la posibilidad, necesidad y sentido de una teología latinoamericana." *Teología y mundo contemporáneo: Homenaje a Karl Rahner en su 70 cumpleaños*. Edited by A. Vargas-Machuca. Madrid: Universidad Pontificia Comillas y Ediciones Cristiandad, 1975, 325–50; *ET* I: 271–301.

"En torno al concepto y la idea de liberación." I. Ellacuría et al., *Implicaciones sociales y políticas de la teología de la liberación*. Andalucía: Escuela de Estudios Hispanoamericanos y Instituto de Filosofía, Consejo Superior de Investigaciones Científicas, 1989, 91–109. *Revista Latinoamericana de Teología* 30 (1993): 213–32; *ET* I: 629–57.

"La UCA ante el doctorado concedido a Monseñor Romero." *ECA* 437 (1985): 167–76. In English, "The UCA Regarding the Doctorate Given to Monseñor Romero," *Envío* 9 (1990): 15–18.

"Utopía y profetismo desde América Latina: Un ensayo concreto de soteriología histórica." *Revista Latinoamericana de Teología* 17 (1989): 141–84; *ET* II: 233–93. Also published as "Utopía y profetismo." *ML* I: 393–442. In English, "Utopia and Prophecy in Latin America." Translated by James R. Brockman. *MLT*: 289–328.

"El verdadero pueblo de Dios, según Monseñor Romero." *ECA* 392 (1981): 529–54; *ET* II: 357–96. In English, the conclusion is published as "Persecution for the Sake of the Reign of God." In *Companions of Jesus: The Jesuit Martyrs of El Salvador.* Maryknoll, NY: Orbis Books, 1990, 64–75.

"Voluntad de fundamentalidad y voluntad de verdad: Conocimiento-fe y su configuración histórica." *Revista Latinoamericana de Teología* 8 (1986): 113–31; *ET* I: 107–37.

"Zubiri en El Salvador." *ECA* 361–62 (1978): 949–50; *EF* III: 203–6.

"Zubiri, filósofo teologal." *Vida Nueva* 1249 (1980): 45; *EF* III: 271–73.

"Zubiri sigue vivo." *Vida Nueva* 1396 (1983): 55; *EF* III: 353–55.

"Zubiri, vasco universal." *El Diario Vasco* (October 3, 1980): 22; *EF* III: 275–78.

Secondary Literature

Abbott, Walter M. *The Documents of Vatican II.* New York: America Press, 1966.

Aquino, María Pilar. *Our Cry for Life: Feminist Theology from Latin America.* Maryknoll, NY: Orbis Books, 1993.

Ashley, J. Matthew. "Ignacio Ellacuría and the *Spiritual Exercises* of Ignatius of Loyola." *Theological Studies* 61 (2000): 16–39.

Assmann, Hugo. *Teología desde la praxis de la liberación: Ensayo teológico desde la América dependiente.* In English, *Theology for a Nomad Church.* Translated by Paul Burns. Maryknoll, NY: Orbis Books, 1975.

Bell, Daniel M., Jr. *Liberation Theology after the End of History: The Refusal to Cease Suffering.* London and New York: Routledge, 2001.

Bernstein, Richard J. *Praxis and Action: Contemporary Philosophies of Human Activity.* Philadelphia: University of Pennsylvania Press, 1971.

Berryman, Phillip. *Stubborn Hope: Religion, Politics and Revolution in Central America.* Maryknoll, NY: Orbis Books, 1994.

Boff, Clodovis. *Theology and Praxis: Epistemological Foundations.* Translated by Robert Barr. Maryknoll, NY: Orbis Books, 1987.

———. "Methodology of the Theology of Liberation." In *Mysterium Liberationis: Fundamental Concepts of Liberation Theology,* ed. Jon Sobrino and Ignacio Ellacuría. Maryknoll, NY: Orbis Books, 1993.

Brackley, Dean. *Divine Revolution: Salvation and Liberation in Catholic Thought.* Maryknoll, NY: Orbis Books, 1996.

———. "Rutilio and Romero: Martyrs for Our Time." The Annual Archbishop Romero Lecture. Notre Dame: LANACC, Kellogg Institute, 1997.

Brockman, James. *The Word Remains: A Life of Oscar Romero.* Maryknoll, NY: Orbis Books, 1982.

Burke, Kevin. *The Ground beneath the Cross: The Theology of Ignacio Ellacuría.* Washington, DC: Georgetown University Press, 2000.

———, and Robert Lassalle-Klein, editors. *Love That Produces Hope: The Thought of Ignacio Ellacuría.* Collegeville, MN: Liturgical Press, 2006.

Burrell, David B. "An Introduction to *Theology and Social Theory: Beyond Secular Reason.*" In *Modern Theology* 8, no. 4 (October 1992): 319–29.

Castellón Martín, José Joaquín. *Ellacuría y la filosofía de la praxis.* Huelva: Hergué, 2003.

Castro de Zubiri, Carmen. *Biografía de Xavier Zubiri*. Málaga: Ediciones Edinford, 1992.

Cavanaugh, William T. *Torture and Eucharist: Theology, Politics, and the Body of Christ*. Oxford: Blackwell, 1998.

———. "Dying for the Eucharist or Being Killed by It? Romero's Challenge to First-World Christians." *Theology Today* 58, no. 2 (July 2001): 177–90.

———. "The Ecclesiologies of Medellín and the Lessons of the Base Communities." *Cross Currents* 44, no. 1 (Spring 1994): 67–84.

———. "The World in a Wafer: A Geography of the Eucharist as Resistance to Globalization." *Modern Theology* 15, no. 2 (April 1999): 181–96.

Chopp, Rebecca S. *The Praxis of Suffering: An Interpretation of Liberation and Political Theologies*. Maryknoll, NY: Orbis Books, 1986.

Cruz, Jesús Saez. *La accesibilidad de Dios: Su mundanidad y transcendencia en Xavier Zubiri*. Salamanca: Publicaciones Universidad Pontificia, 1995.

Duffy, Stephen J. *The Graced Horizon: Nature and Grace in Modern Catholic Thought*. Collegeville, MN: Liturgical Press/Michael Glazier, 1992.

Dussel, Enrique. *Philosophy of Liberation*. Maryknoll, NY: Orbis Books, 1985.

Gibellini, Rosino. *The Liberation Theology Debate*. London: SCM Press, 1987.

Godzieba, Anthony J. "Fear and Loathing in Modernity: The Voyages of Capt. John Milbank," *Philosophy and Theology* 9, no. 2 (1995): 419–33.

Goizueta, Roberto. *Caminemos con Jesús: Toward a Hispanic/Latino Theology of Accompaniment*. Maryknoll, NY: Orbis Books, 1995.

González, Antonio. *Estructuras de la praxis. Ensayo de una filosofía primera*. Trotta: Madrid, 1997.

———. "Aproximación a la obra filosófica de Ignacio Ellacuría." *Estudios Centroamericanos* 505–6 (1990): 980–89.

———. *La novedad teológica de la filosofía de Zubiri*. Madrid: Fundación Xavier Zubiri, 1993.

Gracia Guillén, Diego. *Voluntad de verdad: Para leer a Zubiri*. Barcelona: Editorial Labor Universitaria, 1986.

———. "Filosofía práctica." In *La pasión por la libertad: Homenaje a Ignacio Ellacuría*, ed. José A. Gimernat and Carlos Gómez. Estella (Navarra): Editorial Verbo Divino, 1994.

———. "El tema de Dios en la filosofía de Zubiri." In *Estudios Eclesiásticos* 56 (1981): 61–78.

———. "Xavier Zubiri." In *Dictionary of Fundamental Theology*, ed. René Latourelle. New York: Crossroad, 1995, 1165–69.

Gutiérrez, Gustavo. *El Dios de la Vida*. Lima: Centro de Estudios y Publicaciones, 1989. In English, *The God of Life*. Translated by Matthew J. O'Connell. Maryknoll, NY: Orbis Books, 1991.

———. *Hablar de Dios desde el sufrimiento del inocente*. Lima: Instituto Bartolomé de Las Casas, 1985. In English, *On Job: God-Talk and the Suffering of the Innocent*. Translated by Matthew J. O'Connell. Maryknoll, NY: Orbis Books, 1987.

———. *Teología de la liberación, Perspectivas*. Lima: Centro de Estudios y Publicaciones, 1971. In English, *A Theology of Liberation*. Translated by Caridad Inda and John Eagleson. Maryknoll, NY: Orbis Books, 1973, 1996.

Hauerwas, Stanley. *After Christendom? How the Church Is to Behave If Freedom, Justice, and a Christian Nation Are Bad Ideas*. Nashville: Abingdon Press, 1991.

Hemming, Laurence Paul, ed. *Radical Orthodoxy? A Catholic Enquiry.* Aldershot/ Burlington: Ashgate, 2000.

Hennelly, Alfred T., ed. *Liberation Theology: A Documentary History.* Maryknoll, NY: Orbis Books, 1990.

———. *Theologies in Conflict: The Challenge of Juan Luis Segundo.* Maryknoll, NY: Orbis Books, 1979.

Hinkelammert, Franz. *Cultura de la esperanza y sociedad sin exclusión.* San José, Costa Rica: DEI, 1995.

Iglesias, Fernando Llenin. *La realidad divina: El problema de Dios en Xavier Zubiri.* Oviedo: Seminario Metropolitano, 1990.

Ignatius of Loyola. *The Spiritual Exercises of Saint Ignatius: A Translation and Commentary.* Translated by George Ganss. St. Louis: Institute of Jesuit Sources, 1992.

Iriarte, Candido Aniz. "Punto de partida en el acceso a Dios: Vía de la religación, de Zubiri." *Estudios filosóficos* 35 (1986): 237–68.

Isasi-Díaz, Ada María. *En La Lucha = In the Struggle: Elaborating a Mujerista Theology,* 10th anniversary edition. Minneapolis: Fortress Press, 2004.

King, Martin Luther, Jr. *A Testament of Hope: The Essential Writings of Martin Luther King Jr.* Edited by James M. Washington. San Francisco: Harper & Row, 1986.

Klaiber, Jeffrey. *The Church, Dictatorships, and Democracy in Latin America.* Maryknoll, NY: Orbis Books, 1998.

Kloppenburg, Bonaventura. *Christian Salvation and Human Temporal Progress.* Chicago: Franciscan Herald Press, 1979.

———. *The People's Church: A Defense of My Church.* Chicago: Franciscan Herald Press, 1978.

———. *Temptations for a Theology of Liberation.* Chicago: Franciscan Herald Press, 1974.

Lamb. Matthew. "The Theory-Praxis Relationship in Contemporary Christian Theology." In *CTSA Proceedings* (1976): 147–78.

Lassalle-Klein, Robert. "The Jesuit Martyrs of the University of Central America: An American Christian University and the Historical Reality of the Reign of God." Ph.D. diss., Graduate Theological Union, Berkeley CA, 1995.

Lee, Michael E. "Liberation Theology's Transcendent Moment: The Work of Xavier Zubiri and Ignacio Ellacuría as Non-Contrastive Discourse." *Journal of Religion* 83, no. 2 (April 2003): 226–43.

Lindbeck, George A. *The Nature of Doctrine: Religion and Theology in a Postliberal Age.* Philadelphia: Westminster Press, 1984.

Lobkowicz, Nicholas. *Theory and Practice: The History of a Concept from Aristotle to Marx.* New York: University Press of America, 1967.

Loewe, William P. "Beyond Secular Reason? Reflections in Response to John Milbank's *Theology and Social Theory.*" *Philosophy and Theology* 9, no. 2 (1995): 447–54.

Lonergan, Bernard. *Insight: A Study of Human Understanding.* New York: Philosophical Library, 1957.

López Vigil, María. *Oscar Romero: Memories in Mosaic.* Washington, DC: EPICA, 2000.

Martínez Santamarta, Ceferino. *El hombre y Dios en Xavier Zubiri.* Salamanca: Ediciones Universidad de Salamanca, 1981.

Meier, John P. *A Marginal Jew: Rethinking the Historical Jesus*. New York: Doubleday, 1991.

―――. "The Bible as a Source for Theology." *CTSA Proceedings* 43 (1988): 1–14.

Míguez Bonino, José. *Christians and Marxists: The Mutual Challenge to Revolution*. Grand Rapids: Eerdmans, 1976.

Milbank, John. *Theology and Social Theory: Beyond Secular Reason*. Cambridge: Blackwell, 1990.

―――. "Enclaves or Where is the Church?" *New Blackfriars* 73 (June 1992): 341–52.

Milbank, John, Catherine Pickstock, and Graham Ward. *Radical Orthodoxy: A New Theology*. New York: Routledge, 1999.

Millás, José D. *La realidad de Dios: Su justificación y sentido en Xavier Zubiri y Javier Monserrat*. Rome: Gregorian University, 2004.

McGovern, Arthur. *Liberation Theology and Its Critics: Toward an Assessment*. Maryknoll, NY: Orbis Books, 1989.

Neuhaus, Richard John. *The Catholic Moment*. San Francisco: Harper & Row, 1987.

Nichols, Aidan. "*Non tali auxilio*: John Milbank's Suasion to Orthodoxy." *New Blackfriars* 73 (June 1992): 326–32.

Novak, Michael. *Will It Liberate? Questions about Liberation Theology*. New York: Paulist Press, 1986.

O'Malley, John W. *The First Jesuits*. Cambridge: Harvard University Press, 1993.

Pelikan, Jaroslav. *The Christian Tradition: A History of the Development of Doctrine*, vol. 1: *The Emergence of the Catholic Tradition (100–600)*. Chicago: University of Chicago Press, 1971.

Pintor-Ramos, Antonio. "Dios como problema en Zubiri." *Universitas Philosophica* 2 (June 1985): 29–44.

Pixley, George V. *On Exodus: A Liberation Perspective*. Translated by Robert Barr. Maryknoll, NY: Orbis Books, 1987.

Rahner, Karl. *Foundations of the Christian Faith: An Introduction to the Idea of Christianity*. Translated by William V. Dych. New York: Crossroad, 1978.

―――. *Theological Investigations*. 23 vols. New York: Crossroad, 1979.

―――. *The Practice of Faith*. Edited by Karl Lehman and Albert Raffelt. New York: Crossroad, 1986.

Ratzinger, Joseph. *The Ratzinger Report*. San Francisco: Ignatius Press, 1985.

Romero, Oscar Arnulfo. *Voice of the Voiceless: The Four Pastoral Letters and Other Statements*. With introductory essays by Jon Sobrino and Ignacio Martín-Baró. Translated by Michael J. Walsh. Maryknoll, NY: Orbis Books, 1985.

Rovaletti, María Lucrecia. *La dimension teologal del hombre: Apuntes en torno al tema de la religación en Xavier Zubiri*. Buenos Aires: Editorial Universitaria de Buenos Aires, 1979.

Samour, Héctor. *Voluntad de liberación. El pensamiento filosófica de Ignacio Ellacuría*. San Salvador: UCA Editores, 2002.

―――. "Filosofía y liberación." *Estudios Centroamericanos*, 637–38 (November–December 2001): 1119–38.

Schillebeeckx, Edward. *Christ the Sacrament of the Encounter with God*. New York: Sheed & Ward, 1963.

Segundo, Juan Luis. *Faith and Ideologies*. Translated by John Drury. Maryknoll, NY: Orbis Books, 1984.

————. *The Liberation of Theology*. Translated by John Drury. Maryknoll, NY: Orbis Books, 1976.

Senet de Frutos, Juan Antonio. *Ellacuría y los derechos humanos*. Bilbao: Desclée de Brouwer, 1998.

Sigmund, Paul. *Liberation Theology at the Crossroads*. Oxford and New York: Oxford University Press, 1990.

Sobrino, Jon. *Companions of Jesus: The Jesuit Martyrs of El Salvador* (Maryknoll, NY: Orbis Books, 1990.

————. *La fe en Jesucristo: Ensayo desde las víctimas*. Madrid: Editorial Trotta, 1999. In English, *Christ the Liberator: A Historical-Theological Reading of Jesus of Nazareth*. Translated by Paul Burns. Maryknoll, NY: Orbis Books, 2001.

————. *Jesucristo Liberador: Lectura historica-teológica de Jesús de Nazaret*. Madrid: Editorial Trotta, 1991. In English, *Jesus the Liberator: A Historical-Theological Reading of Jesus of Nazareth*. Translated by Paul Burns and Francis McDonagh. Maryknoll, NY: Orbis Books, 1993.

————. *El principio misericordia: Bajar de la cruz a los pueblos crucificados*. San Salvador: UCA Editores, 1992.

————. *Witnesses to the Kingdom: The Martyrs of El Salvador and the Crucified Peoples*. Maryknoll, NY: Orbis Books, 2003.

————. "The Crucified Peoples: Yahweh's Suffering Servant Today." In *1492–1992: The Voice of the Victims. Concilium*, special edition, ed. Leonardo Boff and Virgilio Elizondo; trans. Dinah Livingstone. London: SCM Press, 1990.

————. "Ignacio Ellacuría, el hombre y el cristiano." In *Fe y justicia*. Bilbao: Editorial Desclée de Brouwer, 1999, 11–109.

Sobrino, Jon, and Rolando Alvarado, eds. *Ignacio Ellacuría: Aquella libertad esclarecida*. San Salvador: UCA Editores, 1999).

Sokolowski, Robert. *The God of Faith and Reason: Foundations of Christian Theology*. Washington, DC: Catholic University of America Press, 1982, 1995.

Sols Lucia, Jose. *La teología historica de Ignacio Ellacuría*. Madrid: Editorial Trotta, 1999.

Stout, Jeffrey. *Democracy and Tradition*. Princeton, NJ: Princeton University Press, 2004.

Tanner, Kathryn. *God and Creation in Christian Theology*. New York: Blackwell, 1988.

Torres, Sergio, and John Eagleson, editors. *Theology in the Americas*. Maryknoll, NY: Orbis Books, 1976.

Tracy, David. *The Analogical Imagination: Christian Theology and the Culture of Pluralism*. New York: Crossroad, 1981.

————. "Traditions of Spiritual Practice and the Practice of Theology." *Theology Today* 55, no. 2 (1998): 235–41.

Trujillo, Alfonso Lopez. *De Medellín a Puebla*. Madrid: Biblioteca de Autores Cristianos, 1980.

————. *Liberation or Revolution?* Huntington, IN: Our Sunday Visitor, 1977.

Vekemans, Roger. *God and Caesar: The Priesthood in Politics*. Maryknoll, NY: Orbis Books, 1972.

————. *Teología de la Liberación y Cristianos por el Socialismo*. Bogota: CEDIAL, 1976.

Volf, Miroslav. "*Liberation Theology after the End of History*: An Exchange," *Modern Theology* 19, no. 2 (April 2003): 263.

Whitfield, Teresa. *Paying the Price: Ignacio Ellacuría and the Murdered Jesuits of El Salvador.* Philadelphia: Temple University Press, 1995.

Williams, Rowan. "Saving Time: Thoughts on Practice, Patience and Vision." *New Blackfriars* 73 (June 1992): 319–26.

Zubiri, Xavier. *El hombre y Dios.* Edited by Ignacio Ellacuría. Madrid: Alianza Editorial Fundación Zubiri, 1984.

———. *Inteligencia sentiente.* Madrid: Sociedad de Estudios y Publicaciones, 1980.

———. *Naturaleza, historia, Dios.* Madrid: Editora Nacional, 1944.

———. "El problema teologal del hombre." In *Teología y mundo contemporáneo: Homenaje a Karl Rahner en su 70 cumpleaños.* Edited by A. Vargas-Machuca. Madrid: Universidad Pontificia Comillas y Ediciones Cristiandad, 1975, 55–64.

———. *El problema teologal del hombre: Cristianismo.* Edited by Antonio González. Madrid: Alianza Editorial Fundación Zubiri, 1997.

———. *Sobre la esencia.* Madrid: Sociedad de Estudios y Publicaciones, 1962.

Study Guide

Chapter One
Liberation Theology: A Soteriological Debate

1. According to liberation theologians, how is what Christians call "salvation" related to human liberation?

2. Though the Vatican documents on liberation theology are not condemnations, they express caution about several themes. What are they?

3. How does Ellacuría's location affect the way that he does theology?

Chapter Two
Principle and Foundation of Ellacuría's Soteriology

1. What are some of the significant problems that Ellacuría and Zubiri diagnose in modern Western thought? How does the notion of "sentient intelligence" address them?

2. How does Ellacuría's proposed three-fold method for theology differ from other proposals for how theology should be carried out?

3. How does the notion of participating in the removal of sin from the world differ from talking about the forgiveness of sin?

Chapter Three
Locus Salvificus: *Jesus Crucified and the Crucified People*

1. What is the difference between searching for the "historical Jesus" and Ellacuría's attempt to "historicize" the portrait of Jesus in the Gospels? Do they have different implications for Christian life today?

2. Why does Ellacuría believe it important to think of the removal of sin as an ongoing process rather than a one-time event?

3. If the poor bear the weight of salvation today, do they replace the cross of Jesus as salvific? Can one speak of Jesus' cross as a definitive event while still speaking of the poor in this way?

4. Does using the language of the Reign of God suggest something involving the present that heaven does not?

5. How are the concepts of utopia and propheticism related to the Reign?

Chapter Four
Ecclesial Praxis as Real Discipleship

1. How is talk of Christian praxis different from that of Christian practice(s)? For Ellacuría, how is praxis related to his larger vision of historical reality?

2. What does it mean to call the church itself a sacrament of salvation? Is this title ontological (it simply *is* sacrament) or praxical (it is sacramental in what it *does*)?

3. How does Ellacuría unite the concepts of contemplation and work for justice?

4. What qualities of Oscar Romero serve as a model for Christians today?

Chapter Five
Transforming Realities and Contesting Orthodoxies

1. What does John Milbank mean when he says that theology today is trapped in a modern secular metanarrative? Does Ellacuría rely on a Christian metanarrative?

2. How does Ellacuría's call for a faith that does justice call for more than "giving each person their due"?

3. Are there ways that radical orthodoxy's call to sacramental imagination and Ellacuría's attention to faith in historical reality are complementary? Can one fully exist without the other?

About the Author

The son of Puerto Rican parents, Michael E. Lee was born in Miami, Florida. He holds graduate degrees from the University of Chicago and the University of Notre Dame. His research interests include: Roman Catholic soteriology, spirituality, Latin American liberation theology, and U.S. Latino/a theology. Currently Dr. Lee is Assistant Professor of Systematic Theology at Fordham University, where he is also affiliated with its Institute for Latin American and Latino Studies. Dr. Lee is an administrative team member of the "Christ" topic area for the Catholic Theological Society of America (CTSA), and on the governing board of the Academy of Catholic Hispanic Theologians of the U.S. (ACHTUS). He lives in New York City with his wife, Natalia, and their son, William.

Index

Of Related Interest

Dean Brackley, S.J.
THE CALL TO DISCERNMENT IN TROUBLED TIMES
New Perspectives on the Transformative Wisdom
of Ignatius of Loyola

As the centerpiece of Crossroad's expanding offerings in Jesuit spirituality and thought, we offer this remarkable book from Dean Brackley, a leader in social justice movements and professor in El Salvador. Brackley takes us through the famous Ignatian exercises, showing that they involve not only private religious experience but also a social, moral dimension, including care for others.

"Challenging, yet infused with passion and hope, this book will provide valuable insight both to students of Ignatian spirituality and, more generally, to those who wonder how Christian spirituality can continue to shape a creative and faith-filled response to our crucified world."
— J. Matthew Ashley, Associate Professor of
Systematic Theology, University of Notre Dame

978-0-8245-2268-1, paperback

crossroad

Of Related Interest

Kevin Mongrain
THE SYSTEMATIC THOUGHT OF
HANS URS VON BALTHASAR
An Irenaean Retrieval

Is there a single driving force unifying the diverse writings of Hans Urs von Balthasar? Kevin Mongrain points to von Balthasar's retrieval of Irenaeus of Lyons. In Irenaeus, von Balthasar found inspiration for a genuinely Christian theology that resists the recurring danger of gnosticism while honoring the Mystery of God.

"With astonishing rhetorical skill and an enviable command of Balthasar's vast corpus, Mongrain convincingly shows that Irenaeus is both the most crucial early Christian writer for Balthasar and a man whose basic mental outlook and theology of history closely parallel Balthasar's own."
— Edward T. Oakes in *Theological Studies*

978-0-8245-1927-2, paperback

A Herder & Herder Book

crossroad

Of Related Interest

Johan Baptist Metz
FAITH IN HISTORY AND SOCIETY
Toward a Practical Fundamental Theology

New Translation by J. Matthew Ashley

Since its first appearance in 1977, this book continues to be the single most important text for understanding the theology of Johann Baptist Metz, one of the founders of the "new political theology."

"*Faith in History and Society* is the most important statement to date of the meaning of political theology! Metz's major themes — praxis, apocalyptic narrative, and the memory of suffering — are here related and developed into a genuinely new and stunning political theology."
— David Tracy, University of Chicago Divinity School

978-0-8245-2554-5, paperback

A Herder & Herder Book

Check your local bookstore for availability.
To order directly from the publisher,
please call 1-800-707-0670 for Customer Service
or visit our Web site at *www.cpcbooks.com*.
For catalog orders, please send your request to the address below.

THE CROSSROAD PUBLISHING COMPANY
16 Penn Plaza, Suite 1550
New York, NY 10001

crossroad